ANARCHIST DEVELOPMENT IN CULTURAL STUDIES

2013.1: Blasting the Canon

Anarchist Developments in Cultural Studies (ADCS) is an international peer-reviewed and open-access journal devoted to the study of new and emerging perspectives in anarchist thought. ADCS is an attempt to bring anarchist thought into contact with innumerable points of connection. We publish articles, reviews/debates, announcements, and unique contributions that: (1) adopt an anarchist perspective with regards to analyses of language, discourse, culture, and power; (2) investigate various facets of anarchist thought and practice from a non-anarchist standpoint, and; (3) investigate or incorporate elements of non-anarchist thought and practice from the standpoint of traditional anarchist thought.

Published + Distributed, 2013, by punctum books
Brooklyn, New York – United States
Email. punctumbooks@gmail.com
Web. http://punctumbooks.com

General Contact: Duane Rousselle, Duane.Rousselle@egs.edu
Book Design & Typesetting: Eileen Joy
Copy-Editing: Sheridan Phillips
Other Technical Services: Angry Nerds (Aragorn!)
www.AngryNerds.com
Cover Design (unless otherwise stated): iç mihrak
http://icmihrak.blogspot.com

ADCS is part of the Cultural Studies working group of the North American Anarchist Studies Network (www.naasn.org)

ISSN: 1923-5615

ANARCHIST DEVELOPMENTS IN CULTURAL STUDIES

2013: Issue 1: Blasting the Canon // ISBN: 978-0615838625
Issue Editors: Ruth Kinna and Süreyyya Evren

TABLE OF CONTENTS

REVIEW/DEBATE: *BLACK FLAME*

INTERVIEW

UNSCIENTIFIC SURVEY

Anarchist Developments in Cultural Studies
ISSN: 1923-5615
2013.1: Blasting the Canon

Introduction
Blasting the Canon

Ruth Kinna & Süreyyya Evren*

This issue was inspired by Süreyyya Evren's doctoral research into postanarchism and the conversations that resulted from it about the construction of the anarchist past, the theoretical integrity of 'classical anarchism'—particularly as it is understood in postanarchist writings—and the nature of anarchist history.[1]

*Ruth Kinna is a political theorist at the University of Loughborough, UK. She is the author of the *Beginner's Guide to Anarchism* (Oneworld, 2005), editor of the journal *Anarchist Studies* and the recently published *Continuum Companion to Anarchism* (2012). With Laurence Davis, she co-edited the collection *Anarchism and Utopianism* (Manchester, 2009). She is also co-editor, with Alex Prichard, Saku Pinta and David Berry of *Libertarian Socialism* (Palgrave, 2012), which explores canonical issues by examining the inter-relationships, tensions, overlaps, and ruptures in anarchism and Marxism.

*Süreyyya Evren (b. 1972) writes on anarchism, contemporary art, and literature. He has published several books in Turkish and several articles in English and German. He is the editor and founder of the post-anarchist magazine *Siyahi* (Istanbul, 2004-2006). Together with Duane Rouselle, he edited the *Post-Anarchism Reader* (Pluto, 2011) and founded the postanarchist journal *Anarchist Developments in Cultural Studies*.

[1] Süreyya Turkeli, "What is Anarchism? A Reflection on the Canon and The Constructive Potential of Its Destruction," PhD diss. (Loughborough University, 2012).

The questions that this research raised were less about the persuasiveness of postanarchist treatments of nineteenth-century anarchists, which had already been explored in some detail, than about the ways in which the tradition of classical anarchism was constructed in postanarchist critique. Not only did it appear that this construction failed to capture complexity, fluidity, and creativity of anarchist practices, it also seemed that it contributed to the reification of a highly partial reading of nineteenth century traditions. The canon was central to this analysis, because the notion that there was a 'classical' tradition already assumed that 'anarchism' might be defined by the writings of a narrow range of writers—typically, Proudhon, Bakunin, and Kropotkin—and by an equally narrow selection of texts, theorised in a particular manner, using frameworks of analysis that were inherently distorting. The anarchist canon emerged from the analysis of a tradition scrutinised by philosophers who found anarchism wanting and by sympathetic historians who adopted highly personalised accounts of anarchist thought (Tolstoy: 'The Prophet'; Bakunin: 'The Destructive Urge').[2]

Paul Eltzbacher's work[3] provided a useful starting point for the discussion, not because his account of the seven sages of anarchism was particularly well known (on the contrary, it's a classic that few now read), but because of the influence it exercised at the time it was written (1911) and, perhaps, structurally, on subsequent works, notably Woodcock's *Anarchism*.[4] Eltzbacher's legalistic approach is difficult to love: Gustav Landauer believed that it missed entirely anarchism's 'unspeakable mood.'[5] Yet it is also misunderstood. Marie Fleming argued that Eltzbacher's analysis of anarchism as anti-statism was reductive and that anarchism could only be understood contextually: as a movement that emerged 'in response to specific social-economic grievances in given historical circumstances.'[6]

---

[2] For a discussion of anarchism and analytic philosophy see Benjamin Franks, "Anarchism and Analytic Philosophy," in Ruth Kinna, ed., *Continuum Companion to Anarchism* (London: Continuum, 2012), 53–74.
[3] Paul Eltzbacher, *Anarchism: Seven Exponents of the Anarchist Philosophy* (London: Freedom, 1960); available at Project Gutenburg: http://www.gutenberg.org/ebooks/36690.
[4] George Woodcock, *Anarchism A History of Libertarian Ideas and Movements* (New York: Meridian Books, 1962).
[5] Gustav Landauer to Paul Eltzbacher, April 2, 1900, in Gustav Landauer, *Revolution and Other Writings: A Political Sampler*, ed. and trans. Gabriel Kuhn (Oakland: PM Press, 2010), 303.
[6] Marie Fleming, *The Odyssey of Elisée Reclus: The Geography of Freedom*

Her view not only emphasised anarchism's European origin but perhaps attributed to Eltzbacher an ambition not his own. As Michael Schmidt and Lucien van der Walt argue, Eltzbacher's aim was to understand anarchism *ideologically* ('scientifically,' to use his terminology) and to try to discover the common threads that made sense of the application of the label 'anarchist' to the set of writers who were already commonly identified with this epithet.[7] If his work helped establish a particular definition of anarchism and tie this definition tightly to a canon, his concern was to bring clarity to ideas that were not well understood.[8] And however faulty his framework, (van der Walt outlines what he sees as the shortcomings in his contribution) Eltzbacher rejected the idea that anarchists must necessarily be sub-divided into irreconcilable schools, an approach pioneered by other early analysts like Ernst Zenker,[9] and he recognised that a full understanding of anarchism depended on a familiarity with an international movement and with a body of literatures, typically circulating in newspapers, often authored anonymously.

One of the objections to the approach Eltzbacher pioneered is that it failed to provide an intelligible account of anarchist politics. Indeed, described as anti-statism, anarchism appears compatible with multiple currents of thought, including neo-liberal strains that socialist anarchists flatly reject. For Kropotkin, who applauded Eltzbacher's efforts to provide an intellectually rigorous analysis of anarchism, anarchism referred to a set of practices rather than an ideology. He attempted to describe these by probing the affinities between the nineteenth-century groups he was involved with and a diverse set of popular movements, cultural currents, thinkers, and events.[10] This analysis was itself a political act, part of an effort to normalise anarchist ideas by demonstrating the principles that anarchists espoused had a popular root, and, at the same time, a contribution to a struggle with social democracy that was designed to show that socialism

---

(Montreal: Black Rose Books, 1988), 23.
[7] Michael Schmidt & Lucien van der Walt, *Black Flame: The Revolutionary Class Politics of Anarchism and Syndicalism, Vol. 1: Counter-Power* (Oakland: AK Press, 2009), 17–18, 35–45.
[8] Eltzbacher, *Anarchism*, 1.
[9] Ernst Victor Zenker, *Anarchism; a Criticism and History of the Anarchist Theory* (London & New York: The Knickerbocker Press, 1897).
[10] Peter Kropotkin, 'Anarchism,' in R.N. Baldwin, ed., *Kropotkin's Revolutionary Pamphlets* (New York: Dover, 1972), 283–300.

and socialist transformation might take different forms to those prescribed by the then dominant party machines. This approach enabled him to show that it was possible to think about anarchism as a distinctive strand within the revolutionary socialist movement and to assert the superiority of particular adjectival forms (as the best vehicles for realising popular aspirations) without imposing rigid theoretical, disciplinary, cultural, or temporal boundaries on the ideas and practices that fell within it. Similarly, it enabled him to acknowledge that anarchist ideas were not especially nor fundamentally European and to identify a host of anarchistic practices without relinquishing the notion that anarchism described a distinctive politics and a normative, ethical stance.

Eltzbacher's identification of the seven sages has undoubtedly contributed to canonical thinking and to the perception that anarchism might be defined exclusively with reference to the ideas of a few great men. Introductions to anarchism often survey selected figures, sometimes explicitly prioritising ideas, sometimes contextualising them in historical movements, and not unusually divorcing the theory from the practice. It's easy to dismiss everything about the canon, yet before rejecting it altogether it seems important to consider what precisely we are blasting, when we blast it. Even Wyndham Lewis, in his most fearsome attack, coupled blast with blessing.[11] It seems from the unscientific survey conducted for this issue that respondents feel similarly. The results suggest that the idea of a theoretical tradition continues to resonate, albeit for an unrepresentative and (of course!) statistically insignificant sample. And it's interesting to find that of Eltzbacher's seven sages (Kropotkin, Bakunin, Proudhon, Tucker, Stirner, Tolstoy, and Godwin), the first-named three are still ranked in the top slots one hundred years after he devised his list. Does it follow from these results that the idea of a canon is integral to anarchist conceptions of anarchism? The selection criteria used by participants and the commentaries on the selections, as well as the selections themselves, suggest that this is not the case; that there is a good deal of disagreement about what anarchism might mean, even within the confines of 'classical' thought; and that an appreciation or interest in

---

[11] Wyndham Lewis, *Blast 2* (London: John Lane, the Bodley Head, July 1915), 94–95; available at the Modernist Journals Project: http://dl.lib.brown.edu/mjp/render.php?id=1144595337105481&view=mjp_object.

anarchist thinking is entirely compatible with critique and active engagement.

The contributors to this issue suggest a number of different purposes for blasting the canon. For Michelle Campbell, the inspiration is to allow more voices in—her choice is Voltairine de Cleyre, a notable exponent of anarchism without adjectives; Elmo Feiten's blast is directed at canonical construction and focuses on Max Stirner, a bugbear of recent canon-builders and, as Feiten argues, a spook even in sympathetic accounts of his work. James Miller examines the significance of the prefixes that attach to terms and the political, social, and activist identities they create. Nathan Jun and Robert Graham both attempt to blast what they see as the static or programmatic and authoritative ordering of anarchist voices: this is the focus of their critique of Lucien van der Walt. For his part, van der Walt suggests that their resistance is fraught with difficulty: blasting one canon usually results in the creation of an alternative, rather than the rejection of canons themselves. Yet as Leonard Williams argues, the process of selections does not necessarily lead to definitive choice. Distinguishing between theory and the practice of canon-building, he defends the practice of 're-presenting' the 'ideas, values, and spirit found within anarchism' and blasts only the 'prescriptive conditions for admission to the club.' A history of underground literatures, handwritten, typed, mimeographed, which reproduce images, extracts from poetry, songs, literature, and political thought, all lovingly chosen to propagate anarchist ideas, underwrites his account.

The role of history in canonical thinking is tackled by Matthew Adams. His blast is against canonical approaches that treat the past as something to be surpassed, and he shows how an appreciation of historical context and the conditions in which anarchists operated help us think productively about their attempts to articulate a distinctive anarchist culture. Canonical figures are not written out of history, but they no longer play a representational role. In history, canonical thinking tends towards the deployment of discrete categories, the invention of useful shortcuts for critique. However, as Jim Donaghey also argues, it is possible to develop non-canonical approaches. In his analysis of anarchism and punk, the alternative he proposes is rooted in the embrace of antimony, tension, and overlap. Ryan Knight's essay touches on similar themes but makes the point through textual interpretation, contrasting small-'a' treatments of Bakunin to Bakunin's writings. What emerges is not a canonical, big-'A' Bakunin, but a Bakunin who looks remarkably like the small-'a' anarchists who define themselves in opposition. To blast the canon, in this way, is to open a dialogue and invite discussion of continuities, not with a view to advancing positions on the past, but as Mümken proposes in his interview with Gabriel Kuhn, to 'reflect on the social transformations, theoretical developments, and practical experiences of the last decades.'

Anarchist Developments in Cultural Studies
ISSN: 1923-5615
2013.1: Blasting the Canon

This Canon Which Is Not One

Leonard A. Williams*

ABSTRACT
Thinking about an anarchist canon focuses on a number of issues: whether or not such a canon exists; questions of identity and boundary maintenance; concerns about representation. This essay addresses these questions by exploring not only what *constitutes* a canon, but also how one *emerges* and what *purposes* it might serve. We generally turn to a canon as an aid for either understanding or changing the world before us. Anarchist canons thus develop not only around texts and theorists, but also around events and practices—yet, no canon can claim universality; each one is inherently limited and skewed. How then can we avoid the dangers posed by a reified canon? These risks can be mitigated, initially, by regarding a canon as a tool kit enabling us to understand the tradition and gain some leverage for contributing to it. Second, we can subject any canon that does emerge to questioning and challenge. A third approach is to pay attention to activists' concerns and the cultural products that reflect on their practices. Finally, whenever we encounter an established canon, we must test its worth by assessing whether or not it speaks to our condition.

KEYWORDS
canon, tradition, representation, anarchism, theory, practice

In an often-cited passage, David Graeber (2004: 3) notes that, in many accounts, anarchism has been treated as a set of ideas basically similar to Marxism. In other words, "anarchism is

* Leonard A. Williams teaches political science at Manchester University in North Manchester, Indiana, USA. Interested in political ideologies, he is writing a book on contemporary anarchist thought (when time and energy permit).

presented as the brainchild of certain nineteenth-century thinkers—Proudhon, Bakunin, Kropotkin, etc.—it then went on to inspire working-class organizations, became enmeshed in political struggles, divided into sects." This similarity to Marxism, especially its academic variant, also extends to the apparent establishment and persistence of a canon of classic works. Indeed, Süreyyya Evren has observed that it is common for reference books on anarchism to start with an exposition of key theorists and conclude with a discussion of the practical applications of their theories. If, however, "anarchist practices are a form of thinking: a thinking on freedom, equality, solidarity, action," then "anarchist political philosophy can't be understood by referring to representative thinkers only, it requires analysis of the common points of this elusive complex network of radicalisms and resistances" (Alpine Anarchist Productions 2010).

When *Anarchist News* ("The Anarchist Canon Is" 2010) asked for opinions on the anarchist canon, the comments revealed an equally elusive and complex network of responses. Some comments presented lists of key anarchist thinkers; others voiced objections to those named on the lists, saying that some of the figures mentioned were not even anarchist at all. Still other comments expressed (more or less vulgarly) the thought that the whole enterprise was worthless. Thinking about the existence, form, and significance of an anarchist canon thus raises a number of issues. One issue is whether or not a canon actually exists. Another issue involves questions of identity and boundary maintenance: Who is and who is not an anarchist? What is and what is not anarchist in spirit? Still another issue addresses Graeber's and Evren's significant concerns about representation: whether or not an institutionalized, fixed, or reified anarchist canon privileges certain texts and perspectives over, and to the exclusion of, others.

Before proceeding further, we must first decide what constitutes a canon. Without belaboring the point, we can understand a canon as a list of authors or books that one should read in order to be knowledgeable about, or answer questions about, a particular domain of experience. We can see canonical influences evident in some of the anthologies of anarchist writings. For example, the editor of one anthology (containing writings that stretch from those by Godwin and Stirner to ones by Cohn-Bendit and Goodman) audaciously asserted that what "anarchists have actually said and done in respect to specific economic, social, and political issues is best learned from the texts contained in this book" (Shatz 1971: xi). More modestly, Daniel Guérin (2005: 3), though he intended not to beatify anyone, nevertheless saw fit to begin his anthology with works what he called the "pioneers"—namely Stirner, Proudhon, and Bakunin.

Commonly understood, then, the canon of classic works in the anarchist tradition certainly would include those by Proudhon, Bakunin, and Kropotkin, supplemented perhaps with those by Goldman, Malatesta, Landauer, or any number of other famous names. More recent additions to such a list might include works by folks like Ward, Bookchin, or Chomsky. Like all canons, though, this particular list of authors and texts is highly selective and limited in coverage; inherently, no canon can be truly comprehensive—which is one of the reasons why the presence of any canon is problematic.

There is some debate, though, about whether or not an anarchist canon actually exists. In making the case for a post-anarchism, for instance, thinkers such as Saul Newman (2010) have criticized classical anarchism—embodied in the works of Proudhon, Bakunin, and Kropotkin—for its Enlightenment orientation and essentialism. In challenging such claims, Nathan Jun (2012) has replied that "classical anarchism" was a fiction. His claim was that no common, coherent perspective can be found among the ideas of these supposedly classical anarchists. Evren (2008) similarly quarreled with assertions about classical anarchism in noting that, in order to be supported or even fully understood, they first required the construction of a critical genealogy of the anarchist "canon."

Further, one can point to some recent introductions to anarchism that abjure a focus on particular thinkers and instead prefer to focus on movements and values—works by Colin Ward (2004) and Cindy Millstein (2010) are notable in this regard. For such writers, conceiving of anarchism as a set of classic works is highly problematic. Even though nineteenth-century canonical works may have marked the beginning of the tradition, "an isolated philosophical reading of Anarchist 'classics'" cannot give one an accurate picture of anarchism that is best conceived as "a creed that has been worked out in action" (Meltzer 1996: 13, 17). In this context, anarchists are linked not by common authors or texts, but by the common themes underlying their social and political practices. Randall Amster (2012) agrees, but then further confuses matters by using the term "canon" to refer not to a set of authors or texts, but to these common themes or values that anarchists have embraced in practice. Given that anarchists themselves have used the term in different ways and have taken multiple stances on the question of a canon, let us shift gears from determining what *constitutes* a canon to understanding what *purposes* a canon might serve.

Although the construction of any particular canon is a significant and complex historical question, any anarchist canon (to the extent that one exists) would offer the elements of an answer to this sort of question: *What is anarchism all about?* Certainly, people who self-identify as anarchists have to answer this question in face-to-face conversations with some frequency. Yet, there are limits to the educative value that these conversations might have—if only because anarchism itself is a non-creedal, non-authoritarian perspective. As we are often reminded, anarchism is not a fully specified, ideological doctrine; it advocates no universal program or authoritative set of principles. Every program or principle that may be presented always seems to be subject to critique and exception. Any one person's take on anarchism seems to be just that—an idiosyncratic understanding of what constitutes anarchism or a personal assessment of its worth.

In taking the discussion of anarchism beyond one's particular horizons, or if a person wanted to be modest in one's pronouncements about anarchism, she or he might end up saying something like: *This is what I think anarchism is all about, but if you want to know more, here are some books (or pamphlets, zines, films, CDs, websites, and the like) that have helped me understand it. Perhaps they can help you understand anarchism.* Even in this modest version, the participants in the dialogue (knowingly or not) are gesturing toward a broader understanding of the anarchist tradition. They do so by ruling some works to be within the tradition and others to be outside it, and those that are within the tradition necessarily bear some relationship to canonical works and conceptions. Thus, as John Dunn (1996) suggested with regard to the history of political thought, a canon itself serves as a cognitive resource for understanding a given domain or tradition. In sum, any reference to a canon provides the curious person with a ready orientation to a particular world, with a more or less reliable map of a given territory.

We can also understand a canon in a Wittgensteinian (1958) fashion. From this point of view, a canon would function something like a tool kit. Canonical works would give one a vocabulary for talking about anarchism, as well as a sense of its basic values and concerns. One draws on this vocabulary in making sense of anarchism when the topic comes up, or in commenting on certain social and political events. Using canonical authors or texts as shorthand forms of communication, it becomes possible for one to connect with like-minded people. Hence, immersing oneself in a canon is also like learning a language game, enabling one to function in a particular milieu. Familiarity with a canon (whether conceived as the source of a tradition or as the distillate of one) brings one into a community, helps one enter a form of life. Further, becoming versed in a canon is also like learning how to count; it enables one to carry on. One can take additional steps in learning about the tradition, passing its lessons and values on to others, and even making one's own contributions to it.

Thinking about an anarchist canon in this way makes the canon a means by which a community establishes its boundaries, that is, proclaims or asserts its identity. For a tradition and community as diverse as anarchism, though, it would be wrong to try to establish permanent boundaries or markers. It may well be helpful to think that there are multiple canons within a broadly conceived anarchist "tradition"—individual canons either existing in isolation or in intersecting webs (Jun 2012: 134). For example, it makes sense to believe that there are different canonical works for social ecologists and for primitivists. Their respective canons would diverge (including Bookchin rather than Zerzan, for example, and vice versa), to be sure, but they might also intersect a bit (e.g., adding Mumford), even as their respective interpretations of intersecting works would undoubtedly vary. A canon might thus be seen as the textual or intellectual equivalent of an affinity group. It can even function as part of a tactical formation in a demonstration (Winston 2011; "A Book Bloc's Genealogy" 2012). Even so, recognizing diversity and multiplicity does not mean that we have rejected the very idea of a canon or caused any particular canon (of thinkers or texts) to disappear. For instance, Albert Meltzer, a critic of academic approaches to understanding anarchism, took care to cite Godwin, Proudhon, and Hegel as anarchism's philosophical precursors, and then went on to detail what he saw as anarchism's specific tenets and values. In doing so, he further noted that three important lines of theory and practice stemmed from Godwin, only one of which led to a revolutionary "'mainstream' Anarchism [that] was coherent and united, and was given body by the writings of a number of theoreticians such as Peter Kropotkin, Errico Malatesta, Luigi Galleani, and others" (Meltzer 1996: 17).

As the general issue of an anarchist canon percolates among scholars and activists, I have found it helpful to think about it partly through the lens of a similar, longstanding debate within academic political theory. The study of political theory, particularly within departments of political science, has long been identified with the study of canonical texts in Western political thought—what John Gunnell (1979) labeled the Tradition. Conceived as a series of classic works extending "from Plato to NATO," the works in this theoretical canon were exclusively the product of dead, white, European males. Until feminist and radical scholars began to challenge such canonical approaches—in literature, philosophy, and political theory—theorists largely continued to teach their subject through this lens. Although subject to critique, and occasionally revised or supplemented, the canon of texts remains an important starting point for understanding political thought. Even the most committed critics of the canon still refer to it and make use of it, if only to criticize it, as they nevertheless pursue other lines of thought.

Why should this be the case? One possible reason points to the stickiness of canons and traditions themselves, particularly when they are the subjects of inquiry. Each generation of theorists teaches the next in the way it was taught. There is also something comforting about having a canon, for it at least provides a ready description of what it is one does. Political theorists, in this context, read and talk about a particular set of old books. A second reason often given is that the canonical tradition survives because the texts themselves serve as an important source of instruction. George Kateb (2002), for example, sees canonical texts as a resource for those seeking to answer questions related to political theory (whether one regards them as "perennial" or not).

A final reason for exploring a canon involves conceiving the enterprise of political thinking in a more pragmatic context. James Tully (2002), for one, argues that the point of doing historical work in political theory is to show that hegemonic forms of thinking were situated responses to particular problems. Reading canonical works assists one in thinking about how our social and political practices develop or evolve, so that a historical survey of previous forms of political thought helps one identify alternatives to the current order. A further reason for thinking through a tradition that Tully offers is to identify the language games (i.e., vocabulary, examples, analogies, and narratives) through which political debates and struggles operate. Surveying our languages and practices, both historical and contemporary, can help us understand the interplay of problems and solutions related to governance and freedom.

There are dangers in embracing a canon, however. One such danger lies in institutionalizing, fixing, or reifying that canon.

With such a canon in place, we run the risk of misrecognizing our introductory exposure to a domain of theory or practice for the whole experience. We must avoid mistaking the map for the territory or taking the part for the whole. This is the sort of mistake that some anarchist thinkers refer to as representation—any situation in which one speaks on behalf of another, speaks about another, or speaks for another. For example, Todd May's (1994: 130) poststructuralist anarchism is built around the ethical principle that "practices of representing others to themselves—either in who they are or what they want—ought, as much as possible, to be avoided." Friendly suggestions are one thing, he suggests, but psychoanalytic interpretations are something else. Doubtless, political or governmental expressions of interest (statements about what the people of this community want) go even further; indeed, they constitute acts of authority or domination. No wonder, then, that Mikhail Bakunin rejected any authority that was externally imposed or presumed to be infallible. In any context—whether of Church or State, in therapy or the academy—his observation, "It is the characteristic of privilege and of every privileged position to kill the mind and heart of men," continues to ring true (Bakunin 1882).

May's observations remind us that we should not assume that the family resemblances that allow us to identify schools of thought, political or religious ideologies, and the like also permit us to treat these phenomena as monolithic. When those in the mainstream media invoke stereotypical frames of "anarchists," as Chris Hedges (2012) recently did, it should make one cringe. One might well reply with patient discussion of the realities of anarchist practice (Graeber 2012) or mount some form of retaliatory attack (Anonymous 2012). Regardless of what would be the most effective response, the controversy sparked by Hedges' column illustrates that the tendency to represent others to themselves is not unidirectional. When frames of "anarchists" are employed in this representational manner, some anarchists return the favor by invoking equally representational frames of "liberals" or "pacifists," "journalists" or "academics." Is the representation of comrades by our political antagonists to be decried as misleading and stereotypical, while our representation of those same antagonists to be embraced as truth spoken to power?

In drawing and maintaining boundary lines between the opponents and defenders of the various systems of domination, anarchists and other radicals seem to be involved in battles over representation—what A.K. Thompson (2010) has called "semiotic street fights" and Graeber (2009) discussed under the heading of "mythological warfare." In affirming anarchism's principled opposition to representation, then, we seem to be asserting that anarchism (unlike other forms of radicalism) is neither doctrinaire nor prescriptive, but open-ended and personal in nature. The more general goal in opposing representational practices per se, particularly those commonly employed in the media and the academy, is to avoid dictating to others what they in fact believe, feel, say, or mean by virtue of certain statements, actions, or practices. This is an admirably non-authoritarian stance, but if taken too far, it could have the effect of making it hard to say anything at all about anything of importance. At the same time we acknowledge that anarchism is inchoate and mutable, we could very likely find ourselves in a situation in which we forgo the right to speak about others except in individualistic, idiosyncratic terms. Critique, whether in the form of word or deed, would be impossible.

In this context, say, I would not be able to discuss the practices of academics, because in claiming there is a class of people called "academics," I have flattened, universalized, and otherwise unduly represented them. If I were to make claims about "platformists" or "insurrectionists"—or any other group— would I not similarly erase the diversity of views and experiences to be found among the people identifying with or active among the group? If one cannot discuss the generic for fear of committing representation, if one must instead remain in the grip of the unique and idiosyncratic, then it seems to me that conversation (let alone reflection or theory) becomes impossible. The only alternatives left would be either an autistic silence or a reliance on the ostensive—neither of which would help us advance the political aims to which we may be committed. Remaining mute before experience can amount to complicity with the evils we wish to prevent, and we cannot simply point to capitalism or domination and expect to be understood.

Again, we turn to a canon of works (in whatever form or medium) largely as an aid for understanding and changing the world before us. A canon lets us enter into a discursive context, reinterpreting it while in the course of engaging with it. The question of the canon's origins remains, however. A typical suggestion is that the canon has been determined by some authoritative panel of experts, perhaps even a vanguard. One imagines a committee of learned folk, suitably credentialed, setting forth a list of Great Books to which we must attend if we want to count ourselves as educated or cultured beings. It is rather farfetched to imagine such a panel of elder activists and theorists (or some combination thereof) coming together to debate which texts should be in a collection of the Great Books of the Anarchist World. Even though we speak of an anarchist canon, it is without question not a product of some authoritative body—no such body exists. Anarchists most likely would neither permit the establishment of one nor, if such a body were to appear, pay it any mind.

Perhaps canons emerge as parts of a spontaneous order, through the sort of repeated individual conversations mentioned above. Suppose one activist or theorist in a given milieu tells another that certain works of Noam Chomsky explain it all; the latter in turn tells another and another, and so forth. Repeated requests for Chomsky's works at book fairs and infoshops are made, along with other anarchist writers or artists who (for one reason or another) have become similarly prominent in the minds of people interested in anarchism. People outside the milieu hear about the recommendation through curious interaction, occasional eavesdropping, or governmental surveillance, say. Word spreads that one must read Chomsky, if one ever wants to understand how folks in the milieu view things. (The process continues, operating perhaps like a face-to-face equivalent of the algorithms used by Amazon.) Before we realize the gravity of our actions, "Chomsky" has thus become canonized. The people who follow will be forever induced, encouraged, pressured, or perhaps even forced to read Chomsky in order to join an affinity group or contribute to a journal, to participate effectively in the conversation, or to be welcomed within the anarchist milieu. The more voluntaristic this process of canonization is, obviously, the more acceptable it would be from an anarchist viewpoint. Even so, it seems likely that one person's or one group's freely given consent would become another's externally imposed requirement; an unfettered preference eventually mutates into an authoritative mandate.

Of course, it is entirely possible that canons do not appear in this spontaneous fashion. Regardless of how they emerge, the point is that once they are more or less formed, canons are certainly reaffirmed and reconstituted with every bit of research or commentary that is produced thereafter. As we saw above, even anarchist theorists and activists who want to write only about shared values nonetheless often make reference to canonical figures in the tradition. In this respect, the canons that emerge are not unlike the established social relationships or orthodox ideological perspectives that anarchists often oppose.

For canons to exist and persist, people—researchers and commentators, theorists and activists—need to turn to a relatively common set of works when seeking orientation or guidance. In accepting or presuming the existence of any particular canon, then, people help ensure that the canon's contents have been shaped (to a degree) by their background perspectives and by the problems they seek to solve. As such, no canon can claim universality; each and every one is inherently selective, limited, and skewed.

To this point, I have been treating the notion of a canon as if it were restricted to books and authors. Though the term is commonly understood in this fashion, it certainly has broader applicability once one recognizes that canons function much like paradigms or research programs in science—that is, canonical works function as a set of exemplary achievements (Wolin 1968; Kuhn 1970; Lakatos and Musgrave 1970). We turn to such exemplars when we have lost our way, however temporarily, and need orientation for our thinking and acting.

We thus find anarchist canons developing not only around texts and theorists, but also around practices. Consider how we tell the history of anarchism by referring to archetypal events: the Paris Commune, Haymarket, the Spanish Civil War, May 1968, the Zapatista rebellion, Seattle, etc. We gain grounding and inspiration by revisiting the challenges comrades faced and the actions they took in those circumstances and others. Consider, too, how we discuss anarchist tactics by repeatedly invoking such common methods as trashing, spiking, and the efforts of the Black Bloc; not to mention, squats, street parties, and the TAZ, or even free skools, infoshops, and the DIY movement (Franks 2006). By reading or hearing about how others have employed these tactics, we gain a repertoire of practices to experiment with and a set of experiences to share and compare. Further, in the context of prefigurative social relationships, note the discussions of archetypal organizational efforts from Reclaim the Streets to Food Not Bombs, from Earth First! to Critical Mass, from the Situationist International to the CrimethInc. Ex-Workers Collective (Shantz 2011).

How might such practices become canonical? One option is that self-identified anarchists develop a tactic or start a project, tell or write about it in anarchist forums, and thereby, get tagged with the label *anarchist*. Another option is that anarchists draw important values and lessons from the theoretical perspectives found in canonical texts and then implement them in practice. In the abstract, neither the inductive nor the deductive answer is wholly correct. Just as with a textual canon, any concrete answer requires a more detailed genealogy in order to be acceptable. What is certain is that, once again, such a canonical tool kit results when people turn to a relatively common set of practices that provide some orientation or guidance about how to act in social and political contexts. As Ward (1996: 19) observed: even though many "obscure revolutionaries, propagandists and teachers who never wrote books" certainly advanced the anarchist cause; references to the "famous names of anarchism" recurred in his book "simply because what they wrote speaks, as the Quakers say, to our condition."

Because we are in face-to-face and virtual conversation (both unmediated and mediated) with others, because we seek to build and to influence a range of social relationships, it is hard to avoid the conclusion that representation happens. Because we look around for guidance and orientation, because we seek to furnish and replenish our tool kits of concepts and practices, it seems that canons emerge as part of what seems to be a natural process. How then can we avoid the danger that a reified canon poses?

Uri Gordon (2008), in the introduction to his book, offered some useful reflections on the relations between theory and practice that may be helpful in this context. Because of their commitment to non-authoritarian values, anarchist theorists have to be very careful to avoid both representation and vanguardism in their thinking and writing. One common way of preventing these errors is for the writer to present an autobiographical sketch, thereby providing the reader with the coordinates necessary to locate the writer in sociopolitical space. This usually takes the form of a list of formative experiences and associations, of specific actions and movements of which the writer has been part. Whether or not activist bona fides have been put forth, writers often employ another device to soften the effect of their analyses—namely, presenting a list of caveats. Sometimes the caveats tell the reader what is not meant or intended by certain expressions or concerns; at other times, they put the project into the context of very limited or circumscribed aims. Here, among anarchists, it is frequently helpful to cite Graeber's (2004: 12) insightful comment that theoretical interpretations should be properly understood "not as prescriptions, but as contributions, possibilities—as gifts." In short, the basic lesson is for theorists to heed the milieu—or rather, milieux. As we know, anarchism collectively consists of a diverse set of schools and practices— none of which has any widely accepted, valid claim to representing or being *anarchism* per se. The risks posed by reference to an anarchist canon can be ameliorated if the theorist generally stays close to the practical concerns of activists.

The primary means for addressing our representational quandary seems to be one of giving critical support to the idea of an anarchist canon. Whenever a canon develops, and it likely will, one should approach reading it not as a prescriptive condition for admission into the club. Being an anarchist is not a matter of having one's library card punched in all the right places. Instead, the canon should be seen as a means of enabling scholars and activists to gain an understanding of the tradition (finding our roots) and acquire some leverage for creatively contributing to it. Canonical works do not so much *represent* (stand for) anarchism as much as they provide the means through which we can *re-present* (offer anew) some of the ideas, values, and spirit found within anarchism. In short, one should take a pragmatic approach that initially accepts the canon as an ever-available, but only apparently fixed, point of entry through which the canon itself can be transformed—as Derrida (1988: 62) observed, "iterability alters."

The second path of escape might be to continue to subject any canon that emerges to questioning and challenge. In this sense, we can use the canon not only as a point of entry, but also as a line of flight. Within the broad context of anarchism, advocates of particular (sub)traditions routinely argue with each other about the relative merit of this or that text, this or that way of thinking, this or that strategy or tactic. The existence of contending schools of thought, and the diversity of reasoning they embody, thus presents one possible way of avoiding the danger of reification. Further, particular challenges to any potentially institutionalized canon need to be encouraged on behalf of works, thinkers, and schools that are left out or left behind by the partisans of the canon. Feminists and critical race theorists have served that function for other canonical domains, as well as for anarchism, and they should continue to do so. Moreover, the gaps in the canon are a valuable source for creative renewal and revitalization of the broader tradition. Consider, for example, the insight and energy brought to anarchism from the rediscovery of Stirner's thought or Situationist practices. In general, we challenge or change a tradition largely by remembering what we have forgotten about it, by bringing to the forefront what we have otherwise left behind.

A final path for confronting the canon is for scholars and theorists, text-based as they are, to keep in mind that anarchism has long been conceived as an action-oriented tradition. Even as a mode of thought or ideology, its concerns have largely been practical ones. Theorists should pay attention to activists' expressed concerns and to informed reflections on their practices. In addition, theorists need to pay attention to the debates that often emerge among activists in the different milieux. In this sense, commentators and observers should plan to take polemics seriously, heeding and engaging with the controversies occurring among activists in different locales. Face-to-face interaction with activists helps, to be sure, but so does paying attention to the cultural products that regularly emerge in the course of various practices.

Taking such an approach to thinking about the canon also requires some self-reflexive thought about the extent to which it either violates or remains true to the anarchist spirit, however understood. Certainly, intellectual work—thinking and writing— has not been absent from various anarchist traditions past and present. Many anarchists of the nineteenth and twentieth century were writers as well as activists; many anarchists today are little different. We know of their struggles and concerns through their writings, art, conversations, deeds, and memories which have engaged and inspired us. Yet, some anarchist theorists and commentators want to insist that treating anarchism as an ideology or a political theory is a mistake from the outset. Amid assertions that all of the "isms" are "wasms," the goal seems to be to remind us that promoting anarchy is an activity, not a body of doctrine. Some activists further take on an anti-intellectual posture, criticizing those engaged in scholarship either as insufficiently anarchist or as excessively careerist, and encouraging anarchists to engage in action and nothing but action. The focus of our efforts should be on *doing*, conceived as the practical negation of an existing state of affairs (Holloway 2005: 23). In this context, "what anarchism needs is what might be called Low Theory: a way of grappling with those real, immediate questions that emerge from a transformative project" (Graeber 2004: 9).

Even as we pursue the paths highlighted above, anarchists should be careful not to exchange one form of reified thinking for another. One should not fetishize a "lower" theory that emerges from activist participation any more than one should fetishize a "higher" form of theorizing that might be evident in a canon. Properly understood, the longstanding truism about the necessary interrelationship between revolutionary theory and practice still retains some validity. How, in the final analysis, is it possible to explore a heterodox perspective via more or less canonical writers, texts, or practices? Is it even possible to hold canonical writers, texts, or practices in a critical or tentative embrace?

In some respects, the answers to these questions remain empirical or practical matters. We cannot provide them in any absolute or eternal fashion. In the experimental approach taken by some Quakers, we have to draw upon the continuing revelations that come to us in the course of our daily social and political lives. Whenever we encounter a particular element of an established canon, or confront the entirety of canonical works or practices, we must always test its worth by assessing whether or not it speaks to our condition. In other words, the arguments made for any principle or practice must stand on their own merits, independent of whether or not they were drawn from or shared by a figure from the canon (Philp 2008: 146). We must challenge the works and practices we encounter to take proper account of the lessons that we have drawn from our own experience and judgment.

REFERENCES

Alpine Anarchist Productions. 2010. "Alpine Anarchist Meets Süreyyya Evren," *Alpine Anarchist Productions* [website], August: http://www.alpineanarchist.org/r_evren_english. html.

Amster, Randall. 2012. *Anarchism Today*. Santa Barbara: Praeger.

"The Anarchist Canon Is." 2010. *Anarchist News*, November 18: http://anarchistnews.org/node/12725.

Anonymous. 2012. "Denial of Service Attack Against Chris Hedges Panel." *Infoshop News*, February 18: http://news.infoshop.org/article.php?story=20120218135548492.

Bakunin, Mikhail. [1882] 2009. "God and the State," *The Anarchist Library*, February 14: http://theanarchistlibrary.org/library/michail-bakunin-god-and-the-state.

"A Book Bloc's Genealogy." 2012. *Anarchist News*, January 8: http://anarchistnews.org/node/21353.

Derrida, Jacques. 1988. *Limited Inc*. Evanston: Northwestern University Press.

Dunn, John. 1996. *The History of Political Theory and Other Essays*. Cambridge: Cambridge University Press.

Evren, Süreyyya. 2008. "Notes on Post-Anarchism," *The Anarchist Library*: http://theanarchistlibrary.org/library/sureyyya-evren-notes-on-post-anarchism.

Franks, Benjamin. 2006. *Rebel Alliances: The Means and Ends of Contemporary British Anarchisms*. Oakland: AK Press.

Gordon, Uri. 2008. *Anarchy Alive! Anti-Authoritarian Politics from Practice to Theory.* London: Pluto Press.

Graeber, David. 2004. *Fragments of an Anarchist Anthropology.* Chicago: Prickly Paradigm Press.

Graeber, David. 2009. *Direct Action: An Ethnography.* Oakland: AK Press.

Graber, David. 2012. "Concerning the Violent Peace-Police: An Open Letter to Chris Hedges." *n+1,* February 9: http://nplusonemag. com/concerning-the-violent-peace-police.

Guérin, Daniel. 2005. *No Gods, No Masters: An Anthology of Anarchism.* Oakland: AK Press.

Gunnell, John. 1979. *Political Theory: Tradition and Interpretation.* Cambridge: Winthrop.

Hedges, Chris. 2012. "The Cancer in Occupy." *Truthdig,* February 6: http://www.truthdig.com/report/item/the_cancer_of_occupy_201 20206/.

Holloway, John. 2005. *Change the World Without Taking Power: The Meaning of Revolution Today.* London: Pluto Press.

Jun, Nathan J. 2012. *Anarchism and Political Modernity.* New York: Continuum.

Kateb, George. 2002. "The Adequacy of the Canon." *Political Theory* 30 (August): 482–505.

Kuhn, Thomas. 1970. *The Structure of Scientific Revolutions.* 2nd enlarged ed. Chicago: University of Chicago Press.

Lakatos, Imre, and Alan Musgrave. 1970. *Criticism and the Growth of Knowledge.* Cambridge: Cambridge University Press.

May, Todd. 1994. *The Political Philosophy of Poststructuralist Anarchism.* University Park: Pennsylvania State University Press.

Thompson, A.K. 2010. *Black Bloc, White Riot: Anti-Globalization and the Geneaology of Dissent.* Oakland: AK Press.

Ward, Colin. 1996. *Anarchy in Action.* London: Freedom Press.

Ward, Colin. 2004. *Anarchism: A Very Short Introduction.* Oxford: Oxford University Press.

Winston, Ali. 2011. "Explainer: What Is a 'Book Bloc'?" *The Informant,* June 20: http://informant.kalwnews.org/2011/06/ex plainer-what-is-a-book-bloc/.

Wittgenstein, Ludwig. 1958. *Philosophical Investigations,* trans. G.E.M. Anscombe. 3rd ed. New York: Macmillan.

Wolin, Sheldon. 1968. "Paradigms and Political Theories." In *Politics and Experience,* eds. Preston King and B.C. Parekh, 125–152. Cambridge: Cambridge University Press.

Anarchist Developments in Cultural Studies
ISSN: 1923-5615
2013.1: Blasting the Canon

Canon and Identity
Thoughts on the Hyphenated Anarchist

James J. Miller*

ABSTRACT
The topic of canon is more than a discussion revolving around texts, historical figures, or someone's status in relation to that canon. This paper argues that the canon itself includes a way of applying and understanding one's identity in the canon. I explore the ways that identities are negotiated within the canon and seek an understanding of the workings of the canon. Taking the relations between anarchism, queer theory, feminism and religion as texts, this paper analyzes the canon and suggests directions for making the canon more anarchist by understanding the canon and its relationship to identity through the folklore of myth.

KEYWORDS
canon, narrative, identity, queer theory, religion, folklore, action

Generally, when one is in a conversation with a colleague or comrade about canon, the discussion revolves around texts, historical figures, or someone's status in relation to that canon. Questions of place in the canon or validity in the canon are the most frequent topics. There has been much ink spilled on the

---

* James J. Miller holds an MA in folk studies and is currently pursing a PhD in humanities at the University of Louisville, Kentucky, USA. His research focuses on narrative, radical politics, intentional communities, and vernacular religion. James teaches at Western Kentucky University and is currently focusing his research on the radical elements in monastic and ascetic communities in the United States. He lives in Bowling Green, Kentucky with his wife, friends, and cats.

content of the canon, who is a part of the canon, and what this body of information has meant. I am not sure that many words, print or otherwise, have been spent on our understanding of the meaning of the term canon from an anarchist perspective. This is a category or genre that tends to be assumed, understood as natural and allowed to pass by. This paper argues that this is one of the primary problems with the canon, and it seeks an understanding of the workings of the canon and to suggest directions for making the canon more anarchist.

Canon is often understood as the best of the best, necessary writers, the starting points or the formative texts and peoples associated with a genre, discipline or ideology. This includes essays, zines, groups, events, books and the people who wrote and produced these items. These items do not act on their own—they are interlaced and constitute a larger narrative. The zine or text has to be understood in a context. The canon and what we believe is a part of it are the building blocks for a narrative about us; those who adhere to the canon. The canon is the stuff of analysis, from which we build critiques and future actions and through which we define ourselves. The canon can be understood as a narrative that constructs our identity. It is part of the story we tell about ourselves. Because of the link between narrative and identity, we should understand the canon as a myth.

Myth is, as morphology, often used in differentiating ways. This paper will borrow and use the definition of William Bascom from the field of folklore. A myth in this paradigm is an origin story that is not necessarily given a truth value (Bascom 1965, 4). The myth is the narrative that is used to form and constitute and define a group, and most often is constituted as an origin story. The creation narratives present in many cultures are myths that define humanity, its features, goals and ends for the communities that have created these myths. Other narratives are added to this base narrative to create a full story arch for the community.

Looking at the canon as a narrative arch, we can then use canon to understand the identity of a community. Treated as a myth, the canon, then, is both a prescriptive narrative and descriptive narrative. One uses the canon to understand what is anarchist and what is not anarchist. The individual is defining identity through this set of texts, authors, ideas and even actions as relationships to others in a narrative structure with the accompanying tropes, devices and nuances. I can use the canon to describe texts that are anarchist and prescribe anarchist actions or create new texts by applying these narratives as a filter. Further, the way texts are used and understood will be a part of the canon as well. Rogers Abrahams says that, "identity has become the encompassing term for cultural, social, and spiritual wholeness. It also emerges in discussions of territorial integrity, often as a rhetorical ploy in struggles for maintaining domain" (Abrahams 2003, 198). This is an apt and useful definition for canon, as the canon is not only what we use to include and create, but also to preclude and destruct.

Identity then, is what is at stake when defining the canon and thus what our understanding of canon is shaping. How we understand the canon will dictate how we understand identity, both for ourselves and others. In everyday speech we use this idea to define who is or is not anarchist and how we are to understand ourselves in relationship to them, their writing and their actions. When I define the anarchist canon, I am describing what it is to be an anarchist for me and often for others. At the same time, I am defining what it is not anarchist and the "other" in relation to this identity. Asserting an identity and applying the canon then both constitutes the "I" and the "you" or "other."

Because canon structures identity, it also contributes to the construction of narratives. These narratives then, have a reciprocal effect on the canon, defining what can and cannot be included. "Identity seems to be built on notions of an ideal life-plan or an archetypal map of the actual world" (Abrahams 2003, 199). This life plan or map is a projected narrative on history and the future. The narrative force of the canon shows that it deals with more than our texts and historical figures and that actions; lifestyles, choices and developments are also part of the canon. It has the power to map out a person's life, the life of a movement, the life of a particular action or event or even how I judge and categorize the lives and narratives of others. The anarchist narrative, however I form it, becomes my standard for critiquing and judging just like a canon.

Insofar as students of expressive culture have looked for texts, objects, and figures that represent such larger wholes, identity has been used more to refer to groups rather than individuals. But unlike other such keywords as tradition or authenticity, the semantic domain of identity is not tied to styles, but rather to (apparent) matters of substance, states of being, or existence in its display (Abrahams 2003, 205).

The role that canon plays in identity-formation thus helps illuminate how we constitute ourselves and the process of our becoming. This means that the idea of canon itself has to be treated gravely: the discussion is not just about content, but about the evaluation of identity. The canon can constitute a system for comparison, inclusion and exclusion within the content.

What my group defines as the canon or the content for the identity for the group is much deeper than a bit of history or a reading list. This defines the ideas, methods and identities that are performable for acceptance and solidarity. As much as anarchism seeks to redefine social and political affiliations and roles, it is itself subject to the ways these forces produce identity. To reiterate the point made earlier: identity can be prescriptive. When one seeks to become a part of the group there are forms, texts, actions and the like to which one must adhere in order to be filed into the ranks and before one can be called comrade. Likewise, if one already accepts these texts, ideas or actions then they can be described as being a part of the group. One may not self identify with a particular group but may be judged to be in the group, at least by definition, descriptively.

The issues raised by identity and canon are complex and in order to understand them better, I want to use a couple short examples. I am going to look at three areas within the anarchist paradigm—queer theory, feminism and religion—that are somewhat contested within and between different groups. This paper is not seeking a complete history of the identity formation within these groups; rather, a few examples of how these identities are contested and are made problematic will suffice to explore the processes inherent in the anarchist canon. This paper seeks to recognize how the canon's content can be used and applied in order to reveal a "canonical method" in anarchism.

One of the most apparent features of anarchism, even for outsiders, is the naming structure. Naming is definitely a part of identity formation and recognition. Terms or titles designate, or index, a canon or a set of attributes associated with the referent of that term. Walk up and down the rows at an anarchist book fair and terms like anarcho-queer, anarcha-feminist, anarcho-syndicalist, Christian anarchism, Islamic anarchism, etc. pop up. These are titles that index definitions and bracket identities off from each other. A second common feature is the hyphenation of terms. These terms are interesting for our study as they represent a negotiation of the narratives. They have developed to describe a new identity, the result of a sort of Gestalt convergence that has reached a point in which it needs to be named.

Terms are not just shifts within the anarchist paradigm—they are the attempts to meld, mix, and negotiate identity across groups or canons. These hyphens mix two terms that have their own somewhat discrete canon. For example: Queer theory has its own history and canon apart from the anarchists, as does feminism. For a particular group of individuals, neither term 'queer' nor 'anarchist' adequately describe their experience. The new hyphenated term, 'anarcho-queer,' not only brings together two groups it also signals the emergence of a new identity, outside the binomial represented linguistically by their juxtaposition.

There is a set of negations going on here. The hyphenated term is a space in which canons can be negated and added to in order to create a new canon or myth and in turn to construct one's identity within a group. In placing terms together, there are at least two canons that are being negated in part. I cannot assume that the anarcho-queer theorist is the same as a queer theorist, because in this term there is an indication that they are not only or fully a queer theorist. There is a negation of part, known or unknown, of the canon of queer when I add anarchist. My preconceived notion is negated and a space is formed that can be filled with new information. This is the creating of a void, as one who reads or hears these terms needs to be informed about this new identity. The same can be said about the anarchist canon in relation to the anarcho-queer theorist. There is something about anarchism that does not fully describe the anarcho-queer theorist, and to read the standard anarchist canon would not lead me to an anarcho-queer critique; it is lacking. Anarchism's completeness in relation to the subject is negated by the hyphenated term in this context.

Anarcha-feminist as a term has developed through critiques of freedom, action and issues of inclusion and exclusion. The zine *What the Fuck is Anarcha-feminism* illustrates how these new terms assert a new identity in the face of feminism. This zine is basically a list of negations of the expectations of someone adopting a feminist identity and functioning with a popular feminist canon. The negations are presented both through a textual critique as well as a list of terms that describe anarcha-feminism (e.g., london anarcha-feminist kolektiv n.d.). A new canon and a new way to read the old canon (thus creating a new canon) negates and asserts parts of the old canon to create a new one. Ideas of actions, goals, and methods redefine the narrative. Popular ways of action in feminism such as voting are negated and brought into question. Anthologies like *Colonize This!* (Hernández and Rehman 2002) disrupt and negate the old narrative along race and color lines as well. These identities are asserted because the canon currently holding the monopoly on identity is thought to leave out or neglect a key part of someone's identity and struggle.

Colonize This! is "a collection of writings by young women of color that testifies to the movement—political and physical—of a new generation of global citizens, activists, and artists" (Hernández and Rehman 2002, xi). This text fills the void in the literature, one that was presumably created by the exclusion, or passive negation, of a dominant group. This text challenges the assumption that 'feminism' prior to this text was full or complete, as well as many of the paradigm's conclusions and actions that flowed from it. Narratives by women of color index a history of white middle class feminism and the ways that it excluded narratives that did not fit its canon. That isn't to say that these feminists as a whole outright rejected these narratives but that their feminism had blind spots and omissions.

Sheila Jeffreys in *Unpacking Queer Politics* describes the early relationships with lesbian feminism and queer politics and states, "Queer politics, then, was created in contradistinction to lesbian feminism. The dreadfulness of lesbian feminism was its founding myth" (Jefferys 2003, 35). In this example, the negation of the one narrative creates the next. The myth or the starting narrative is born out of redefinition or the negation of another myth. This process is a part of an identity-formation process. This new term outraged lesbian feminists who see the term as exclusionary, not inclusive. In this case, canon or identity is being negated and supplemented in order to fully express and index a new emergent reality. But a new term will have the same problems of the old one: "When used to refer to self or group of identification, the word seems to emancipate, yet when used to refer to others it too often imprisons" (Abrahams 2003, 207). Identity and language of identity in one swipe both include and exclude. The limitation reflects the tendency to treat labels and titles as complete and discrete.

How can there be a relationship between terms when the starting premise is so hostile? One recent book which is not in the anarchist canon per se, *Feminism is Queer* (2010) sheds light on this question. The book was written by Mimi Marinucci and is subtitled "The Intimate Connection between Queer and Feminist Theory." It attempts to overcome the problems inherent in the application of terms derived from identity and the use of canon. It suggests that one might have a personal narrative that feminists and queers describe, and which are useful to the individual. But Marinucci questions the extent to which one can really be in both camps. And more importantly for our discussion, whether one can one be in both camps and, simultaneously, an anarchist? The discussion highlights a paradox: the need to negotiate identity within different frameworks for identity to be fully actualized and the simultaneous exclusionary effects of identify-forming descriptive terms for individuals seeking actualization.

Marinucci ponders the suggestion that feminism "as a form of identity politics, will inevitably fail because the identity categories, such as sex and gender, that promise to unite a group of people are always mitigated by additional categories that ultimately divide members of the group"—an application of Simone de Beauvoir's point that making categories (or identities) is a part of the human condition (Marinucci 2010, 68). This is a catch that actually applies to all identity categories. This problem of inclusion militates against the statement— the title of Marinucci's book—that "feminism is queer." The statement that feminism equals queer is an equivocation and the book needs the qualification in its subtitle to soften the ontological implication. Negations brought about by assertions of category would ultimately destroy one or the other identity.

The logic of this argument suggests that it is impossible to make the anarcho-queer compatible with anarcho-feminism. However, compatibility is not necessary as long as the narratives do not completely negate each other. This I think is the final conclusion/ lesson of *Feminism is Queer*. The relationship between these theories, both historical and contemporary, can produce the necessary links for unity. Nevertheless, the question remains: how do communities with differentiating basic myths, backgrounds and identities work together without negating each other and inclusively? Is this an issue of terms that only new terms can fix? My answer is no: we will only fall into the problems with the terms described above. Could more inclusive terms be used? No, because at some point, terms would become so broad as to lose their ability to describe, prescribe and define a referent. If all texts we liked were a part of the anarchist canon the designation and language may lose its meaning.

Paulo Freire offers some insight into why these identities and names are important to us as theorists: "If true commitment to the people, involving the transformation of the reality by which they are oppressed, requires a theory of transforming action, this theory cannot fail to assign the people a fundamental role in the transformation process" (Freire 2000, 126) He continues: "It is essential that the oppressed participate in the revolutionary process with an increasingly critical awareness of their role as subjects of the transformation" (Freire 2000, 127). Language gives subjects a way to understand themselves, and they are able to manipulate their self-understandings through the use of language. The names and markers we give to ourselves and others signify our role both in the process of change and in the process of oppression. The terms and signals we use for ourselves place us within the narrative of the canon.

If the canon is understood as a way to fit into a larger set or related narratives, then many of these smaller categories are not as important as when we are defining freely our relationships within these networks. This is one way to get to praxis and to keep other valid narratives from negating our own to the point that solidarity breaks down. Much more could be said in relationship to the histories and relationships between anarcha-feminism and anarcho-queer as well as queer and feminist theory. The point here is that identity understood within the lens of praxis can allow us to use these theories as tools for connections and less as distinct categories of difference. The hyphenated term indicates an identity outside of the canon but related to it. This approach can be used for other groups who may be able to work with the anarchist canon or narrative, even though they do not identify with it.

With the previous example we saw seemingly opposing groups being brought together through a process of definition in relation to a larger narrative. Another way that this negotiation between identities can be achieved is through the associations of the narratives. These groups can make their identity and their narrative acceptable to anarchists by showing that the anarchist canon is integral or reflected in their tradition. This is also apparent in Marinucci's work insofar as she attempts to ground the narratives of feminism and queer theory within each other by showing their intimate link and avoiding negations. Another group that employs this approach is the religious anarchists.

Alexandre Christoyannopoulos quotes Ciaron O'Reilly to argue that Christian anarchism, a religious anarchism, "is not an attempt to synthesize two systems of thought," but is rather a "realization that the premise of anarchism is apparent in Christianity." So what is the premise or kernel that is found that links his belief to anarchism? For him it seems to be an issue of the state—in his view, Christianity, in its final logical end, would abolish the state (Christoyannopoulos, 2011, 6). The anarchist feature of a stateless society is said to be an integral part of the Christian religion, in this argument, and is thus linked to the anarchist canon. Is that enough?

For some the answer is no. For most of the "no's," I would assume it is the assertion of a deity or the other ideas associated with Christianity, real or imagined, that presents the obstacle.

Here we find that a link to the canon is not enough; the canon has to be applied correctly and has to have specific aesthetic attributes. Abolishing the state isn't enough; the rejection of authority has to be pushed further. That push, or method, for applying the canon is often more a part of the canon that we want to admit. The anarchist canon is more than the set of goals; there is a way in which it needs to work. The Christian anarchist has stated that within their group the same end is desired, but the deity remains. Is the acknowledgement of the deity sufficient to place the identity outside the anarchist fold? Is the negation of a deity a part of the canon itself or is it a logical outcome of how the canon is used? These have to be worked out in a discussion of the canon.

The Christian anarchist sees the idea of God and the canon differently to the non-religious anarchist. To this argument, Christoyannopoulos reiterates Dorothy Day's response that God, if in existence, is not something you can reject (Christo-yannopoulos 2011, 6). It would be akin to being against gravity because it pulls you to the ground and oppresses you. The canon not only prescribes what and who, but how we think. In this we see the way a deity is understood in specific terms by the anarchist canon. For the Christian Anarchist, deity is a starting point, and for the anarchist canon, deity is a point to contest.

The religious anarchist, like other types of anarchist, may arrive at their anarchist conclusions from routes outside the anarchist canon. From a religious perspective, one could pull the rejection of property from St John Chrysostom or St Basil the Great. St Basil the Great rejected property above need as theft, irrational, and in some cases, murder (see Schroeder 2009). These two 4th-century writers are not included in the anarchist canon. Is the canon open to include, even as a side note, other texts that come to similar positions or conclusions? Can the parts of the canon one uses be different if the conclusions are similar or the same as the anarchist? If the canon one pulls from is different, can one still be called an anarchist? I think it would be problematic to claim that all anarchists come to their conclusions about the deity in the same way: Harold Barclay does a good job outlining the complexities and currents within the canonical anarchist thinkers' writings on religion in his essay "Anarchist Confrontations with Religion" (in Jun and Wahl 2010). There needs to be a method of negotiating the canon itself which is flexible, but which also retains much of its original make-up in order to account for the complexities of multiple identities.

The hyphenated terms are used to close the gap between two

narratives in the attempt to bring them together, while the non-hyphenated terms make a claim to an inherent link in the ideologies. We can also see this process in the book *Feminism is Queer*. The Christian anarchist is making a similar move in claiming that "Christianity is Anarchist." Other religions may also make a similar claim. The terms themselves are a part of the formation of canon in that these terms reflect how canon is being put together and how the canon will be interpreted within these communities. As an author, I am sympathetic to the non-hyphenated term in that I would like to assume that I can claim a link without dealing with another narrative.

The non-hyphenated term may have more to do with my existence in a context in which other parts of my identity are not questioned or directly marginalized. As a white, heterosexual, male, my personal narrative is not challenged by the overarching myth in the anarchist canon. As much as I attempt to work against some of the difficult elements in the anarchist canon, the religious aspect is what I find problematic. This explains my concern with Christian and religious anarchisms and the canon. The choices in terms may also reflect one's allegiances and solidarity networks, and act as a way to identify others with similar goals and needs within the structure of canon. These terms and their application is then a part of the canon itself.

CONCLUSION

How we use and apply the aspects of the anarchist canon as a part of the canon itself. How far do I have to push the tenets of anarchism? How much can I supplement the canon with writers, tactics, figures, and other texts that are important to aspects of my own identity without either negating others' identities or having my own negated? As anarchists we have to look at more than just the content of the canon. Viewing the canon through identity politics helps us to understand how we are interacting with each other in profound ways: negotiating, negating, validating, and recreating ourselves and others.

In what ways can we negotiate the canon and construct identity without negating others identity? How much solidarity are we willing to lose, gain, or overlook? In this essay, I have tried to give an overview of what the canon is as canon. In the relationships and histories of anarcha-feminism, anarcho-queer, and religious anarchist identities, we see the ways in which the use of canon as a myth and constructed identity defines, validates, and negates narratives within and between these groups. As we consider the canon, these realities and questions must be a part of the process and discussion in order to ensure that the canon is truly anarchist. Cindy Milstein writes that anarchism is "a compelling political philosophy because it is a way of asking the right questions without seeking a monopoly on the right answers" (Milstein 2010, 73). In order to take this definition seriously, not only does the content of the canon need to be anarchist, but the way we interact with that content, the praxis of the canon, must be inclusive, radical and be truly anarchist.

REFERENCES

Abrahams, Roger D. 2003. "Identity." In *Eight Words for the Study of Expressive Culture*, ed. Burt Feintuch, 198–222. Chicago: University of Illinois Press.

Barclay, Harold. 2010. "Anarchist Confrontations with Religion." In *New Perspectives on Anarchism*, eds. Nathan J. Jun and Shane Wahl, 169–185. Lanham: Lexington Books.

Bascom, William. 1965. "The Forms of Folklore Prose." *The Journal of American Folklore* 78.307: 3–20.

Christoyannopoulos, Alexandre. 2011. *Christian Anarchism: A Political Commentary on the Gospel*. Exeter: Imprint Press.

Freire, Paulo. 2010. *Pedagogy of the Oppressed*. New York: Continuum.

Jeffreys, Sheila. 2003. *Unpacking Queer Politics*. Cambridge: Polity Press.

london anarcha-feminist kolektiv. n.d. "what the fuck is anarcha-feminism anyway?": http://www.grassrootsfeminism.net/cms/sites/default/files/anarchafeminism.pdf.

Marinucci, Mini. 2010. *Feminism is Queer: The Intimate Connection Between Queer and Feminist Theory*. New York: Zed Books.

Milstein, Cindy. 2010. *Anarchism and Its Aspirations*. Oakland: AK Press.

St Basil the Great. 2009. *On Social Justice*, ed. and trans. C. Paul Schroeder. Yonkers: St Vladimirs Seminary Press.

Anarchist Developments in Cultural Studies
ISSN: 1923-5615
2013.1: Blasting the Canon

The Possibilities of Anarchist History
Rethinking the Canon and Writing History

Matthew S. Adams[*]

ABSTRACT

While the study of anarchism has undergone a renaissance in recent years, historical scholarship has been a relatively minor aspect of this renewed focus. Presenting an historiographical examination of the main forms of writing on anarchist ideas, this article argues that the predominance of 'canonistic' approaches to anarchism is in part a consequence of the disciplinary dominance of political theory in the study of anarchism. Despite anarchism's complex intellectual history, intellectual historians continue to overlook this rich political tradition. The article concludes by reflecting on the possibilities offered by an intellectual history of anarchism informed by recent methodological developments in cultural history. Not only does this allow us to see beyond the canon, but it also offers new insights on anarchism's most influential thinkers.

KEYWORDS

anarchism, classical anarchism, post-anarchism, canonization, political theory, social history of ideas, intellectual history, cultural history, Peter Kropotkin

[*] Matthew S. Adams completed a PhD on the intellectual history of British anarchism at the University of Manchester in 2011 and is currently teaching modern history at Durham University, UK. His work has appeared in the journals *Anarchist Studies*, *European Review of History*, *History of Political Thought* and *History of European Ideas*. He wishes to thank Ruth Kinna, Catherine Feely, and Martin Adams for their useful comments on earlier drafts of this article.

INTRODUCTION: ANARCHISM AND THE HISTORY OF HISTORY

In the year that Proudhon published his most famous work, *Qu'est-ce que la propriéte?*, Thomas Carlyle was busy delivering a series of lectures that set out the necessary path for the study of history. Published the following year as *Heroes, Hero-Worship and the Heroic in History* (1841), the book set out Carlyle's position that certain 'heroic' individuals were able to recognise the underlying reality of human affairs and act with confidence and audacity—interventions that structured the historical process. 'All things that we see standing accomplished in the world,' he suggested, are the 'material result, the practical realisation and embodiment, of Thoughts that dwelt in the Great Men sent into the world.'[1] History, understood as the narrativization of this process, should therefore concern itself with the thoughts and deeds of these gifted individuals.

Carlyle's strictures for the proper study of history will no doubt seem unsatisfactory to readers of *Anarchist Developments in Cultural Studies*. The glaring gender bias aside, the idea that history is best understood through the actions of Bismarcks and Bonapartes is likely to be dismissed as wholly inappropriate for fathoming the complexities of the past. Yet Carlyle's musings on method exercised a significant role in the early development of history as a discipline, and, in a way, his understanding of history as defined by the actions of 'great men' has endured in certain forms of anarchist scholarship. That is, at least, how critics of the canonisation of anarchism would probably conceive the issue, seeing the reduction of anarchism to the writings of a select band of thinkers as subliminally buying into Carlyle's understanding of the proper method for studying history. 'Great man' history would become entrenched with the professionalization of history, not necessarily a consequence of familiarity with Carlyle's work itself, but parallel developments in Germany echoed many of his assumptions. Leopold Von Ranke was motivated, like Carlyle, by the desire to uncover a providential hand in the unfolding of human history and railed against the destabilising impact of the dual revolution, which helps explain their focus on the heroic. For Ranke, however, this was less the actions of individuals than those of the 'Great Powers' whose actions textured the historical

---

[1] Thomas Carlyle, *On Heroes, Hero-Worship and the Heroic in History: In One Volume* (London: Chapman & Hall, 1898), 1. For a useful discussion of Carlyle's understanding of history, consider John Morrow, *Thomas Carlyle* (London: Continuum, 2006), 161–191.

fabric.[2] Seen in broad terms the distinction meant little, although it does help us see Ranke, fittingly, in the context of a pre-unification Germany fixated by questions of tradition and power. Although Ranke's influence was largely methodological, his call for historians to infiltrate the archive reflected the focus on political history as the principal type of scholarship, and it was this defence of empiricism as much as his own work in diplomatic history that informed the subsequent development of history—especially in Britain.[3]

The professionalization of history therefore runs parallel to the development of modern nationalism, but less indulging readers might object that this narrative of personified great powers has little do with anarchism, a political movement whose *raison d'être* is a deep suspicion of such interpretations of politics and history. For Peter Kropotkin though, someone who took a deep interest in history, the changing fashions of historical scholarship were relevant to his broader political project. Writing at the turn of the twentieth-century, when diplomatic history was at its height, Kropotkin polemically suggested that the type of history represented by Ranke was becoming increasingly passé. Pursuing his ontological theory that modern scientific developments had served to decentre the universe, Kropotkin ventured that 'the sciences that treat man' displayed a similar fragmentation:

Thus we see that history, after having been the history of kingdoms, tends to become the history of nations and then the study of individuals. The historian wants to know how the members, of which such a nation was composed, lived at such a time, what their beliefs were, their means of existence, what ideal society was visible to them, and what means they possessed to march towards this idea . . . . And

---

[2] John Burrow, *A History of Histories* (New York: Alfred A. Knopf, 2008), 431.
[3] Ranke's empiricism is captured in his oft-quoted dictum that history 'merely wants to show how, essentially, things happened': quoted in John Warren, 'The Rankean Tradition in British historiography, 1850 to 1950,' in Stefan Berger et al. (eds.), *Writing History: Theory and Practice* (London: Bloomsbury Academic, 2010), 25 [22–39]. This is often also translated as, 'Its aim is merely to show how things actually were': see John Tosh, *The Pursuit of History: Aims, Methods and New Directions in the Study of Modern History* (London: Longman, 1989), 11.

by the action of all those forces, formerly neglected, he interprets the great historical phenomena.[4]

Crucially, these were not the individuals of Carlyle's dyspeptic historical narratives, but the actions of those hitherto hidden from the historian's gaze. It was a method that Kropotkin would later strive to apply himself in his monumental *The Great French Revolution* (1910), a book that reiterated his view that the 'beating heart' of the Revolution lay in the streets of Paris, not in the National Assembly.[5] Although conspicuously short on evidence, Kropotkin's argument that the historical epistemology had shifted downwards in the rank of orders was not an exaggeration. True, 'high politics, constitutional, diplomatic and military history' continued to dominate the intellectual landscape, but it is possible to trace the emergence of precursors to the economic, social, and cultural histories that would rise to prominence in the mid-twentieth century, and undermine the hegemony of historical scholarship that took political elites as their starting point.[6]

'Classic' cultural history emerged with Johan Huizinga and Jacob Burckhardt, which looked to the canon of high art, great literature, and philosophical speculation to uncover deeper truths about the middle ages.[7] Tellingly, there were tentative steps in the direction of labour history, notably in the work of the Webbs and the Hammonds, a development that acted in concert with the emergence of the working-class as a political agent.[8] The growing

---

[4] Peter Kropotkin, 'Anarchism: Its Philosophy and Ideal,' in George Woodcock (ed.), *Fugitive Writings* (Montréal: Black Rose Books, 1993), 99–121.

[5] Peter Kropotkin, *The Conquest of Bread* (Cambridge: Cambridge University Press, 1995), 27.

[6] Burrow, *A History of Histories*, 438.

[7] Peter Burke, *What is Cultural History?* (Cambridge: Polity, 2004), 7.

[8] Sidney Webb (1859-1947) and Beatrice Webb (1858-1943) were the husband and wife team who helped found the Fabian Society and played an important role in the foundation of the London School of Economics and Political Science in 1895. Both published widely on economic and social issues, and historical study featured prominently in their approach, with economic history featuring from the outset on the curriculum of the LSE. Their co-authored book *The History of Trade Unionism* (1894) was an influential, and frequently reprinted, work. John Lawrence Hammond (1872-1949) and Barbara Hammond (1873-1961) were another husband and wife team who co-wrote pioneering historical works, especially in the fields of labour and social history. Their most significant books were the trilogy *The Village Labour: 1760-1832: A Study*

influence of Marxism would later concretize this disciplinary boundary and would also greatly influence the emergence of social history as the century progressed, although this sub-discipline also had German roots, in Karl Lamprecht's rejection of the 'Rankean orthodoxy' and its concentration on 'great men.'[9] Understanding the past through the machinations of political elites was falling from favour.

This overview of the development of history as a discipline is, inevitably, cursory. In the twentieth century, with disciplinary specialization, it becomes less fitting to talk of a dominant historical epistemology as historians began to splinter into various factions and make claims for the primacy of their own approach to the past. This process began at the end of the nineteenth century, indeed, the words 'specialism' and 'special-ization' date from the 1860s and 1870s, a fact that makes Kropot-kin's pursuit of a synthetic philosophy appear somewhat out of time.[10] While historical practice has diversified, the study of anarchist history has remained largely impervious to these disciplinary changes. Given that these territorial debates have usually taken place in an overtly academic context this is not necessarily surprising, although it is peculiar that while the renewed interest in anarchism has tended to cut across disciplines—as the existence of *ADCS* testifies and the articles in *Anarchist Studies* repeatedly affirm— there have not been parallel developments in historical writing on anarchism. David Goodway lamented this fact in 1989, noting that:

> Anarchist historiography is a frustrating field, tradition-ally tending to be hagiographic or . . . antiquarian in approach. When it comes to their own past—or, indeed, the past in general—anarchists have not subjected it to radical analysis or acted as the innovators they have been in other disciplines.

There was, however, cause for optimism, and Goodway opined that the major innovation in 'historiography *tout court*' was the

---

in the Government of England before the Reform Bill (1911), *The Town Labourer: 1760-1832: the New Civilization* (1917), and *The Skilled Labourer, 1760-1832* (1919).

[9] Peter Burke, *History & Social Theory* (New York: Cornell University Press, 1992), 14.

[10] Stefan Collini, *Absent Minds: Intellectuals in Britain* (Oxford: Oxford University Press, 2006), 454.

growing intellectual self-confidence of social history, promising exciting research into anarchism as a popular movement.[11] His paean for social history was itself a product of the time, but Goodway's criticism of the lack of historical attention paid to anarchism is an enduring issue. In what follows I want to consider the relation between the underdeveloped nature of anarchist historiography, something that is thankfully beginning to change, and the prominence of the canon in commentaries on anarchist ideas. The idea of the anarchist canon, it is argued, has its roots in the disciplinary dominance of political theory in anarchist studies' recent past.[12] That analyses of anarchism published between the early 1970s and mid-1990s were primarily concerned with positioning anarchism in relation to more established political ideologies and strived to uncover anarchism's contribution to the grander questions of human existence, the effect has been to perpetuate the canonical approach, rather than appreciate the vicissitudes of its history.

A casualty in this has been historical scholarship sensitive to the contextual formulation of anarchist arguments, an approach that would focus less on anarchists' relation to the supposedly timeless problematics of philosophy and more on the immediately significant issues confronting anarchist thinkers. To appreciate the complexities of this contextualism is to uncover a fresh way of approaching anarchism's past, one that holds before it the chance to nuance our understanding of the canon, or, if necessary, reject it completely. With this objective in mind, this paper closes with a brief statement in the spirit of Goodway's twenty-three years ago, of some of the potential avenues for anarchist history, and a reflection on promising recent developments—especially apparent in the context of transnational history.

CONSUMING ANARCHIST IDEAS AND FORGING THE CANON: POLITICAL THEORY, HISTORY AND ANTHOLOGY

---

[11] David Goodway, 'Introduction,' in David Goodway (ed.), *For Anarchism: History, Theory, and Practice* (London: Routledge, 1989), 7 [1-22].

[12] Nicolas Walter offered a useful, if now somewhat dated, bibliographic overview to writing on anarchism in 1971. The essay lamented the paucity of historical writing on anarchism, but was confident that this would change imminently. See Nicolas Walter, 'Anarchism in Print: Yesterday and Today,' in David E. Apter and James Joll (eds.), *Anarchism Today* (London: Macmillan, 1971), 127–144.

Given the links between German philosophy and the 'great man' approach to the past—Carlyle was himself heavily influenced by the idealist tradition—it is fitting that one of the first to conceive anarchist history in canonical terms should be German. Even more significant is the fact that Paul Eltzbacher's book, first published in 1900 as *Der Anarchismus* and then translated into English by the American individualist-anarchist Steven Byington in 1908 as *Anarchism*, should be republished in 2004 with the catechismal title *The Great Anarchists: Ideas and Teachings of Seven Major Thinkers.*[13] Eltzbacher's rather dry analysis of anarchism centred upon what has since become a familiar collection of names. William Godwin is placed, at least in chrono-logical terms, at the apex of the tradition, followed by Proudhon, Stirner, Bakunin, and Kropotkin. Included at the end are Benjamin Tucker—perhaps contributing to Tucker's willingness to print the book in his publishing house—and Leo Tolstoy, a figure who has a more ambiguous relationship to anarchism than the rest, with the possible exception of Stirner. These names largely comprise what has come to be seen as the anarchist canon, although there have been skirmishes in the border areas as various historians make particular claims for individual thinkers, or dispute the inclusion of others. George Woodcock's highly influential survey *Anarchism: A History of Libertarian Ideas and Movements* (1962), itself approaching canonical status, followed Eltzbacher in identifying Godwin, Stirner, Proudhon, Bakunin, Kropotkin, and Tolstoy as innovators of anarchism while demoting Tucker. The popularity of Woodcock's book, when juxtaposed against the development of anarchist studies over the last twenty-years, goes some way to explain the predominance of a rather hermetic pantheon of key thinkers.

The modest revival of interest in anarchist ideas between the 1970s and early 1990s was primarily a result, in academic circles at least, of the renewed gaze of the political theorist. A result of this was that texturing the contours of the anarchist tradition and

---

[13] Paul Eltzbacher, *Der Anarchismus* (Berlin: Topos Verlag, 1900); Paul Eltzbacher, *Anarchism* (London: A.C. Fifield, 1909); Paul Eltzbacher, *The Great Anarchists: Ideas and Teachings of Seven Major Thinkers* (New York: Dover, 2004). I am indebted to two works in particular for their discussion of approaches to anarchist history: see Ruth Kinna, *Anarchism: A Beginner's Guide* (Oxford, 2005), 3–43 (especially 10–15), and Lucien van der Walt and Michael Schmidt, *Black Flame: The Revolutionary Class Politics of Anarchism and Syndicalism* (Edinburgh: AK Press, 2009), 34–40.

clarifying the contextual forces that shaped anarchist ideas in the first place became less important than uncovering the contribution of anarchists to political thought in general. Perhaps spurred by works like Robert Paul Wolff's *In Defense of Anarchism* (1970), a book that was silent on the history of anarchist thought, there was a movement towards tying down the tradition with the hope of judging its general contribution to human knowledge. R.B. Fowler's article 'The Anarchist Tradition of Political Thought' (1972), which remains influential, paved the way, buying into Eltzbacher's canon, albeit peculiarly jettisoning Tucker in favour of Alexander Herzen.[14] April Carter's *The Political Theory of Anarchism* published the year before Fowler's article held a more catholic view of the anarchist canon, even if it did continue to set the analysis in the frame of canonical liberal theory, incorporating overlooked figures like Alexander Berkman, as well as being sensitive to the contemporary anarchisms of Alex Comfort and Paul Goodman, amongst others.[15] Nevertheless, the common approach, encapsulated in David Miller's *Anarchism* (1984) and George Crowder's *Classical Anarchism* (1991), was to use a select number of anarchist theorists to reach an adequate definition and critically assess its prospects. Both begin by posing this question of 'definition,' and each ends with a reflection on the 'anarchist case,' which is met with scepticism.[16] This attempt to reach an abstract delineation of anarchism has proven influential, both with those following in Miller and Crowder's train, and with those seeking to challenge their assessment of anarchist theory.[17] By orienting themselves in this

---

[14] R.B. Fowler, 'The Anarchist Tradition of Political Thought,' *The Western Political Quarterly* 25.4 (Dec. 1972): 738 [738–752]. For Fowler's current use, consider Kinna, *Anarchism*, 11, and Schmidt and van der Walt, *Black Flame*, 81 n228. D. Novak's article on anarchism is a precursor, which, although following Eltzbacher's canon, looks further back to early religious movements as possible 'intellectual predecessors.' This article is, however, largely forgotten: see D. Novak, 'The Place of Anarchism in the History of Political Thought,' *The Review of Politics* 20.3 (July 1958): 319 [307–329].
[15] April Carter, *The Political Theory of Anarchism* (London: Harper Torchbooks, 1971). The bibliography is indicative (see 113–116), but so is the 'suggested reading' section, which continues to rely on the classics: Proudhon, Kropotkin, Bakunin, and Tolstoy (see 111).
[16] David Miller, *Anarchism* (London: J.M. Dent, 1984), 2; George Crowder, *Classical Anarchism: The Political Thought of Godwin, Proudhon, Bakunin, and Kropotkin* (Oxford: Clarendon, 1991), 170.
[17] This influence can be seen in Michael Freeden's positive referencing of

literature, even to criticise it, the effect has been to perpetuate a canonical way of viewing anarchism. It is also apparent that both works, especially *Anarchism*, rely heavily on Woodcock's canonical history, and whilst Miller's work has dissenting chapters on the New Left, syndicalism, and individualist anarchism, the focus remains squarely fixed on Proudhon, Bakunin and Kropotkin.

Other works of political theory tend to follow suit. Alan Ritter's *Anarchism: a Theoretical Analysis* (1980) homes in on Godwin, Proudhon, Bakunin, and Kropotkin to support its supposition that 'communal individuality' lies at the heart of anarchism.[18] And more recently, David Morland's *Demanding the Impossible: Human Nature and Politics in Nineteenth-Century Social Anarchism* (1998) focuses squarely on Proudhon, Bakunin, and Kropotkin as exemplars of mature anarchist theory, alongside offering a deeper prehistory of anarchism in the *philosophes* of the eighteenth-century. The effect, and this is a feature of Crowder's work also, is to deepen the philosophical context of the canon, but leave its boundaries intact. Although this apparent historical contextualisation might seem to shift these works away from political theory *per se*, there are subtle differences between the primarily textual approach adopted and the contextual focus of the historian. Most obviously, their emphasis on texts as self-sufficient source material presupposes a certain timelessness in Western philosophy, making deeper contextualisation redundant. The emphasis is on the resonances between the philosophy of the Enlightenment (itself a dubious catchall term) and the anarchist tradition, and it is suggested that 'Rousseauian positions' are 'paralleled by Godwin and Proudhon,' or that Rousseau's ideas 'formed a platform for [sic] which the anarchists develop[ed] their attack on the state.'[19] The difficulty with this approach, and why these works are representative of political theory rather than the history of ideas, is that they tend to dehistoricise anarchism by approaching its history as one of eternal questions and answers.[20] It is supposed that Rousseau's theorisation of freedom

---

both texts in his important study of political ideologies. See Michael Freeden, *Ideologies and Political Theory: A Conceptual Approach* (Oxford: Oxford University Press, 2008), 311, 312.

[18] Alan Ritter, *Anarchism: A Theoretical Analysis* (Cambridge: Cambridge University Press, 1980), 3.

[19] Crowder, *Classical Anarchism*, 29. It is worth noting, however, that Crowder is generally sceptical of the influence of Rousseau on anarchism.

[20] For a classic dissection of this approach, see Quentin Skinner,

can be mapped onto Kropotkin's with comparative ease, meaning that concepts like 'freedom' become static, something that makes sense across temporal and spatial contexts and can be translated between cultures with ease.[21] Obviously, while important connections exist between Rousseau and the formation of the anarchist tradition, the historian would no doubt sound caution in overemphasising these points of contact.[22] Since Kropotkin's engagement with Rousseau is in fact surprisingly limited, the value of approaching this relationship in a more critical manner seems self-evident.

The relationship between the 'classical' tradition and the Enlightenment has informed the most significant intellectual development in anarchist studies in recent years and one that *ADCS* explored in its first issue: the emergence of post-anarchism.[23] Developing the idea that Godwin, Proudhon, Bakunin, and Kropotkin were unabashed children of the Enlightenment, a number of commentators have viewed this heritage through the multifocal lens of poststructuralist philosophy. Spying a troubling connection between the classical tradition and Enlightenment humanism—seen by Saul Newman in four principal themes: essentialism, a 'universality of morality and reason,' faith in 'natural laws,' a 'dialectical view of history,' and a 'certain positivism'—the post-anarchist critique challenges the emancipatory potential of anarchism on the basis of its adherence to these rationalist shibboleths.[24] The crux of this critique is a familiar one, captured in Crowder's diagnosis of

---

'Meaning and Understanding in the History of Ideas,' *History and Theory* 8.1 (1969): 3–53.

[21] Crowder, *Classical Anarchism*, 7–16. Anarchists are also frequently guilty of this ahistoricism and often tend to amplify it, encapsulated in Kropotkin's reflection that 'Anarchist philosophy' was advanced by Zeno and can also be seen in the Hussites and Anabaptists. See P.A.K., 'Anarchism,' in *The Encyclopaedia Britannica: Eleventh Edition: Volume 1* (Cambridge: Cambridge University Press, 1910), 915 [914–919].

[22] For a useful discussion of this, see C. Alexander McKinley, *Illegitimate Children of the Enlightenment: Anarchists and the French Revolution, 1880-1914* (Oxford: Peter Lang, 2008).

[23] For an invaluable introduction, see, in particular: Süreyyya Evren, 'Introduction: How New Anarchism Changed the World (of Opposition) after Seattle and Gave Birth to Post-Anarchism,' in Duane Rousselle and Süreyyya Evren (eds.), *Post-Anarchism: A Reader* (London: Pluto Press, 2011), 1–19.

[24] Saul Newman, *The Politics of Postanarchism* (Edinburgh: Edinburgh University Press, 2011), 6.

Kropotkin's troubling scientism, allegedly resulting in a Hegelian view of history that imparted contradictory conclusions for social emancipation.[25] Accepting that anarchism is 'imbued with a type of essentialism or naturalism that forms the foundation of its thought,' post-anarchists tend, nevertheless, to depart from the Crowder/Miller explanation in believing that something is salvageable from this wreck.[26] For Newman, the reflexivity of post-anarchism shows that 'anarchism has something to teach itself'; for others, post-structuralism offers the opportunity to 'reformulate the claims of anarchism.'[27]

Despite this iconoclastic urge, post-anarchists have largely left the anarchist canon untroubled. Post-anarchist texts have been less concerned with complicating the history of anarchist ideas than extracting a kernel of anarchist theory, an echo of the political theory works outlined above. For some critics of the post-anarchist position, this lack of necessary care in fathoming the depth and variety of anarchism's intellectual history means that the post-anarchist critique itself rests on unstable foundations.[28] As Jesse Cohn and Shawn Wilbur complained, many post-anarchist texts adopt a 'reductive' interpretation of anarchism centred on a 'limited number of "great thinkers"' and are insensitive to the 'margins' of the tradition—a lacuna given that many of these 'second wave' anarchists were themselves intent on addressing the weaknesses of the past.[29] What is particularly significant in this is that even in one of the most significant innovations in anarchist theory, there remains a discernible thread between the generations in their identification

---

[25] Crowder, *Classical Anarchism*, 156–169. Similar assessments appear in: Miller, *Anarchism*, 75, and Richard Sonn, *Anarchism* (New York: Twayne, 1992), 37. For an alternative view, consider Matthew S. Adams, 'Kropotkin: Evolution, Revolutionary Change and the End of History,' *Anarchist Studies* 19.1 (2011): 56–81.
[26] Todd May, *The Political Philosophy of Poststructuralist Anarchism* (Philadelphia: University of Pennsylvania Press, 1994), 63.
[27] Newman, *Politics of Postanarchism*, 182; Andrew M. Koch, 'Post-Structuralism and the Epistemological Basis of Anarchism,' in Rousselle and Evren, *Post-Anarchism*, 39 [23–40].
[28] Consider Allan Antliff, 'Anarchy, Power and Post-Structralism,' in Rousselle and Evren, *Post-Anarchism*, 160–167, and Benjamin Franks, 'Post-Anarchism: A Partial Account,' in Rousselle and Evren, *Post-Anarchism*, 168–180.
[29] Jesse Cohn and Shawn Wilbur, 'What's Wrong with Postanarchism?', *The Anarchist Library*: http://theanarchistlibrary.org/library/jesse-cohn-and-shawn-wilbur-what-s-wrong-with-postanarchism.

of a canon of great texts. Indeed, if anything, in terms of political theory, between Eltzbacher and Todd May the canon has shrunk: Tucker and Tolstoy are elided, and the heart of anarchism is seen in the work of Proudhon, Bakunin, and Kropotkin. And even for these three thinkers the coverage varies, for while Kropotkin's primary works are all available in English, for both Proudhon and Bakunin there is thinner coverage, resulting in the peculiar situation where commentators identify Proudhon as one of anarchism's canonical thinkers but are often only familiar with his *Qu'est-ce que la propriété?* and occasionally *Idée Générale De La Revolution au XIXe Siecle.*[30] Lip service is paid to the idea that anarchism is a mutable political tradition along the lines that 'anarchism is a diverse series of philosophies and political strate-gies', but the inquisition is primarily levelled at a recognisably select group of thinkers.[31] That said, given that post-anarchists are primarily concerned with theorising a step beyond the historical tradition, the lack of attention paid to adding nuances to this history is unsurprising.

While it has been claimed thus far that the endurance of the canon has primarily been a result of the primacy of political theory in the field of anarchist studies, it should be noted that there are important exceptions to this trend. Anarchist writers like Nicolas Walter, for instance, never lost sight of the impor-tance of recognising the efforts of those often overlooked in scholarly writing on anarchism, particularly those whose efforts tended to bridge the divide between scholarship and activism, encapsulated in his occasional essays on Joseph Lane and Lillian Wolfe.[32] Looking back further, a rich historical imagination is noticeable in other anarchists. Kropotkin, for instance, usually started his books and articles by locating anarchism in the

---

[30] A useful and brief historical overview that comments on the French and English sources is Alex Prichard, 'The Ethical Foundations of Proudhon's Anarchism,' in Benjamin Franks and Matthew Wilson (eds.), *Anarchism and Moral Philosophy* (Basingstoke: Palgrave Macmillan, 2010), 86–112.

[31] Saul Newman, 'Anarchism and the Politics of Ressentiment,' in John Moore (ed.), *I am Not a Man, I am Dynamite: Friedrich Nietzsche and the Anarchist Tradition* (Autonomedia: Brooklyn, 2004), 109 [107–126].

[32] See Nicolas Walter, 'Joseph Lane' and 'Lillian Wolfe,' in David Goodway (ed.), *The Anarchist Past and Other Essays* (Nottingham: Five Leaves, 2007), 209–219 and 231–237. Walter's historical interests are also apparent in David Goodway's other collection of his writings: see Nicolas Walter, *Damned Fools in Utopia and Other Writings on Anarchism and War Resistance* (Oakland: PM Press, 2011).

broader currents of socialist thought and in *Modern Science and Anarchism* offered a detailed overview of Western intellectual history.[33] In *Anarchism and Anarcho-Syndicalism*, Rudolf Rocker followed Kropotkin's lead in tracing a comparatively detailed pre-history of anarchism, producing an evolutionary account of its development.[34] The most significant historical voice during this period was, however, Max Nettlau. Often described as the 'Herodotus of anarchism,' Nettlau was an avid collector of the fragmentary sources of anarchism's past and used these materials to produce a range of histories, biographies, and bibliographies, the latter deemed by Kropotkin a 'most important' and 'reasoned' work.[35] Nettlau's major work, a monumental seven-volume history of anarchism, reflected his thoroughness and placed the major anarchist theoreticians in an obsessively detailed historical context. That Nettlau's name remains relatively unfamiliar, however, sadly denotes the impact of his work. As Heiner Becker noted in the introduction to the heavily edited edition of Nettlau's history published by *Freedom Press*, one of the few pieces of his writing translated into English, 'he is virtually unknown,' despite being '*the* pioneer in the field of the historiography of anarchism.'[36]

Moreover, emerging concurrently with the attentions of the political theorist, there was also a modest revival in anarchist history—a revival that bore a vague imprint of the burgeoning interest in social history praised by Goodway. Dealing with the British movement, John Quail's *The Slow Burning Fuse* (1978) and Hermia Oliver's *International Anarchist Movement in Late Victorian London* (1983) were both shaped by the *raison d'être* of social history, the 'premise . . . that ordinary people not only have a history but contribute to shaping history more generally.'[37]

---

[33] See Peter Kropotkin, 'Modern Science and Anarchism,' in George Woodcock (ed.), *Evolution and Environment* (Montréal: Black Rose Books, 1995), 15–107.

[34] Rudolf Rocker, *Anarchism and Anarcho-Syndicalism* (London: Freedom Press, 1973).

[35] Nicolas Walter, 'A flawless reminder of life left of left,' *Times Higher Education Supplement*, October 10, 1997: 27; Kropotkin, 'Anarchism,' 919.

[36] Heiner M. Becker, 'Introduction,' in Max Nettlau, *A Short History of Anarchism* (London: Freedom Press, 1996), ix [ix–xxiii].

[37] Peter N. Stearns, 'Social History Present and Future,' *Journal of Social History* 37.1 (Autumn, 2003): 9 [9–19]; John Quail, *The Slow Burning Fuse* (London: Paladin, 1978); Hermia Oliver, *International Anarchist Movement in Late Victorian London* (Beckenham: Croom Helm, 1983).

Quail makes this point at the outset, noting that his book is not concerned with 'the literati'; rather:

> It is as a movement in relation to the ebb and flow of popular revolt that this book concerns itself with the British anarchists. Only in relation to this does it consider Anarchist philosophy and its philosophers.[38]

Oliver's book, although somewhat dismissive of Quail's 'spirited' work, generally follows suit in seeking to unearth 'new matter' rather than dwell on the prominent figures, which explains, the author notes, 'why less is said about Kropotkin' in his book.[39] Nineteen years previously, James Joll had offered a detailed if rather freewheeling history, *The Anarchists* (1964), that sought to blend an assessment of anarchism's canonical figures (Godwin, Proudhon, Bakunin, and Kropotkin) with an appreciation of wider themes in anarchist history—propaganda by the deed, the complexities of syndicalism, and the Spanish Revolution.[40] In a sense, this brief flurry of historical activity was a response to the canonical approach of political theory. This is certainly true of Quail and Oliver's books with the former noting that 'recent years has seen . . . assorted attempts to assess Anarchist ideas of a rather patchy quality.'[41] While Joll sought to bridge the gap by offering a historically grounded interpretation of anarchist ideas, both Quail and Oliver's texts were more radical in calling for a focus on the day-to-day activities of anarchist activists. The influence of social history is seen in the emphasis on the ephemera of the movement—the papers, forgotten pamphlets, and smoky meetings—that gave anarchism its practical impetus with relatively little interest shown in the content of these ideas themselves. Despite this brief flurry of historical activity, the comparative obscurity of these texts is a testament to the continued primacy of political theory in anarchist studies. While Quail's book continues to exercise some influence, both Oliver's and Joll's have drifted into the shadows, notwithstanding the latter's role as a prominent popular historian of socialism.

Historical writing on anarchism never completely disappeared and, amongst anarchists themselves, the history of their movement remained of interest, but in the context of the renewal of

---

[38] Quail, *Slow Burning Fuse*, xiv, xiii.
[39] Oliver, *International Anarchist Movement*, n.p.
[40] James Joll, *The Anarchists* (London: Methuen).
[41] Quail, *Slow Burning Fuse*, xiii.

interest in anarchism in the second half of the twentieth century, it remained of minor importance. The spate of biographies on anarchist figures[42] and predominantly biographical exegesis of anarchist ideas[43] in these years should be mentioned, although invariably these shored up the canonisation underway in political theory.[44] In addition, some of these works were of debatable quality, especially the dated rash of 'psychohistories' prominent in Bakunin scholarship.[45] Even more significant, as Woodcock

---

[42] Consider E.H. Carr, *Michael Bakunin* (London: MacMillan, 1937)—this text was reprinted in 1975; Edward Hyams, *Pierre-Joseph Proudhon: His Revolutionary life, Mind and Works* (London: J. Murray, 1979); Anthony Masters, *Bakunin: The Father of Anarchism* (London: Sidgwick & Jackson, 1974); Martin A. Miller, *Kropotkin* (Chicago: Chicago University Press, 1976); George Woodcock and Ivan Akakumović, *The Anarchist Prince: A Biographical Study of Peter Kropotkin* (London: T.V. Boardman, 1950); George Woodcock, *Pierre-Joseph Proudhon: A Biography* (London: Routledge & Kegan Paul, 1956).

[43] In this category I would place works like K. Steven Vincent's excellent study of Proudhon, which is more focused on Proudhon's intellectual development than providing a comprehensive biography. See K. Steven Vincent, *Pierre-Joseph Proudhon and the Rise of French Republican Socialism* (Oxford: Oxford University Press, 1985). In a similar vein, although less successful, consider Richard B. Saltman, *The Social and Political Thought of Michael Bakunin* (Westport: Greenwood, 1983); Stephen Osofsky, *Peter Kropotkin* (Boston: Twyne Publishers, 1979).

[44] An exception to this is the recovery of Gustav Landauer's anarchism. Yet, despite the glut of biographical works on him during these years, he rarely found himself manoeuvred into the dominant canon itself, and it is only recently that major attention has been devoted to him. The main biographies date from the 1970s: see Ruth Link-Salinger Hyman, *Gustav Landauer: Philosopher of Utopia* (Indianapolis: Hackett, 1977); Eugene Lunn, *Prophet of Community: the Romantic Socialism of Gustav Landauer* (London: University of California Press, 1973); Charles B. Maurer, *Call to Revolution: the Mystical Anarchism of Gustav Landauer* (Detroit: Wayne State University Press, 1971). Landauer's own work was only made available with Gustav Landauer, *For Socialism,* trans. David J. Parent (St. Louis: Telos Press, 1978). This lacuna was recently partly filled by Gabriel Kuhn's excellent collection: Gustav Landauer, *Revolution and Other Writings: A Political Reader,* trans. Gabriel Kuhn (Oakland: AK Press 2010). I consider Landauer's influence in the British context in a forthcoming article: see Matthew S. Adams, 'Art, Education, and Revolution: Herbert Read and the Reorientation of British Anarchism,' *History of European Ideas* (Nov. 2012); doi: 10.1080/13825585.2012.736220.

[45] In particular, see: Arthur Mendel, *Michael Bakunin: Roots of Apocalypse* (New York: Praeger, 1981). Also connected to this approach, consider Aileen Kelly, *Mikhail Bakunin: A Study in the Psychology and Politics of*

noted in the revised edition of his classic history of anarchism—
revised, it should be said, to reach a more optimistic evaluation of
anarchism's future—was the emergence of the anarchist anthology. Attempting to mirror the 'strikingly protean fluidity' that
Woodcock identified as a source of anarchism's strength, his own
contribution to the genre The Anarchist Reader (1977) operated on
a basis of inclusivity, giving space to thinkers marginalised in his
history like Alexander Berkman and showing sensitivity to
contemporary developments by including Herbert Read, Alex
Comfort, and Murray Bookchin.[46] The serious lacuna in this, as
has been noted, is the absence of women.[47] Although Woodcock
included one selection from Emma Goldman, given anarchism's
history of challenging gender inequalities and the historically
influential role of women in the movement, this is a peculiar
blind spot. It is one compounded by the facts that the Goldman
text included is, despite her copious writings on sexual politics,
an excoriation of the 'Bolsheviki,' and that as the book was
published in the late-1970s, Woodcock seemed impervious to the
backdrop of radical feminism that was then a prominent feature
of the political terrain.[48]

The anthologisation of anarchist texts has gone some way to
destabilising the canon, but as with Woodcock's selection, these
books have their own problems. Daniel Guérin, who was subsequently to publish his own influential reader, voiced scepticism
at the value of these efforts:

> It is doubtful whether this literary effort is . . . very effec-
> tive. It is difficult to trace the outlines of anarchism. Its
> master thinkers rarely condensed their ideas into syste-
> matic works. If, on occasion, they tried to do so, it was
> only in thin pamphlets designed for propaganda and
> popularization in which only fragments of their ideas can
> be observed. Moreover, there are several kinds of anar-
> chism and many variations within the thought of each of
> the great libertarians.[49]

Utopianism (Oxford: Clarendon, 1982).
[46] George Woodcock, Anarchism: A History of Libertarian Ideas and Movements (London: Penguin, 1986), 414; George Woodcock (ed.), The Anarchist Reader (Hassocks: Harvester Press, 1977).
[47] Kinna, Anarchism, 13.
[48] Emma Goldman, 'The Failure of the Russian Revolution,' in The Anarchist Reader, 157 [153–162].
[49] Daniel Guérin, Anarchism: From Theory to Practice (New York:

Despite his doubts, his two-volume selection *No Gods No Masters* (1998)[50] innovatively attempted to historicise the anarchist tradition while highlighting the significance of fragmentary texts in appreciating the diversity of anarchist history. As the quotation above suggests, Guérin trod familiar ground in offering Stirner, Proudhon, Bakunin, and Kropotkin as the 'master thinkers' of the tradition, but included lesser known texts from their respective *oeuvres*; for instance, Kropotkin's speech from a Lyon court before his imprisonment in 1883 and letters from Bakunin regarding his *contretemps* with Marx. The historical value of Guérin's collection is particularly evident in the second volume, which incorporates missives from the Kronstadt naval base and the Spanish Revolution, alongside the work of syndicalist Fernand Pelloutier and the synthesist Voline. Again, however, the deafening silence in the text is women, with Goldman the sole female voice, but reduced to offering reflections on Kropotkin and Kronstadt.[51] Three American antholo-gies both perpetuated and addressed these failures. Leonard Krimerman and Lewis Perry's *Patterns of Anarchy* (1966) adopted a refreshingly open interpretation of anarchism, featuring individualist thinkers like Stephen Pearl Andrews, religious libertarians like Dorothy Day, and a section on critiques of anarchist theory.[52] Marshall Shatz and Irving Horowitz's editions were similarly varied, and although there was a continued weighting on Guérin's 'masters,' they notably included Goldman's work on sexual politics as a contribution in its own right.[53] The inadequacies of the anthology format were addressed recently in Robert Graham's monumental two-volume documentary history of anarchist ideas, a book that not only places considerable emphasis on anarchism's heritage of addressing

---

Monthly Review Press, 1970), 3.

[50] The original text was entitled *Ni Dieu ni maitre: anthologie de l'anarchisme* and was published in four volumes.

[51] Daniel Guérin (ed.), *No Gods No Masters: An Anthology of Anarchism: Book Two* (Edinburgh: AK Press, 1998), 163–208, 49–51, 104–119, 165–180. Goldman on Kropotkin can be found in Guérin, *No Gods No Masters: Volume One*, 287–294.

[52] Leonard I. Krimerman and Lewis Perry (eds.), *Patterns of Anarchy: A Collection of Writings on the Anarchist Tradition* (New York: Anchor), 207–222, 372–378, 491–553.

[53] Marshall S. Shatz (ed.), *The Essential Works of Anarchism* (New York: Bantam, 1971), 312–355; Irving Louis Horowitz (ed.), *The Anarchists* (1964; London: Aldine Transaction, 2004), 266–283.

gender inequalities, but also strives to blast the canon open by challenging its Eurocentrism, including sections on anarchism in China and Latin America.[54]

To survey all the works written on anarchism in the last fifty years is impossible, but from the précis above a number of themes emerge. Again, it is worth repeating that what historically has been a weakness in writing on anarchism is changing. In a sense, the very ability to reflect on the canon as a potentially problematic feature of our perception of anarchism presupposes a disenchantment that has already spurned a number of works. Certainly, from the brief flowering of anarchist histories informed by the democratising impetus of social history in the late 1970s and early 1980s, it is clear that resistance to reducing anarchism to a select band of thinkers is an established trend. Discussions of the canon, therefore, should not be cause for pessimism as such, but instead offer opportunities to reflect on how we engage with the historical tradition of anarchism and seek new ways to comprehend this protean set of ideas. More recently, the rise of transnational histories of anarchism, which appreciate the polyglot milieus in which anarchists are usually found, as well as the fecund international networks that spark innovations in anarchist ideas, is symbolic of the resistance to reductive approaches to the subject.[55] Similarly, it is possible to point to influential works on anarchism that imaginatively blend methodological perspectives from political theory with a keen historical sense, of which Benjamin Franks' *Rebel Alliances* is a good example.[56] And, while I have homed in on the supremacy of

---

[54] Robert Graham (ed.), *Anarchism: A Documentary History of Libertarian Ideas, Volume One: From Anarchy to Anarchism (300CE to 1939)* (London: Black Rose Books, 2005), 236–252, 336–366, 319–335. See also Robert Graham (ed.), *Anarchism: A Documentary History of Libertarian Ideas: Volume Two: The Emergence of The New Anarchism (1939-1977)* (London: Black Rose Books, 2008).

[55] I am thinking of Benedict Anderson, *Under Three Flags: Anarchism and the Anti-Colonial Imagination* (London: Verso, 2005); David Berry and Constance Bantman (eds.), *New Perspectives on Anarchism, Labour and Syndicalism: The Individual, the National and the Transnational* (Newcastle: Cambridge Scholars Publishing, 2010); Steven Hirsch and Lucien van der Walt (eds.), *Anarchism and Syndicalism in the Colonial and Postcolonial World, 1870-1940: The Praxis of National Liberation, Internationalism, and Social Revolution* (Leiden: Brill, 2010); Schmidt and van der Walt, *Black Flame*.

[56] Benjamin Franks, *Rebel Alliances: The Means and Ends of Contemporary British Anarchisms* (Edinburgh: AK Press, 2006).

political theory as one of the reasons for the canonisation of the 'classical anarchists,' it is worth pointing out that these works have done an impressive job of keeping anarchism alive in the scholarly imagination and posing many pertinent questions regarding how we understand this tradition. It should also be noted that it has not solely been the preserve of the historian to rescue neglected anarchists from obscurity and that important attempts have been made by those working broadly in the field of political theory to highlight the usefulness of reflecting on anarchism's neglected actors.[57]

Nevertheless, I think that it is justified to say that historical scholarship has been a noticeably minor aspect of the renewed interest in anarchism and that there is a strong connection between this and the solidity of the canon. In 1971, Nicolas Walter reflected on the likely development of anarchist studies and found cause for optimism:

> In general, it looks as if during the 1970s we may expect further historical and biographical description of anarchism as a phantom of the past; we should also hope for more important (and more difficult) social and political analysis of anarchism as a spectre haunting the present; we may then look forward to a fresh expression of anarchism as a vision of the future.[58]

His anticipation of a turn to the political analysis of anarchist ideas was borne out, but his rather dismissive appreciation of anarchist historical studies was not. Apart from an ephemeral flowering of work informed by social history and the current exciting emergence of transnational histories of anarchism, the field of anarchist history has been relatively barren. This is very noticeable in the context of anarchist ideas where, as to be expected, political theorists have spilt the most ink, and historians have been largely absent. Given the rich complexity of anarchism's intellectual history, something that is either implicit or explicit in all the works surveyed here, it is surprising that

---

[57] A good example of this is Ruth Kinna, 'Guy Aldred: Bridging the Gap between Marxism and Anarchism,' *Journal of Political Ideologies* 16.1 (2011): 96–114. A similar intention can be seen in a number of the articles in the following edited collection: Laurence Davis and Ruth Kinna (eds.), *Anarchism and Utopianism* (Manchester: Manchester University Press, 2009).

[58] Walter, 'Anarchism in Print,' 139.

there has not been a more pronounced movement in this direction.

INTELLECTUAL AND CULTURAL HISTORY: NEW HISTORIES OF ANARCHIST IDEAS

For Goodway in 1989, growing familiarity with the methods of social history offered the prospect of novel approaches to anarchism's past. In reality, this pronouncement was rather after the event. Steps towards social histories of anarchism had already been taken, and by this time there was a new *enfant terrible* on the scene that was already displacing social history as the vogue sub-discipline: cultural history. While this trend has since become entrenched in mainstream historiography, in the context of anarchist history the new horizons it opened up have not been acknowledged.[59] And, with our present interest in the endurance of the canon, the general approach of cultural history offers a way of reconceptualising how we write about the 'masters' of anarchist theory. With this in mind, I want to briefly make a case for a blend of intellectual and cultural history in what follows, taking anarchist ideas as worthy objects of historical study, but sensitive to notions of political culture.[60] The upshot of this is, inevitably, an emphasis on the context in which ideas grow. This is a worthy quest and an objective that intellectual histories of anarchism usually affirm, denying the validity of considering 'works merely as self-contained texts' and emphasising the importance of placing 'thinkers and their works in their specific historical and personal context as well as in their broader traditions.'[61] Often though, these contexts are seen as common-sensical and self-evident, meaning that appeals to the importance of contextual factors in appreciating anarchist intellectual history are rather weakly substantiated. What cultural history offers—as, indeed, did social history before it—is a fresh way to think about the contexts that inform the emergence of political ideas, and, as a result, suggest a path for new histories of anarchism.

---

[59] On cultural history's growth, see Peter Burke, 'Strengths and Weaknesses of Cultural History,' *Cultural History*, 1.1 (2012): 1–13.

[60] Generally, the terms 'intellectual history' and the 'history of ideas' are used interchangeably, with the former more frequently used nowadays. Here, I use both terms to refer to the same historical sub-discipline.

[61] Peter Marshall, *Demanding the Impossible: A History of Anarchism* (London: Fontana, 1993), xiii.

Before this, however, it is worth noting the irony that while those writing on anarchism wring their hands over the exclusivity of their canon, a parallel discussion frequently takes place among mainstream intellectual historians regarding the 'canon of works to which we devote special attention.' The dynamic of this discussion is very similar, an anxiety over undue narrowness and fears regarding the potential 'exclusion of texts from other cultures,' but invariably, the historian is led to confess that 'most often I agree with traditional authorities in identifying works to be included in any . . . list of especially significant texts.'[62] As anarchists puzzle over whether an unhealthy amount of attention is paid to Kropotkin, within the (admittedly rather elitist) confines of intellectual history he barely registers, and neither does anarchism, even in radical attempts to rethink the wider issue of canonisation.[63] While university library shelves strain under the weight of books on Thomas Hobbes and John Locke, the literature on even the most prominent in the anarchist canon pales into insignificance.[64] Against this background, it might be asked whether the tendency towards canonisation in anarchist studies is really such an issue, especially if the treatment of Guérin's 'masters' is reflexive, conscious of the weaknesses of focusing on individuals, and realises that such an amorphous political doctrine as anarchism cannot be reduced to the pen strokes of a single figure. Similarly, if it is also recognised that

---

[62] Dominick LaCapra, 'Rethinking Intellectual History and Reading Texts,' in Dominick LaCapra and Steven L. Kaplan (eds.), *Modern European Intellectual History: Reappraisals & New Perspectives* (London: Cornell University Press, 1982), 51 [47–85].

[63] Consider Siep Stuurman, 'The Canon of the History of Political Thought: Its Critique and a Proposed Alternative,' *History and Theory* 39.2 (May 2000): 147–166. An important exception is J.W. Burrow's impressive *The Crisis of Reason*, which focuses heavily on Bakunin. Nevertheless, this analysis tends to dwell on his paeans for violence as symptomatic of a wider cult of irrationality in fin-de-siècle thought, instead of an analysis of his political ideas. Kropotkin, as he conceded in the preface, is not included in his study, and it is interesting to reflect on the fact that Kropotkin's scientific proclivities and his later move away from aggressive rhetoric would complicate the picture of anarchism presented: see J.W. Burrow, *The Crisis of Reason: European Thought, 1848-1914* (London: Yale University Press, 2000), xiv.

[64] A rather unscientific indication of this can be seen using the university library catalogue aggregator copac (www.copac.ac.uk). Entering the search term 'Kropotkin' returns 202 results and 'Bakunin' 349, in comparison to 1,090 for 'Thomas Hobbes' and 2,696 for 'John Locke.'

any canon of works, as defined by Dominick LaCapra as those texts 'to which we devote special attention' rather than works of oracular value, must be built on correspondingly shifting sands, writing on the anarchist canon can still be a legitimate endeavour. Those writing on anarchist history are beholden to ponder the boundaries of this canon and should be conscious that the ethnocentrism and patriarchy predominating when it was forged influenced its composition, but if this is recognised, there remains much to be said about thinkers seen as canonical that are otherwise neglected in the mainstream.

That said, rethinking the approach to writing the history of anarchist ideas can help in looking beyond the confines of the canon, and resources for this re-evaluation can be found within intellectual history itself. Often, historical appreciations of anarchist ideas veer towards the 'unit-idea' method made famous in Arthur Lovejoy's classic work *The Great Chain of Being* (1936). For Lovejoy, borrowing a metaphor from 'analytic chemistry,' the duty of the intellectual historian is to trace the individual ideas that comprise philosophical systems, often uncovering the truism that 'philosophic systems are original or distinctive rather in their patterns than in their components.'[65] Changing sciences, Lovejoy then proposed that the role of the historian was principally Linnaean:

> A study of sacred words and phrases of a period or . . . movement, with a view to clearing up their ambiguities, a listing of their various shades of meaning, and an examination of the way in which confused associations of ideas arising from these ambiguities have influenced the development of doctrines.[66]

This taxonomic focus is a familiar feature of writing on anarchism, but the pursuit of the unit-idea can lack historical acuity. Ideas can become 'hypostatized as an entity', and doctrines presented as if 'immanent in history', leading to a tendency towards unhistorical comment on earlier 'anticipations'

---

[65] Arthur O. Lovejoy, *The Great Chain of Being: A Study of the History of an Idea* (Cambridge: Harvard University Press, 1961), 3.
[66] Lovejoy, *Great Chain of Being*, 14. I am indebted to Abigail Williams' discussion of Lovejoy's work: see Abigail Williams, 'Literary and Intellectual History,' in Richard Whatmore and Brian Young (eds.), *Palgrave Advances in Intellectual History* (Basingstoke: Palgrave, 2006), 49–65.

of later ideas.[67] The habit of tracing an 'anarchist 'tendency' as far back as Lao Tzu in the ancient world,' which has an impressive lineage in anarchist studies given Kropotkin's faith in it, risks such ahistoricism.[68] Rather, historically grounded writing on anarchism should be more sensitive to the social, cultural, and intellectual contexts in which these ideas grew, thinking more broadly about the particular problems to which anarchist writers were responding. Ironically, given intellectual history's steadfast commitment to its own canon, this approach has the potential to overcome the narrow concentration on a select band of thinkers:

> It is hard to see how we can hope to arrive at . . . historical understanding if we continue . . . to focus our main attention on those who discussed the problems of political life at a level of abstraction and intelligence unmatched by . . . their contemporaries. If on the other hand we attempt to surround these classic texts with their appropriate ideological context, we may be able to build up a more realistic picture of how political thinking in all its various forms was in fact conducted in earlier periods.[69]

For mainstream intellectual history, such a contextualist approach requires the historian to think more widely about the prevailing discourses relevant to a given political thinker and to look to marginal and neglected texts to provide a deeper intellectual context.[70] To understand the thrust of the political

---

[67] Skinner, 'Meaning and Understanding,' 10, 11.

[68] Marshall, *Demanding the Impossible*, xiv. The counter position to this is well set out in Schmidt and van der Walt, *Black Flame*, 33 *passim*.

[69] Quentin Sinner, *The Foundations of Modern Political Thought, Volume 1: The Renaissance* (Cambridge: Cambridge University Press), xi.

[70] It is worth noting that this approach to intellectual history differs slightly from that pursued by prominent historians like Peter Gay and H. Stuart Hughes. While both are interested in the context in which ideas grow, their focus on the *zeitgeist* differs from the specificity of contextualist intellectual history. As Gay wrote in the introduction to his seminal *The Enlightenment*, 'The narrow Enlightenment of the philosophes was embedded in a wider more comprehensive atmosphere, the atmosphere of the eighteenth century, which may be called, without distortion, the Age of the Enlightenment. It was from this age that the philosophes drew ideas and support, this age which they partly led, partly epitomized, and partly rejected': Peter Gay, *The Enlightenment: An Interpretation: The Science of Freedom* (1969; London: W.W. Norton, 1997), x. In a similar vein, consider H. Stuart Hughes, *Consciousness & Society:*

classics, the argument goes, it is necessary to uncover the historically defined issues that motivate an author, which are often not the timeless meditations on the human condition emphasised by political philosophy, but concerns that are more parochial. What this also provides is a bridge between theory and practice, a perennial cause for concern with anarchist writers, for the emphasis is on striving to understand the issues that define political life in the first place and therefore warrant written intervention.[71]

A practical effect of the contextualist method is greater sensitivity to the motivations for political engagement, manifested in a more developed awareness of the ephemeral literature that comprises a thinker's intellectual universe, texts to which they are responding either implicitly or explicitly. This has the potential to nuance our perceptions of the canon in anarchism, rather than rejecting it by posing fresh and potentially illuminating questions concerning a thinker's relation to their immediate environment. Traditionally, this has been something of a weakness in scholarship on anarchism, and the political theorist's tendency to view anarchism in terms of its relation to contemporary issues often abstracts thinkers from the issues they were really facing. A couple of examples from Kropotkin's work help illuminate this point. While Hobbes, T.H. Huxley, and Rousseau are frequently referenced in relation to Kropotkin's *chef-d'oeuvre Mutual Aid*, Henry Maine's name is probably less familiar. Yet *Mutual Aid* draws heavily on Maine's prodigious scholarship on legal history, which was itself a frequently cited body of work in the Victorian intellectual world.[72] Alone this poses tantalising questions about Kropotkin's use of source material in the construction of *Mutual Aid*, considering his deep antipathy to legal conventions and Maine's belief in it as a benchmark of civilization, something compounded by Kropotkin's unhesitating praise for the Oxford professor. Contemplating the shared assumptions between these thinkers casts light on Kropotkin's philosophy, as does musing on the divergences.

The Reorientation of European Social Thought: 1890-1930 (1958; Brighton: Harvester Press, 1979). For this general point, I am indebted to Robert Darnton, 'Intellectual and Cultural History,' in Michael Kammen (ed.), *The Past Before Us: Contemporary Historical Writing in the United States* (Ithaca: Cornell University Press, 1980), 340 [327–353].
[71] Skinner, *Foundations of Modern Political Thought*, xi.
[72] Peter Kropotkin, *Mutual Aid* (1904; London: Penguin, 1939), 76, 107, 107n, 113n, 114, 117, 118, 131n, 190.

Furthermore, given that Maine is sometimes shuffled into the canon of 'anarcho-capitalists,' does this cast any light on the vexed relationship between this brand of thought and the mainstream anarchist movement?[73] Or, consider Toulmin Smith, another figure who Kropotkin lavished praise on in *Mutual Aid*, and who has acquired an equally ambiguous political reputation, depicted variously as a premature 'Thatcherite' libertarian, traditional Tory, and committed mutualist.[74] Indeed, with its rich referencing, *Mutual Aid* offers a unique opportunity in Kropotkin's oeuvre to recreate the intellectual framework of this text, to explore the sources on which his political sociology rested, and understand Kropotkin's relation to the wider intellectual culture in which he lived. Even in the best histories of anarchism, this has tended to be overlooked given the historians' desire to chart the vicissitudes of anarchist theory and rescue this political doctrine from distortion and obscurity. To gain a clearer insight into their work, however, developing a durable context is vital:

> We cannot gain a proper understanding of Arnold or Mill or Spencer without an appreciation of the assumptions they shared with their contemporaries, and of the ways in which they differed from them—how, for instance, they used familiar political vocabularies for new and unexpected purposes.[75]

Substitute Kropotkin, or Bakunin, or Tucker, for the thinkers mentioned above and some of the deficiencies of anarchist history become apparent. While histories of anarchism have contributed a significant amount to unearthing the complexities and ambiguities of this tradition, they have been weaker at tying together an appreciation of anarchism with a view of the wider intellectual and cultural contexts that gave its theorists their élan in the first place.

A legitimate criticism of this intellectual history approach is

---

[73] Brian Doherty, *Radicals for Capitalism: A Freewheeling History of the Modern American Libertarian Movement* (New York: PublicAffairs, 2007), 7, 25.

[74] Kropotkin, *Mutual Aid*, 142n, 144n, 161n, 163n, 209; Ben Weinstein, '"Local Self-Government Is True Socialism": Joshua Toulmin Smith, the State and Character Formation,' *English Historical Review* CXXIII.54 (2008): 1195 [1193–1228].

[75] H.S. Jones, *Victorian Political Thought* (Basingstoke: Macmillan, 2000), xi.

that although it may illuminate the philosophical foundations of anarchism, it tends to fetishise theory. It might add texture to the canon, but it overlooks the fact that not all those identifying as anarchists paused to pen pamphlets. Heiner Becker and Nicolas Walter made this point in their brief article on the history of *Freedom Press*, noting that 'historians . . . tend to concentrate on the easy things: the big names and the great events, the organisations and periodicals which last for a long time, the pamphlets and books which can be found in libraries.'[76] Contextualist intellectual history does offer a route out of this pursuit of 'easy' answers, by privileging the use of minor literature to build a more comprehensive contextual framework.[77] Perhaps an even more helpful way to approach this contextual problem, however, is to turn to perspectives offered by cultural history to re-evaluate these contexts. 'New cultural history,' so called to distinguish it from its Burckhardtian forbear with its bias for high culture, was shaped by a passing engagement with anthropology and places particular emphasis on the importance of symbolic practice, representation, and in a sense, Weberian *Verstehen*.[78] In contrast to the relative austerity of intellectual history, cultural history has been accused of whimsicality by emphasising the subjective nature of experience and concerning itself with creation of cultural meaning by individuals and groups. Histories of table manners, collecting, and clothing are some of the more quirky examples of these new histories, but cultural history has also freshened intellectual history's contextual conundrum.[79] 'Political culture' has emerged as a prominent concept in the study of political ideas, a characteristically loose term that seeks to comprehend the subjective element of political identification. Political culture thus refers to the 'identity and boundaries of the community,' and the site where various political discourses 'overlap.' Rather than taken as self-evident, 'meaning' is tied to this complex of values:

[Political culture] constitutes the meanings of the terms in

---

[76] Heiner Becker and Nicolas Walter, 'Freedom: People and Places,' in *Freedom: A Hundred Years* (London: Freedom Press, 1986), 4 [4–7].

[77] For a useful challenge to Skinner's understanding of contextualism, consider Mark Bevir, 'The Role of Contexts in Understanding and Explanation,' *Human Studies* 23.4 (Oct. 2000): 395–411.

[78] For a general overview of cultural history's history, see Burke, *What is Cultural History?*

[79] Burke, *What is Cultural History?*, 58, 59, 68.

which . . . claims are framed, the nature of the contexts to which they pertain, and the authority of the principles according to which they are pressed, and which these claims are formulated, the strategies by which they are pressed, and the contestations to which they give rise.[80]

While in the nineteenth century cultural history conceived culture as a body of learning and 'high art,' this perspective on culture emphasises the centrality of shared meanings and actors' attempts to define their own communities of meaning. In polemical terms, the upshot of this is a resistance to the Marxian underpinning of social history, which tended to see values as an 'efflux' of material conditions. Instead, cultural historians often stress the autonomous nature of values, and point to the power of these in motivating action in the social sphere at some remove from material factors. The validity of this critique is a moot point and not one to be explored here, but the renewed focus on the idea of self-definition and personal identification offers an intriguing way of approaching the study of political ideas that stresses the fluid and sometimes overlapping sources of political identity. For those thinking about anarchist history, this challenges the hermetic approach to the study of anarchism by attaching weight to interactions with representatives of other political traditions, and emphasising the process by which anarchists created their own political culture from a potpourri of prevailing ideas and values. As the example of Maine and Kropotkin suggests, these neglected relations are a potentially fruitful avenue to understanding anarchism's past.

A further development of the cultural history of ideas is sensitivity towards non-textual contexts.[81] Recognising the fact

---

[80] Keith Michael Baker, 'Introduction,' in Keith Michael Baker (ed.), *The French Revolution and the Creation of Modern Political Culture, Volume 1: The Political Culture of the Old Regime* (Oxford: Pergamon Press, 1987), xii [xi–xxiv].

[81] Brian Cowan, 'Intellectual, Social and Cultural History: Ideas in Context,' in *Palgrave Advances in Intellectual History*, 171–188 (esp. 180–183). I am aware of the Derridean pronouncement that 'Il n'ya a pas de hors-texte,' which should not necessarily be taken 'literally.' In the present article, however, the distinction between textual and non-textual refers simply to the intellectual historians' particular focus on political literature and the cultural historians' more varied approach to source material. I take the comment on Derridean literalism from Alex Callinicos, *Theories and Narratives: Reflections on the Philosophy of History* (Durham: Duke University Press, 1995), 3.

that literary fragments do not constitute the *only* context in which to situate ideas, the role of the more elusive 'values, prejudices, and expectations' that sway historical actors comes to the fore. While these 'cultural conventions' are obviously engaged with textually, in practice there tends to be a difference between the kinds of source material privileged by the contextualist historian of political ideas and those that interest the cultural historian.[82] To uncover the assumptions that comprise this framework of values, it is necessary to think more creatively about the material drawn upon, and think more expansively about the contexts in which we place anarchist ideas. Similarly, cultural history is often linked to a growing interest in form rather than simply the philosophical content of ideas. The parallel development of 'book history,' for instance, has placed particular emphasis on engagement with printed matter: 'the book is not so much a category as a process: books happen; they happen to people who read them, reproduce, disseminate, and compose them.'[83] From the perspective of anarchist history, where newspapers are often short-lived, articles anonymous, publishing ventures the product of cooperation between multiple groups and authors, this is clearly a richer history than most. Again, Kropotkin's work offers an illuminating example. Given that the liberal-minded journal *Nineteenth Century* was the conduit for most of Kropotkin's major articles once he began his sojourn in Britain, the impact of this relationship upon his ideas themselves has not been scrutinised. How did the form of his arguments, the rhetorical construction of his writing, and the patina of these articles differ from his early publications and those intended primarily for anarchist audiences? One change is that Kropotkin began to draw on different examples in seeking to boost his persuasiveness, a process mirroring his physical journey from east to west. The imagery of Russian *mirs* was supplanted by the communalism of the French peasantry while living under the Third Republic, before Kropotkin drew on quainter examples of bicycle clubs and friendly societies in the context of Britain, then the most urbanised country in the world.[84] Form is therefore

---

[82] Cowan, 'Intellectual, Social, and Cultural History,' 183.

[83] Leslie Howsam, *Old Books & New Histories: An Orientation to Studies in Book and Print Culture* (London: University of Toronto Press, 2006), 5. I am indebted to Catherine Feely for her advice on book history.

[84] This is briefly explored in Matthew S. Adams, 'Rejecting the American Model: Peter Kropotkin's Radical Communalism,' *History of Political Thought* 36.3 (Autumn 2013).

something often overlooked in anarchist history, and while the social history of anarchism praised by Goodway pursued a parallel path, cultural history's fixation on representation and the multiple contexts that inform the growth and transmission of ideas marks a departure from the focus on 'structures or processes' beloved by social historians.[85] There is, of course, important overlap between these methodological approaches—it would be a distortion to accuse social historians of being uninterested in the matter of values—but the sometimes acrimonious conflicts between them have opened up useful ways to rethink our approach to understanding anarchism's history.

CONCLUSION

'O Reader! — Courage, I see land!'[86]

In this article, I have attempted to avoid the embattled tone that often accompanies considerations of method. My intention was not to offer a 'defence' of history or, as with one recent collection, a manifesto for how it should be written.[87] Instead, it is motivated by a belief that anarchism's is a rich and varied history and by surprise that attention to this has been a somewhat slugg-ish aspect of the general revival of interest in anarchism. It is particularly apparent in the context of anarchism's intellectual history, the field where most activity might be expected, and where, in fact, there has been comparatively little innovation. That Woodcock's history of anarchism, with all its deep erudition and sparkling prose, remains unsurpassed, is symptomatic of this lack of historical attention.

It is this paucity of historical writing, I have argued, that helps explain the dominance of the canon in anarchist studies. The disciplinary ascendancy of political theory emboldened this concentration on a select band of thinkers as representative of the tradition, as the primary concern became conclusive definition and anarchism's status as a political ideology. Post-anarchism, one of the most significant developments in anarchism's recent

---

[85] Peter Mandler, 'The Problem with Cultural History' in *Cultural and Social History*, Vol.1, No.1 (2004), 94-117.

[86] Thomas Carlyle, *The French Revolution: A History, Volume III* (1837; London: Chapman and Hall, 1898), 288.

[87] Richard J. Evans, *In Defence of History* (London: Granta, 2001); Keith Jenkins, Sue Morgan, and Alun Munslow (eds.), *Manifestos for History* (London: Routledge, 2007).

intellectual history has, despite levelling critical attention at the conventional understanding of anarchism, done little to displace this tendency. Again, however, it is important to note that this is beginning to change. Historical sensitivity is now primarily an attribute of those not writing from an explicitly historical perspective, and the attempt to nuance under-standings of anarchism through appeal to its more marginal actors is informed by a rejection of canonical thinking. Similarly, the exciting growth of transnational histories of anarchism demonstrates that what once may have been a weakness is starting to change. The fear then that anarchist studies was buying into a Carlylean 'great man' history by canonising a select group of thinkers overstates the case, and as this special issue testifies, resistance to this process is a well-established, and productive, theme.

Further attempts to move beyond canonistic thinking in scholarship on anarchism, and indeed attempts to offer fresh insights on those predominant members of this perceived elite, should be welcomed. Historical research offers tantalising opportunities in this direction. While those writing on anarchist matters have been focusing on the grand epistemological impacts of poststructuralist philosophy, the more modest developments in mainstream historical writing have passed by largely unobserved. Awareness of these insights is not a guarantor of worthwhile writing, and neither is it necessary to be aware of these disciplinary debates to offer new perspectives on anarchist ideas, but recent attempts to think anew about the nature of historical context and its relationship to political ideas have enlivened the study of mainstream events and movements. Like Goodway's praise for social history at the end of the 1980s, my statement on the benefits of the cultural history of ideas is no doubt belated; by the time Goodway was writing, social history had already been largely displaced by cultural history. Yet greater sensitivity to deepening the textual context of anarchist ideas, appreciating the cultural assumptions underpinning political arguments, being more aware of the form of rhetorical interventions and conscious of anarchists' attempts to fashion a distinctive political culture offers new ways to approach anarchism's history. Such 'thick description,' to borrow a phrase from anthropology much beloved by cultural historians, also presents the opportunity to rethink the canon as shorthand for anarchist philosophy, by rescuing overlooked influences from anonymity and recovering the debates that gave anarchism its theoretical élan in the first place.[88] Then, rather than follow Lord Acton's suggestion to fellow-historian Mandell Creighton—'Advice to persons about to write History: Don't'—historical writing on anarchism might experience the kind of renaissance underway in the social sciences.[89]

---

[88] Clifford Geertz, *The Interpretation of Cultures* (New York: Basic Books, 1973), 3–10.

[89] John Emerich Edward Dalberg, Lord Acton, *Acton-Creighton Correspondence* (1887) 'Letter II,' *The Online Library of Liberty*: http://oll.libertyfund.org/title/2254/212810.

Anarchist Developments in Cultural Studies
ISSN: 1923-5615
2013.1: Blasting the Canon

Voltairine de Cleyre and the Anarchist Canon

Michelle M. Campbell[*]

ABSTRACT

Voltairine de Cleyre (1866-1912) is an important, but often ignored, figure in American classical anarcha-feminism. De Cleyre's works provide an important entrance point through which contemporary anarchist academics and activists can discuss feminism within past, present, and future radical movements. Her writings certainly leave us at the point of commencing an in-depth consideration of what a post-anarchist feminism might look like. Moreover, two of de Cleyre's major contributions to the field include the idea of anarchism without adjectives and her no-frills approach to public speaking and writing, both applicable to contemporary problems within the movement, especially in theoretical contexts. For these reasons, it is essential that Voltairine de Cleyre be consciously included in the anarchist canon.

[*] Michelle M. Campbell is a Master of Arts graduate student at Central Michigan University, Mt. Pleasant, Michigan, USA, and her thesis explores the development of a theory of post-anarchist feminism utilizing contemporary American post-apocalyptic science fiction literature. Michelle teaches freshman composition at CMU, and she has given several guest lectures and department sponsored talks about anarchist theory and anarcha-feminism. She is the president of the Graduate Student Union, a labor union representing almost 450 teaching and administrative graduate students at CMU, and she is also active there on the Academic Senate and Academic Senate Executive Board. She serves as the director of operations for *Temenos*, CMU's graduate creative writing journal. After graduating with her MA in Spring 2013, Michelle hopes to pursue doctoral work while continuing to hone her teaching abilities.

KEYWORDS
Voltairine de Cleyre, anarcha-feminism, post-anarchism, feminism, canon, anarchism without adjectives

Paul Avrich (1978), Voltairine de Cleyre's biographer, once wrote of her: "Voltairine de Cleyre remains little more than a memory. But her memory possesses the glow of legend and, for vague and uncertain reasons, still arouses awe and respect" (Avrich 1978, 6). Unlike Proudhon, Bakunin, Kropotkin, or even Goldman, Most, and Berkman, Voltairine de Cleyre remains a fringe character in the classical anarchist movement.[1] De Cleyre and I grew up sixty miles and one hundred years apart, but I never knew of her existence until a professor forwarded an article to me at the emergence of my fascination with anarchism and feminism. Although during her life de Cleyre lectured around the United States and Europe, wrote prolifically, and taught hundreds, if not thousands, of poor immigrants, her legacy remains ensconced in a few anthologies of selected works and a few Internet websites. She normally appears in bibliographies or list resources with only a few "important" works attached to her name—and often crowded out by other women anarchists of her time, such as the flamboyant Emma Goldman or the Haymarket widow, Lucy Parsons. Often, these women themselves are overshadowed by the men in the movement, especially those from Europe (all of whom, from what I can gather, happened to have luscious beards). But who was Voltairine de Cleyre?

The daughter of a French tinker father and a mother linked to the abolitionist movement, de Cleyre grew up in the heartland of the Midwest. She was born in Leslie, Michigan in November 1886, and her parents moved to St. Johns, Michigan when she was a small child after another one of their children had drowned in a creek. Avrich explains, "As a liberal and freethinker, Hector de Cleyre was an admirer of Voltaire, which, Voltairine tells us, prompted his choice of her name, though 'not without some protest on the part of his wife, an American woman of Puritan descent and inclined to rigidity in social views'" (Avrich 1978, 19). The family was extremely poor, and Voltairine's sister, Addie,

---

[1] To be clear, when I use the term "classic" or "classical" to modify anarchism, I am referring to the period of approximately 1848 to the mid-1930's, in which anarchism developed as a theory and global social movement.

recounted "we were among the *very poor.* There was no 'Welfare' in those days, and to be aided by any kind of charity was a disgrace not to be tho't of. So we were all underfed, and bodily weak" (qtd. in Avrich 1978, 21). Despite this poverty, and the friction it caused between Hector and Harriet de Cleyre, Voltairine grew up to show the capacity for extreme intellect. Avrich describes her as an "intelligent and pretty child, with long brown hair, blue eyes, and interesting, unusual features. She had a passionate love for nature and animals. But, already displaying the qualities that were to trouble her personal relations in later life, she was headstrong and emotional" (Avrich 1978, 24). Voltairine and Addie were voracious readers, and Voltairine began to write at an early age (Avrich 1978, 25). Because of de Cleyre's penchant for intellectual and artistic pursuits, her father, raised as a Catholic, decided she would be best served by an education in a Catholic convent.

Hector de Cleyre believed that an education at the convent in Sarnia, Ontario, would give his daughter the best education possible, while ridding her of bad habits (like reading stories), and promulgating good habits, such as "rule, regulation, time and industry" (Avrich 1978, 30). As Avrich recounts, Voltairine spent "three years and four months at Sarnia, from September 1880 to December 1883," but that didn't mean she agreed with the educational path upon which her father had set her (Avrich 1978, 30). At fourteen years old, Voltairine de Cleyre was already showing signs of the headstrong, fearless woman she would become:

> After a few weeks at the convent she decided to run away. Escaping before breakfast, she crossed the river to Port Huron. From there, as she had no money, she began the long trek to St. Johns on foot. After covering seventeen miles, however, she realized that she would never make it all the way home, so she turned around and walked back to Port Huron and, going to the house of acquaintances, asked for something to eat. They sent for her father, who took her back to the convent. (Avrich 1978, 31)

This proclivity for tenacity and individualism would help to shape both de Cleyre's character as well as her philosophical views concerning anarchism and "The Woman Question" later in her life.[2]

De Cleyre graduated from the convent, with honors, when she was seventeen years old. From there, she returned to St. Johns to live with her mother and sister. For a while, she stayed with an aunt in Greenville, Michigan and later lived in Grand Rapids, Michigan, where she edited a free-thought newspaper. Throughout this time, de Cleyre considered herself a free-thinker, but it was the Haymarket riots, and subsequent "trial" and execution of the Haymarket Martyrs that cemented de Cleyre's philosophical ideals in the direction of classical anarchist thought. Later, she lived in both Philadelphia and Chicago, where she wrote, taught, and lectured, most of the time living in ill health and extreme poverty. She was a contemporary of Emma Goldman and other anarchists residing in the United States at the time—but she was different.

During her lifetime, de Cleyre was well known in anarchist and free-thought circles, and she was extremely productive concerning written discourse, including fiction, non-fiction, and poetry. Avrich writes:

> While lacking Emma's notoriety and dynamic vitality, Voltairine nevertheless emerged as one of the leading figures in the American anarchist movement between 1890 and 1910. In Philadelphia, she was active both among native-born libertarians and among Jewish immigrant revolutionists, serving as a vital link between them. She contributed a steady stream of articles and poems, sketches and stories to a variety of radical journals, of which *Lucifer, Free Society*, and *Mother Earth* were perhaps the most important. (Avrich 1978, 94)

Although de Cleyre wrote about a number of topics, she is best known for her political and philosophical pieces concerning "The Woman Question." Essays, which first began as speeches, such as "Those Who Marry Do Ill," "The Woman Question," and "Sex Slavery," are often overshadowed by equally provocative and well-written pieces concerning anarchism. Essays such as "Anarchism and American Traditions," "Crime and Punishment," and

---

[2] By "The Woman Question," I mean the debates surrounding the question of women's rights in Europe and the United States in the 19th and early 20th centuries. Topics up for debate included marriage, working outside the home, legal rights (such as suffrage), as well as reproductive rights and prevention.

"The Economic Tendency of Freethought" are important pieces of a classical American anarchism.

It is important to understand that, although we often label Voltairine de Cleyre (as well as Emma Goldman, Lucy Parsons, and Louise Michel) as anarcha-feminists, the question of feminism, or "The Woman Question," was extraordinarily different when comparing these women to their first-wave feminist contemporaries. Just a few years after Voltairine de Cleyre's death, R.A.P (Robert Allerton Parker) penned an article for *Mother Earth* titled "Feminism in America." In his article, he described the ambitions of the first-wave feminists in the United States. Parker wrote, "our American feminists are the exponents of a new slavery" (Parker [1915] 2001, 124). He levied several claims against them. The first was that the feminists, championed by Mrs. Charlotte Perkins Gilman, believed "All sexual activity must be sanctified by law and sterilized by respectability," thereby expounding the "prudery and hypocrisy" trapping women into marriage or creating an environment of sexual enslavement (Parker [1915] 2001, 125). The second was that the first-wave feminists "[grew] eloquent over 'work' and 'economic independence'—revealing a pathetic detachment from the woman who does work, who might tell them something of the 'glory of Labor'" (Parker [1915] 2001, 125). Most white, upper-class women with rich husbands who fought for economic independence, Parker pointed out, really were only interested in the middle and upper class positions available, and he accused them of wishing "to become only the clean-handed slaves of the State, the Charities, the Churches, and the 'captains' of industry" (Parker [1915] 2001, 125). Furthermore, suffrage, or the right of women to vote in the United States, was something first-wave feminists used in order to persecute other women, as in California, where the Redlight Abatement Act was championed and voted upon by women to destroy the evils of prostitution (Parker [1915] 2001, 125). This was done in a way that recognized only the "immorality" of the prostitutes, rather than identifying the socio-economic conditions perpetrated by the Church and State, especially the lack of a social safety net and other viable economic opportunities for women that necessitated their induction into the world of sex for money. Of course, Voltairine de Cleyre would make clear in several of her essays and letters that marriage, for all intents and purposes, is (State- and Church-sanctioned) prostitution, too. Parker's article does not explicate every stance of the first-wave feminists, but it does give us enough of a platform from which to differentiate the feminism of Voltairine de Cleyre.

Unlike the first-wave feminists, de Cleyre was not rich and, although she was educated, she lived her entire life in poverty with the lowest classes of immigrants. De Cleyre, too, discusses the issue of economic independence, but very differently than her first-wave feminist contemporaries. Moreover, she was staunchly against the right of women to vote because voting only encouraged the illegitimate authority of the state. Lastly, de Cleyre encouraged women to be knowledgeable about birth control, never to marry, and especially never to live with a man, because doing so only perpetuated the sexual slavery of woman as housekeeper. Of course, this was in direct opposition to the first-wave feminists' cry of modesty and chastity. Unlike first-wave feminists, de Cleyre also was acutely aware of the interaction between the State, Church, and freedom, relative to the ways in which women were trapped into lives of enslavement of marriage, or childbirth, or even working low-wage jobs. For de Cleyre, women were not meant to be modest mothers or wives; rather, they were to behave and be treated as human beings, just as much as any man, regardless of class or wealth.

Voltairine de Cleyre needs to be included in the anarchist canon. In making this argument, I outline the purpose of the canon as a concept, especially in literature, which, I argue, seamlessly translates into the field of anarchist thought. This is especially true since anarchism was, and still is, a mainly intellectual labor, much in the same way as literature and literary criticism. Furthermore, both developed and became enmeshed in cultural discourse in the mid- to late 19th century. After a brief look at the purpose of the canon, I explore the anarchist canon as developed in the 19th and 20th centuries, which still reflects how we study anarchism today. Finally, I explain why Voltairine de Cleyre needs to be included in the anarchist canon, including her contributions to "anarchism without adjectives" and what her anarchist philosophy can tell us today about contemporary politics and post-anarchism. Recognizing de Cleyre's place in the anarchist canon is important because she provides new lines of flight for contemporary anarchist and feminist thought. This is especially important for both academics and activists who feel the need to legitimatize the roots of anarchist thought socially and historically, because de Cleyre's life and works offer numerous ways in which to approach questions beleaguering us still today.

* * *

Even within other circles besides anarchism, de Cleyre is ignored. In her book *Gates of Freedom*, Eugenia C. Delamotte wrote that she hoped her analysis and anthologization of de Cleyre's letters, non-fiction, literature, and poetry would "help to end de Cleyre's long exclusion from the canon of U.S. literatures, an exclusion puzzling not only because of the extent of her work but because of her literary achievement" (Delamotte 2004, 13). Not only is there little mention of de Cleyre in connection with anarchism, she is practically non-existent in terms of feminism, literature, and Michigan or U.S. history. Voltairine de Cleyre needs to be actively included in anarchist canonical studies, specifically because of what we can learn about her anarchism without adjectives and other views in light of contemporary anarchist and post-anarchist study and activism.

Before we begin to discuss the inclusion of de Cleyre in the anarchist canon, it is imperative to situate the anarchist canon in relation to the idea of a canon in general. Because my background is in literature, I have been formally acquainted with canons for years. For many literature degrees, the only required class that cannot be stricken from one's course plan is a course on Shakespeare. I believe that looking at what two authorities in the field of literature, Harold Bloom and Matthew Arnold, have to say about the literary canon will help us to understand the formation, limitations, and pragmatic liminalities of the anarchist canon. Lest we forget, the premise of a canon and formal education are inexorably linked. Formal education, at least in the Western tradition, is generally considered to have begun at institutions centered on religion. The canon was a means to streamline the texts that teachers needed to teach and students needed to study. And, of course, it all came down to what education is still best at these days: control.

Harold Bloom, an authority in the field of literature from Yale University, wrote *The Western Canon*. Although the book concerns literature, a canon is a canon is a canon. Bloom argues that, originally, the canon meant the choice of books in our teaching institutions (Bloom 1994, 3). The canon was a necessity, especially in the last two centuries, because there was not enough time to read everything and even less time to waste wading through bad writing. Bloom writes, "The secular canon, with the word meaning a catalog of approved authors, does not actually begin until the middle of the eighteenth century, during the literary period of

Sensibility, Sentimentality, and the Sublime" (Bloom 1994, 20). This means the canon is a relatively new development in our academic and social consciousness, and one that grew up alongside social theories such as anarchism. Bloom, however, is not beleaguered by many of the questions plaguing anarchists sensitive to things like authority, control, and power. In fact, much of his book is filled with rants about the "resenters," or people like feminists and multiculturalists who are trying to ruin literature with their damned cultural studies. But, in his defense of the canon—and with it Shakespeare, Milton, aestheticism, and elitist white male privilege—Bloom provides us with some tasty tidbits that help to illuminate the questions we ask when we even try to think about opening up, deconstructing, or blasting the canon.

Bloom's stance reveals some very important and intriguing features about the ideology of canons. He writes, "The Western canon, despite the limitless idealism of those who would open it up, exists precisely in order to impose limits, to set a standard of measurement that is anything but political or moral" (Bloom 1994, 35). Bloom approaches this from a standpoint of necessity, but his diction is clear: "impose," "limits," and "standard" are the very words to which most anarchists stand opposed. Imposition, limitation, and standardization all require authority, power, and control. Bloom also explains, "All canons, including our currently fashionable counter-canons, are elitist" (Bloom 1994, 37). So, even in our journey to fillet and splay out the anarchist canon, how do we measure our own elitist intentions? Blasting the canon still requires ammunition, and ammunition is power.

Curiously, Matthew Arnold once wrote a book precisely about the role of canons concerning literature and thought and how they could be used to perfect society. He titled his book *Culture and Anarchy*. Of course, he was using the term anarchy to mean everything that would be bad and horrible in a cold, barren, valueless world. In proposing this dialectic, to put it simply, Arnold argues for a canon of all the good that has been said and written. Arnold levied in the preface to his work that, "culture being a pursuit of our total perfection by means of getting to know, on all the matters which most concern us, the best which has been thought and said in the world" (Arnold [1882] 2006, 5). The alternative to the canon—ignoring all the good that has been said and written—is pure anarchy. But this dialectic is no longer as clear, and perhaps it has never been, as Matthew Arnold portrays. Even though Arnold was in search of perfecting culture through the use of good literature and thought, which would then lead to a classless society, he doesn't come to terms with the fact that any canon rests squarely on the shoulders of the elite and the hierarchy of (usually illegitimate) power in which they are ensconced. How can a canon of imperfect means be used to help perfect society? The answer is clear for neither Arnold nor for contemporary anarchist academics and activists.

The question of whether or not the canon is an appropriate concept for anarchism or post-anarchism is truly a question of pragmatism. While the concept of the canon is not truly ideologically congruent with any anarchist philosophy I have studied, it still exists. The concept of the canon may divide anarchists and freethinkers, especially as we continue to produce more and more information for consumption. Ideologically, it is obvious that the canon as currently conceived is not appropriate for anarchism as conceived contemporaneously. This also links with the practical problem of experts (such as Matthew Arnold, who was a literary critic), the power differential found therein, and the hierarchy necessary to produce, promulgate, and maintain both canonization and expertise. Obviously, there is an overlap between what is ideal and what is practical, and this in many ways mirrors the current symbiotic division between anarchist academics and anarchist activists—it is a disservice to pretend there is neither a problem nor a divide, but my goal has always been to work within the system to change the system. Evolution, not revolution, is what should differentiate our solutions from those of one hundred years ago.

Beginning with Max Nettlau's *Bibliographie de L'anarchie*, first published in 1897, the anarchist canon officially was Eurocentric, and mostly androcentric. While it is certainly true that the collection reflected the availability of texts to European-based Nettlau, and many women who were involved with the movement were not necessarily publishing, it still stands today as one of the most comprehensive guides to specific articles and books across nationalities and approaches of anarchism. While Nettlau's *Bibliographie* was a beginning, the anarchist canon still mostly revolves around those whom Nettlau identified as the major players of anarchism: Proudhon, Bakunin, and Kropotkin. These are the only people who have their own chapters in Nettlau's book. This trinity of European men as the authorities of classical anarchism remains today. In some places, it has been branched out to include Godwin, and later Goldman, Berkman, and sometimes Stirner and Abbot. Still, it is obvious that there is a canon, and it continues to be misrepresentational across the lines of gender, class, and race even today. In contemporary anarchist writings, especially in the field of post-anarchism, almost all of the major players (e.g. Call, May, and Newman) are middle-class educated white men.

I have established that there is such a thing as an anarchist canon. It has existed for a long while and will continue to exist under the present conditions until we have practically, not theoretically, figured out another line of flight. There may be a time when the anarchist canon does not exist, but it is encompassed within so many larger challenges, such as power, hierarchy, the academy, and hegemony, that the only pragmatic solution is to shape it to our ideals and needs, not pretend it does not exist. Therefore, de Cleyre's inclusion in the canon is important because of her views on the intersection of anarchism and feminism, anarchism without adjectives, and her contributions to contemporary anarchist thought and practice.

* * *

Voltairine de Cleyre wrote about and advocated for numerous issues and philosophical considerations. As an anarcha-feminist, de Cleyre is notably best remembered for her radical solutions to questions of gender and sex. According to Sharon Presley, in "No Authority but Oneself," de Cleyre's "importance as a feminist rests primarily on her willingness to confront issues such as female sexuality and the emotional and psychological, as well as economic, dependence on men within the family structure" (Presley 2005, 191). Presley continues, "Voltairine and the anarchist feminists did not just question the unfair nature of marriage laws of that time, they repudiated institutional marriage and the conventional family structure, seeing in these institutions the same authoritarian oppression as they saw in the institution of the State" (Presley 2005, 192). Three of de Cleyre's numerous works discuss these issues particularly important to anarcha-feminism: "The Political Equality of Women," "The Woman Question," and "Those Who Marry Do Ill."

In the essay "The Political Equality of Women," which first appeared in 1894, de Cleyre argued there is no such thing as "rights" because, without the power to enforce certain actions, there can be no respect. She reasoned women must become economically independent in order to have power and thus have the same "rights" as men. She pointed out that, when women stop being and wanting to be the "protected animal," then they will truly become individuals and have equal claim to liberty and equality. De Cleyre wrote, "She is no more the protected animal; she becomes an individual. She suffers, and dreams of 'rights.' She claims some other cause of consideration than that of wife, mother, sister, daughter; she stands alone, she becomes strong, and in recognition of her strength presses her claim of equality" (de Cleyre [1894] 2005, 242–243). Unlike other first-wave feminists, de Cleyre carefully revealed the heart of the issue: equality can only come from within the women's movement, one individual woman at a time. Women should not sit around and wait for equality to be bestowed upon them; rather, they must stand up and claim it. Furthering her feminist position, de Cleyre gave an "insider's" critique of the anarchist movement and offered a solution for all anarchist women.

In "The Woman Question," de Cleyre established that sexism does exist in the anarchist movement even if the men of the movement, and even some women, argue otherwise. She urged all women, especially anarchist women, never to engage in marriage. De Cleyre wrote, "Men may not mean to be tyrants when they marry, but they frequently grow to be such. It is insufficient to dispense with the priest or registrar. The spirit of marriage makes for slavery" (de Cleyre [1913] 2005, 223). De Cleyre saw marriage as the epitome of what the anarchists were fighting against, except, instead of it being a public institution, such as government, it was a private and personal institution. De Cleyre's solution may be even more radical than her critique of marriage, especially for the time. She stated, "I would strongly advise every woman contemplating sexual union of any kind, never to live together with the man you love, in the sense of renting a house or rooms, and becoming his housekeeper" (de Cleyre, [1913] 2005, 223). She encouraged women, instead, to live independent lives and study sex. She emphasized that a woman should never have a child unless it is wanted, and unless the woman is able to provide for it only by herself. This advice still rings eerily true, especially today, in a world that still uses marriage as a tool of the State and Church to regulate bodies. Voltairine de Cleyre's view that marriage is meretricious is a common theme throughout her writings.

In "Those Who Marry Do Ill," for instance, de Cleyre asserted "Because I believe that marriage stales love, brings respect into contempt, outrages all the privacies and limits the growth of both parties, I believe that 'they who marry do ill'" (de Cleyre [1908]

2005, 206). She defined marriage as a sexual and economic relationship where the values of home and family are maintained. In doing so, she explained that moral paradigms are constructed for the benefit of society; thus, those who marry because it is "the right thing to do," are only buying in to a utilitarian paradigm that "best serves the growing need of that society" (de Cleyre [1908] 2005, 197). She observed that marriage restricts the growth of the individual. In addition, the primary purposes of marriage as she viewed it—child rearing and fulfilling sexual appetites—are better served, in the hopes bringing about of lasting love and respect, in rare and impermanent unions.

Generally, Voltairine de Cleyre's anarcha-feminism can be characterized in part by a commitment to the rugged individualism of the American pioneer, as depicted in Turner's "Frontier Thesis." Her philosophy of anarcha-feminism is situated, in part, in a classic liberal understanding of the individual, while, at the same time, exposing the personal as political. Although de Cleyre advocated for sovereignty of the individual, especially of women, she also clearly saw the need for personal responsibility. Unlike many other feminists, de Cleyre did not defer to a cult of womanhood nor did she participate in representational politics on behalf of womankind. Rather, her criticism and precise articulations of the infringement of women's liberty extended just as much to men as to women. De Cleyre not only advocated for the liberty of women, but she also forcefully championed personal responsibility. Like Kropotkin, de Cleyre knew that women could just as easily gain opportunity only to "throw domestic toil on to another woman" (Kropotkin [1906] 1972, 143). Although de Cleyre may be best remembered and revered for her work with feminism, she also became the head of an important movement within anarchist circles.

Early in her anarchist philosophical history, de Cleyre was known for her individualism, but abandoned it in favor of mutualism; however, she never did evolve into a communal (or communist) anarchist as Emma Goldman once reported (Avrich 1978, 147–149). Her upbringing probably caused her retention to values other than communism, as Avrich writes, "As the offspring of small-town America, Voltairine de Cleyre remained distinctly more individualistic in her outlook than the immigrant Kropotkinites among whom she lived. And as she craved independence and privacy in her own life, she prescribed them for society as a whole" (Avrich 1978, 148). Because of her commitment to a rugged individualism, she was often at philosophical odds with other players in the field, such as Emma Goldman. But this came at a time when the anarchist movement, especially in the United States, was beginning to round a corner. The anarchist movement had branched into four major and myriad smaller lineages of philosophical and pragmatic pursuit. The concepts of socialism, communism, individualism, and mutualism began to cause great friction within the movement. Voltairine de Cleyre, like many others, saw this fracturing and worried about a movement that, although infamous, was still relatively small and very young (both chronologically and in the development of theory).

The solution, for de Cleyre, was a concept from the Spanish anarchist movement championed by Ricardo Mella and Fernando Tarrida del Mármol (Avrich 1978, 149). Known as "anarchism without adjectives," "this notion of an unhyphenated anarchism, of an anarchism without labels or adjectives," was developed to counteract the "bitter debates between mutualists, collectivists, and communists in the 1880s . . . which called for greater tolerance within the movement regarding economic questions" (Avrich 1978, 149).

De Cleyre advocated early on for the different factions of anarchism to cooperate. In her essay, "Anarchism," she commented, "Remember, also, that none of these schemes is proposed for its own sake, but because through it, its projectors believe, liberty may be best secured. Every Anarchist, *as* an Anarchist, would be perfectly willing to surrender his own scheme directly, if he saw that another worked better" (de Cleyre 1914, 112). Interestingly, the discontentedness between the factions played out in Voltairine herself. She expounded:

> Personally, while I recognize that liberty would be greatly extended under any of these economics, I frankly confess that none of them satisfies me. Socialism and Communism both demand a degree of joint effort and administration which would beget more regulation than is wholly consistent with ideal Anarchism; Individualism and Mutualism, resting upon property, involve a development of the private policeman not at all compatible with my notions of freedom. (de Cleyre 1914, 112)

Many anarchists of the time were of the mind that it was inappropriate to decide what kind of society and economic modes would engender the ideal anarchist society; rather, to do so would be to project an illegitimate authority upon the future. She explained, "Liberty and experiment alone can determine the best forms of society. Therefore I no longer label myself otherwise than as 'Anarchist' simply" (de Cleyre 1914, 158). It is not only for her promulgation of anarchism without adjectives that de Cleyre should be included in the anarchist canon, but also for her unique position as a born and raised Midwestern American.

Almost all well-known anarchists from the classical period originate from Europe, and this definitely has impacted the portrayal of anarchist philosophy in the canon. Along with Lucy Parsons, Voltairine de Cleyre is one of the few anarchists, and especially women anarchists, who originally hail from the United States. She is, to the best of my knowledge, the only active anarchist of the classical period born in the Midwest, and especially in a small frontier-like town. As stated earlier, this informed both her feminism and "anarchism without adjectives." She always retained an individualism not found in anarchist adherents of European influence. This individualism and commitment to privacy as part of liberty was integral to a feminism promoting economic and sexual independence (as well as independence from the Church and State in private matters, such as birth control). Furthermore, de Cleyre's physical proximity to the Haymarket Affair was important (she was living in St. Johns, Michigan, only about 250 miles away). The Haymarket Riots, and subsequent trial of the Haymarket Martyrs, was the event that instigated her shift from freethinker to anarchist, and she would later be buried in Waldheim cemetery next to the monument dedicated to the men hanged for their anarchist ideals.

* * *

Including Voltairine de Cleyre in the anarchist canon is especially important for post-anarchism, and her contributions to the field are relevant to contemporary imaginings of anarchist theory and practice. "Axiom //. Anarchism Is Not a Men's Movement (That's Capitalism)," of Sandra Jeppesen's "Things to Do with Post-Structuralism in a Life of Anarchy," partly states, "Anarchist theory will have to include intersectional anarcha-feminism, and not as an afterthought or an additional chapter (like, 'Oops! Almost forgot the women/queers/ people of colour/indigenous peoples/people with disabilities'), but in understanding the crucial role women . . . play in anarchist organizing structures, theoretical development, direct action tactics, anti-oppression commitments, cultural production, etc." (Jeppesen 2011, 155). The previous quotation is an exiguous part of a chapter in *Post-Anarchism: A Reader*, one of the most comprehensive anthologies of contemporary anarchist thought. A brief look in the index reveals that essays in this collection mentions fascism more than feminism and Gilles Deleuze more than gender. The upshot is the volume is chock-full of talk of sexuality (including the GLBT community), which is extraordinarily exigent in contemporary anarchist theory. Unfortunately, because of the somewhat limited scope of sexuality studies, feminist inquiry and feminist analysis still stand as the most appropriate theoretical framework through which we should view anarchist studies.

Much more needs to be read and written about the intersection of anarchism and feminism. While some has been written about the theorists themselves, such as de Cleyre and Goldman, it is rare to find scholarship engaging their writings. More often than not, it is the way they lived their lives that intrigues scholars, which then also includes a brief gloss-over of their major contributions. Few know that de Cleyre wrote both poetry and fiction, and that Goldman has essays concerning drama. Who is engaging robustly with these texts and their ideas, instead of with the authors' lives? Perhaps a few, but it is not enough.[3]

This is especially true of post-anarchism. There have been many articles and publications articulating, investigating, and defending theories associated with ideas like power, hegemony, late capitalism, neoliberalism, and the like. Post-anarchism has even opened up a place through which new areas of study like queer anarchism are faring quite well. But where is a post-anarchist reading of contemporary feminism? Where is a post-anarchist analysis of classical anarcha-feminism? There are a few, but certainly not enough. It seems to me that these questions, rather than being repressed, have fallen victim to an affected dispassion: we've been there and done that, and now there are some shiny new French post-structuralists just sitting there waiting to be poked and prodded and played with. Of course, I

---

[3] Recent Voltairine de Cleyre scholars include Sharon Presley, Crispin Sartwell, and A.J. Brigati, and recent Emma Goldman scholars include Candace Falk, Vivian Gornick, Marian Morton, and Martin Duberman. Anarchist biographer Paul Avrich has also undertaken much scholarship on both of de Cleyre and Goldman, and his writings are invaluable for any study of either's life and work.

like a good Deleuzian post-anarchist analysis as much as the next person, but there is other, extremely pertinent, work to be done.

Post-anarchism needs more scholarship and activism utilizing anarcha-feminists like Voltairine de Cleyre. To be clear, there has been some scholarship utilizing Emma Goldman, but since when has heralding one person's ideas as representative of an entire movement spanning multiple nationalities, ethnicities, lifestyles, time periods, etc. ever been a good idea? Goldman receives a goodly portion of the small beam of the limelight because of her flamboyant attitude, evocative media personality, and many arrests, but she should not be the default anarcha-feminist, nor held up as the stereotypical classical anarchist woman. No person should be the default figure of her or his time period or belief system, and this concept is even more heinous when it comes to members of traditionally underrepresented groups.

More needs to be written about contemporary feminism and feminists. Where are the articles and theories about post-anarchist feminism? What would a post-anarchist feminism even look like? What about women in contemporary movements like Occupy? Does the anarchist academic (or activist) still care that women make less than men—that, especially in the United States, women's rights and access to safe contraception and birth control are being eroded daily? What does it matter if we have rousing debates about hegemony and subjectivity using the evocative arguments of dead French theorists if I cannot find gainful employment at the rate of my male counterparts or if I cannot have access to a safe abortion if I have been raped or my life is in danger? Inclusion of Voltairine de Cleyre and her writings in the anarchist canon help us to confront these contemporary questions in our own world and in our own lives. Not only do de Cleyre's writings help to contribute to our understanding of feminism(s), but her works also hold great promise for schisms within contemporary anarchist circles.

Another contribution Voltairine de Cleyre makes to contemporary anarchism is her belief in anarchism without adjectives. This theory was the melting pot between different social and economic thought. Much of today's contemporary anarchist thought focuses only on the social aspects of anarchism—more of a how-to guide for individuals or particular countries, rather than a comprehensive theory or theories including economic tendencies. Although the anarchist movement has attacked neo-liberalism, late-capitalism, and globalization, few major activists or theorists have provided anything but reactionary solutions. If we are to fight against globalization, what are the alternatives? What are the possibilities that could be left in its place? Although such theories may seem prescriptive, the imagination of what could be is important so that, in de Cleyre's words, we can have at the very least the "freedom *to try*" (de Cleyre 1914, 113).

Yet another contribution de Cleyre can make to contemporary anarchist thought as well as to anarchist practice is her "no frills" attitude toward writing and public speaking. Unlike some of her contemporaries, and certainly totally opposite of the majority of the contemporary academic post-anarchist field, de Cleyre had little use for theoretical explications of anarchist thought. Avrich writes, "Pragmatic and skeptical by nature, Voltairine was repelled by stringent dogmas and arid theoretical schemes" (Avrich 1978, 154). He explained how a friend once said "She had little use for people of high-sounding theories. . . . It was activity she was seeking in preference to theories. She was an intellectual, yet without 'assuming the air of intellectuality in order to make others feel inferior in her presence'" (Avrich 1978, p. 154). De Cleyre preferred the company of "simple people, with active comrades, whose hearts are still beating for the Anarchist idea" (Avrich 1978, 154). De Cleyre's philosophy shows us that one can be both an intellectual and an activist, and that the two parties should indeed work together for social and political change. Furthermore, de Cleyre's habit of public speaking to comrades and "simple" people helped to provide the fusion between philosophy and activism she practiced. Most of her essays were actually first speeches. She would speak yearly at the anniversary of the hanging of the Haymarket Martyrs, and she would also speak across the country and at home in Philadelphia to gatherings and clubs. Once, she even took the podium to speak for Emma Goldman when Goldman had been arrested. It was this continual responsibility to people, not only in writing, but also in speech, that helped de Cleyre connect with her audience and stay grounded to the concerns of the masses. Public speaking is a useful form that has fallen by the wayside in the contemporary anarchist movement, and we generally only hear speeches dealing with anarchism at the height of a protest, when an academic is touring his book, or when a conference panel of paper-readers appears on YouTube. De Cleyre's anarchism was a people's anarchism, not an academic anarchism or a reactionary anarchism.

I urge those who read, teach, and talk of anarchism to include de Cleyre in their personal canons. It is as easy as picking up her biography or a copy of her selected works. Although there are not many books about her or anthologies of her work, pieces by and about her are extraordinarily available if one chooses to look. Include her in research or just in a reading group. Much work needs to be done in the field of feminism as related to both contemporary and classical anarchism. Her literary works of poetry, fiction, and non-fiction have barely been touched. There is much work to be done with and because of Voltairine de Cleyre. Without her, the picture of anarchism is much impoverished.

REFERENCES

Arnold, M. [1882] 2006. *Culture and Anarchy*, ed. J. Garnett. Oxford: Oxford University Press.

Avrich, P. 1978. *An American Anarchist: The Life of Voltairine de Cleyre*. Princeton: Princeton University Press.

Bloom, Harold. 1994. *The Western Canon: The Books and School of the Ages*. New York, New York: Harcourt Brace.

Delamotte, E.C. 2007. *Gates of Freedom: Voltairine de Cleyre and the Revolution of the Mind*. Ann Arbor: University of Michigan Press.

De Cleyre, V. 1914. *Selected Works of Voltairine de Cleyre*, ed. A. Berkman New York: Mother Earth Publishing.

De Cleyre, V. [1894] 2005. "The Political Equality of Women." In S. Presley and C. Sartwell, eds., *Exquisite Rebel: The Essays of Voltairine de Cleyre—Anarchist, Feminist, Genius*, 241–243. Albany: State University of New York.

De Cleyre, V. [1908] 2005. "Those Who Marry Do Ill." In Presley and Sartwell, eds., *Exquisite Rebel*, 197–206.

De Cleyre, V. [1913] 2005. "The Woman Question." In Presley and Sartwell, *Exquisite* Rebel, 223–224.

Jeppesen, S. 2011. "Things to Do with Post-Structuralism in a Life of Anarchy: Relocating the Outpost of Post-Anarchism." In D. Rousselle and S. Evren, eds., *Post-Anarchism: A Reader*, 151–167. New York: Pluto Press.

Kropotkin, P. [1906] 1972. *The Conquest of Bread*. Honolulu: University Press of the Pacific.

Nettlau, M. 1897. *Bibliographie de l'anarchie*. Bruxelles: Bibliothèque des Temps Nouveaux.

Presley, S. 2005. "Part V: No Authority but Oneself: Introduction." In Presley and Sartwell, *Exquisite* Rebel, 191–194.

R.A.P. [Robert Allarton Parker]. [1915] 2001. "Feminism in America." In Peter Glassgold, ed., *Anarchy!: An Anthology of Emma Goldman's Mother Earth*, 124–126. Washington, DC: Counterpoint.

Anarchist Developments in Cultural Studies
ISSN: 1923-5615
2013.1: Blasting the Canon

Rethinking the Anarchist Canon
History, Philosophy, and Interpretation

Nathan Jun*

ABSTRACT
How we define the anarchist canon—let alone how we decide which
thinkers, theories, and texts should count as canonical—depends very
much on what we take the purpose of the anarchist canon to be. In this
essay, I distinguish between thinkers, theories, or texts that are
"anarchist," by virtue of belonging to actually-existing historical anarchist movements, and those which are "anarchist" in virtue of expressing
"anarchistic" (or "anarchic") ideas. I argue that the anarchist canon is
best conceived as a repository of historically-expressed anarchistic ideas
and, for this reason, should include both kinds of theories, thinkers, and
texts.

KEYWORDS
anarchism, philosophy, history

I.

The word "canon" (from the Greek "κανών"—"measuring rod")
refers to a standard of judgment or measurement. Thus the
"Biblical canons" of Judaism and Christianity are "fixed collec-
tions of writings that undergird the core beliefs and practices of
those communities . . . [and] are authoritative for worship,
instruction in core beliefs, mission activity, and religious and
practical conduct."[1] The "Western canon," in turn, describes a

---

*Nathan Jun is Assistant Professor of Philosophy and Coordinator of the
Philosophy Program at Midwestern State University in Wichita Falls,
Texas, USA. He is the author of *Anarchism and Political Modernity*

standard set of literary, scientific, historical, philosophical, and religious texts that are considered especially significant in the historical development of Western culture. When anarchists speak of a "canon," we generally have in mind something similar to a Biblical or cultural canon—that is, a standard set of texts (or thinkers, or theories) regarded as authoritative for anarchist thought and practice or especially significant in the historical development of anarchism.

That anarchism should have a canon is not at all surprising. After all, most every political movement, from liberalism to Marxism, has thinkers, theories, and texts that are considered authoritative or historically significant. But how we define the anarchist canon—let alone how we decide which thinkers, theories, and texts should count as canonical—depends very much on what we take the purpose of the anarchist canon to be. Some anarchists would no doubt insist that a thinker, theory, or text must belong to an actually-existing historical anarchist movement in order to qualify, in which case the word "anarchist" is understood as a strictly historical rather than a theoretical or philosophical designation. For others, what matters is that thinkers, theories, or texts express "anarchistic" (or "anarchic") ideas, not that they belong to an actually-existing historical anarchist movement. In this case, the word "anarchist" indicates an anarchistic theoretical or philosophical orientation ("anarchist *in spiritu*") that may or may not coincide with a historical anarchist movement ("anarchist *in littera*").

If the main purpose of the canon is to aid us in defining the parameters of historical anarchist movements, then it should obviously exclude theories, thinkers, and texts that do not belong to such movements. On the other hand, if anarchism is an idea that, as Kropotkin believed, has always existed in humankind,[2] and so is not temporally bound by any particular historical movement, then the canon is better conceived as a repository of anarchistic thinking—expressed *throughout* history—which can be

---

(Continuum, 2012), and the co-editor, with Daniel Smith, of *Deleuze and Ethics* (Edinburgh University Press, 2010) and, with Shane Wahl, of *New Perspectives on Anarchism* (Lexington Books, 2009).

[1] Lee Martin MacDonald, "Canon," in *The Oxford Handbook of Biblical Studies*, eds. J.W. Rogerson and J. Lieu (Oxford: Oxford University Press, 2006): 777 [777–808].
[2] Peter Kropotkin, "Anarchism," in *Encyclopedia Britannica*, 11th edn. (New York: The Encyclopedia Britannica Co., 1910): 914–919, p. 914.

consulted in the present to deepen and enrich our understanding
of anarchism. This is the position I shall defend in this essay.

II.

It is scarcely in dispute among anarchists that there was such a
thing as an actually-existing historical anarchist movement in
19th-century Europe, even if we disagree about when and under
what conditions this movement emerged. One of the most
widely-discussed contributions to this debate in recent times has
been Michael Schmidt and Lucien Van der Walt's *Black Flame:
The Revolutionary Class Politics of Anarchism and Syndicalism,*[3]
which not only claims that anarchism is "a product of the
capitalist world and the working class it created," but traces its
origins with great specificity to Bakunin and the First
International (96, 24). This leads to the controversial implication
that earlier figures, such as Proudhon, were not, in fact,
anarchists (37–38). According to Schmidt and Van der Walt, the
longstanding tendency to place mutualists (such as Proudhon)
and individualists (such as Godwin, Tucker, and Stirner) in the
same camp as "genuine" anarchists (such as Bakunin and Kropotkin) originates with Paul Eltzbacher's *Anarchism: Exponents of
the Anarchist Philosophy* (1900) (35–36). Further, Eltzbacher's
"seven sages" approach, which takes anti-statism to be the
defining feature of anarchist philosophy, proved extremely
influential on several important thinkers, such as Kropotkin,
Rocker, and Nettlau, as well as more recent anarchist historians,
such as Woodcock and Marshall (39–40).

Although this account is indeed controversial, what is truly
contentious about *Black Flame* is its attempt to articulate a unitary definition of anarchism that blurs the distinction between
anarchism as a philosophy and anarchism as a historical movement. When the authors claim that, "'Class Struggle' anarchism,
sometimes called revolutionary or communist anarchism, is . . .
the *only* anarchism," and that "the historical record demonstrates
that there is a core set of beliefs" (19), they are not just trying to
fix the boundaries of the historical anarchist movement of the
19th century. Rather, they are seeking to define anarchism *as
such* in terms of the prevalent theoretical and ideological
tendencies of that movement. What this means, simply put, is

---

[3] Michael Schmidt and Lucien Van der Walt, *Black Flame: The
Revolutionary Class Politics of Anarchism and Syndicalism* (Oakland: AK
Press, 2009); hereafter cited parenthetically by page number.

that thinkers, theories, and texts only qualify as genuinely "anarchist" if they express "revolutionary or communist" anarchist ideas. Put another way, anarchist thought *as such* is strictly coextensive with the ideas expressed in the mainstream of the 19th century anarchist movement.

According to Schmidt and Van der Walt, the goal of this seemingly radical elision is to save anarchism from incoherence and meaninglessness:

> If anarchism can encompass economic liberals, Marxists, radical Christians, Taoism, and more, it is hardly surprising that the standard works on anarchism describe it as "incoherent." Such an approach is not useful. Given that there are few intellectual traditions that do not have at least some negative comments about the state and some positive views on the individual, it is not easy to specify an upper limit on the traditions that may be assimilated, in some form, to the anarchist category. Eltzbacher only had seven selections, but there is no reason to stop there: once Eltzbacher's [anti-statist] definition is accepted, it is a short step to [Peter] Marshall's work, where the "anarchist" gallery includes the Buddha, the Marquis de Sade, Herbert Spencer, Gandhi, Che Guevara, and Margaret Thatcher. And if the notion of anarchism can cover so vast a field—and let us not forget that the case can be made to include Marx and his heirs—then the definition is so loose as to be practically meaningless. (41)

In other words, anarchist theory—and, by extension, the anarchist canon—needs to be historicized in order to bring precision and clarity to an otherwise vague, muddled, and open-ended understanding of "anarchism." Their argument may be summarized as follows:

(1) There is such a thing as a historical anarchist movement which began to exist in Europe in the 1860s.
(2) The mainstream of the historical anarchist movement uniformly understood anarchism as "class-struggle" or "communist" anarchism.
(3) Anarchism just is whatever the mainstream of the historical anarchist movement understood it to be.
(4) Therefore, anarchism just is "class-struggle" or "communist" anarchism.

I take it that this argument would exclude from consideration: (a) anyone who lived prior to the advent of capitalism; (b) anyone who does not explicitly identify as a communist, or with "class struggle" ideas; and (c) anyone who does not explicitly identify as an anarchist, or with anarchist ideas.

All four of the claims above are controversial, but as a philosopher I am especially inclined to question (3). Why ought we to believe "anarchism" *just is* (i.e., is strictly identical to) "whatever the mainstream of the historical anarchist movement understood it to be"? Suppose Jones asks Smith to explain what most Christians believed in 13th-century Europe. Smith might reply with a summary of mainstream Western theology from that period. This is a reasonable enough response, so far as it goes, since Jones has asked a question about history, and Smith has answered accordingly. But suppose Jones asks Smith to define Christianity, and Smith replies by claiming, "Christianity is whatever the mainstream of the Western Church in the 13th century understood Christianity to be." I submit that this is not a reasonable response, as it seems to commit a kind of category mistake. Jones is not asking about the history of Western Christianity—she is asking about the concept of Christianity itself. As such, it seems quite unreasonable for Smith to respond with a claim concerning medieval Catholic history. More damningly, Smith's response to Jones is circular. She is saying, essentially, "Christianity is defined according to the definition of Christianity that was used by the mainstream of the Western Church in the 13th century." But *this* definition assumes the very concept (Christianity) whose definition is in dispute.

Now suppose Jones asks Smith to define "anarchism," and Smith replies by claiming that "anarchism just is whatever the mainstream of the 19th century anarchist movement understood anarchism to be" (premise 3 above). As in the previous example, Smith seems to have committed a kind of category mistake by answering a question about a concept ("anarchism") with a claim about history. Furthermore, Smith's response is circular insofar as it assumes the very concept whose definition is in dispute. This inevitably runs afoul the "No True Scotsman" fallacy. When examples are cited of anarchists (from the 19th century or otherwise) who diverge from the mainstream of the historical anarchist movement, they can be dismissed as "false anarchists," since, *ex hypothesi*, "no true anarchist" would diverge from the mainstream of the historical anarchist movement. Of course, such a conclusion assumes a definition of "true anarchist," and what constitutes an anarchist (let alone a "true anarchist") is the very issue in question.

In short, I do not think it makes sense to define anarchism *as such* strictly in terms of the dominant attitudes, beliefs, opinions, etc. of historical anarchist movement. Yes, "anarchism" refers to a distinct historical tendency within international socialism, and when we talk about "anarchism" in this sense, we are referring very specifically to a bounded historical phenomenon whose origins can be traced to 19th- century Europe. It is the task of historians to set the temporal parameters of this phenomenon and analyze its distinctive characteristics with accuracy and precision. I contend, however, that "anarchism" also refers to a theoretical or philosophical orientation—a term I use deliberately (rather than, e.g., "position") because I believe anarchism represents a range of intersecting attitudes, beliefs, and opinions rather than a comprehensive doctrine or "fixed, self-enclosed social system."[4] When we talk about "anarchism" in this sense, we are not solely, or even mainly, referring to what a particular group of people in a particular historical context happened to think, believe, or feel.

In taking this position, I am ironically of a piece with many of the most notable members of the historical anarchist movement who insisted that anarchism "recognizes only the relative significance of ideas, institutions, and social forms,"[5] that it rejects "acceptance of or rigorous adherence to any one over-arching philosophical system,"[6] and that it "leaves posterity free to develop its own particular systems in harmony with its needs."[7] These "classical" anarchists clearly would not have endorsed a conflation of anarchist theory and anarchist history. Although they liked to think of themselves as children of the *Enragés*,[8] none them would have contended that the socialist movement to which they belonged existed prior to the 19th century. When Kropotkin, Nettlau, Rocker, and others describe anarchist *ideas* as timeless and immortal, they take for granted an

---

[4] Rudolf Rocker, *Anarchosyndicalism: Theory and Practice* (London: Secker & Warburg, 1938), 31.

[5] Rocker, *Anarchosyndacalism*, 31.

[6] *Errico Malatesta: His Life and Ideas*, comp. and ed. Vernon Richards (London: Freedom Press, 1965), 19, 29.

[7] Emma Goldman, *Anarchism and Other Essays* (New York: Mother Earth, 1910), 49.

[8] See C. Alexander McKinley, *Illegitimate Children of the Enlightenment: Anarchists and the French Revolution, 1880-1914* (Berlin: Peter Lang, 2008).

obvious distinction between anarchism as a social and political movement and anarchism as a philosophy. To their minds at least, this allows them to refer to earlier thinkers, theories, or texts as "anarchist" without anachronism.

For the reasons just outlined, anarchist philosophy is better understood as a matter of degree rather than kind; it embodies a spectrum of thought which has manifested itself—in various ways, and to greater or lesser degree—throughout human history. In the next section, I will discuss what I take to be distinctive about anarchism as a philosophical and theoretical orientation. I submit that any theories, thinkers, and texts that reflect this orientation are properly called *anarchistic* (or *anarchic*) and, as I shall argue, that it is profoundly wrongheaded to exclude from the canon those anarchistic or anarchic theories, thinkers, and theories which fall outside of the mainstream of the historical anarchist movement.

III.

Schmidt and Van der Walt are surely right to criticize Eltzbacher's definition of anarchism since, as the classical anarchists themselves repeatedly insisted, anarchism is not reducible to anti-statism. But how exactly should we define anarchism as a general theoretical or philosophical orientation? To provide a detailed answer to this question would far exceed the scope of this essay but, for present purposes, I would suggest that anarchism may be understood as a synergistic fusion of radical antiauthoritarianism and radical egalitarianism. I would further suggest that theories, thinkers, or texts may be judged more or less anarchistic (or anarchic) in orientation depending upon the extent of their commitment to antiauthoritarianism, on the one hand, and egalitarianism, on the other. Let us clarify each of these concepts in turn.

By radical antiauthoritarianism, I mean: (1) unqualified moral opposition to relationships and institutions based on coercion, domination, oppression, and other forms of arbitrary and unjustifiable authority; (2) an active moral commitment to abolishing such relationships and institutions based on coercion, domination, oppression, and other forms of arbitrary and unjustifiable authority; and (3) an active moral commitment to replacing these relationships and institutions with alternatives based on voluntary association and mutual aid. By radical egalitarianism, I mean unqualified moral opposition to all forms of arbitrary and

unnatural political, social, economic, sexual, and cultural inequality.

There are many thinkers who exhibit a commitment to radical
antiauthoritarianism without a corresponding commitment to
radical egalitarianism (e.g., right-wing libertarians); likewise,
there are many thinkers who exhibit a commitment to radical
egalitarianism without a corresponding commitment to radical
antiauthoritarianism (e.g., authoritarian Marxists). An "anarchistic" (or "anarchic") thinker is one who exhibits a commitment
to both of these ideals in tandem. While the manner and degree
to which this commitment is exhibited is important, they are not
absolute criteria for determining whether a thinker qualifies as
"anarchistic"—after all, even important members of the historical
anarchist movement (as cited by Schmidt and Van der Walt)
failed to perfectly live up to their own ideals. In my view, the task
of the anarchist historian of ideas is to "read" theories, thinkers,
and texts "anarchically"—that is, with a mind to discovering
evidence of this synergistic commitment. It is my position that
wherever she finds it she has also found evidence of anarchistic
(or anarchic) thought.

A great deal of research has already been done which demonstrates a commitment to antiauthoritarianism and egalitarianism
on the part of individuals who do not fall squarely within the
"revolutionary communist" current of 19th-century anarchism—
not just Godwin,[9] Stirner,[10] Proudhon,[11] Tolstoi,[12] and Tucker,[13]
but also the Chinese Taoists[14] and Buddhists,[15] the Greek
Cynics,[16] the Jewish[17] and Islamic mystics,[18] the Antinomians,[19]

---

[9] See John Clark, *The Philosophical Anarchism of William Godwin*
(Princeton: Princeton University Press, 1977).
[10] See *Max Stirner*, ed. Saul Newman (Basingstoke: Palgrave MacMillan,
2011); John Clark, *Max Stirner's Egoism* (London: Freedom Press, 1976).
[11] See Alan Ritter, *The Political Thought of Pierre-Joseph Proudhon*
(Princeton: Princeton University Press, 1969).
[12] See Alexander Christoyannopoulos, *Tolstoy's Political Thought*
(London: Routledge, 2012).
[13] See James Martin, *Men Against the State: The Expositors of Individualist
Anarchism in America, 1827-1908* (Auburn: Auburn University Press,
2009), 202–278.
[14] See John Rapp, *Daoism and Anarchism* (New York: Continuum Books,
2012).
[15] See Edward Krebs, *Shifu: The Soul of Chinese Anarchism* (Lanham:
Rowman & Littlefield, 1998), esp. 56–58; see also Arif Dirlik, *Anarchism
in the Chinese Revolution* (Berkeley: University of California Press, 1991),
esp. 70–75, 111–118.
[16] See Donald Dudley, *A History of Cynicism* (London: Methuen, 1974),

Anabaptists,[20] and Diggers,[21] the French *Enragés*,[22] the Young Hegelians,[23] the American individualists,[24] the illegalists and insurrectionists,[25] the Catholic pacifists,[26] the Situationists,[27] and the punks.[28] The claim is not that these individuals are perfectly antiauthoritarian or perfectly egalitarian. What makes their attitudes, beliefs, and ideas distinctively anarchistic, in my view, is a general inclination toward *both* anti-authoritarianism and egalitarianism—again, expressed in various ways and to varying degrees. In direct contrast with Schmidt and Van der Walt, I do not believe that anarchism is *explicitly* socialist in the modern (anti-capitalist) sense of the word. Anarchistic thought can exist, and has existed, in pre-capitalist societies that were nevertheless quite inequitable. Anarchism as a philosophical or theoretical orientation is defined not by opposition to capitalism, but by opposition to morally unjustifiable forms of authority and

---

esp. 211–212.

[17] See Shmuel N. Eisenstadt, *The Jewish Historical Experience in a Comparative Perspective* (Albany: State University of New York Press, 1992), 73–81; see also David Biale, "Gershom Scholem and Anarchism as a Jewish Philosophy," *Judaism* 32 (Winter 1983): 70–76.

[18] See Patricia Crone, "Ninth-Century Muslim Anarchists," *Past and Present* 167 (May 2000) 3–28; see also Hayrettin Yücesoy, "Political Anarchism, Dissent, and Marginal Groups in the Early Ninth Century: The Sufis of the Mu'tazila Revisited," *The Lineaments of Islam*, ed. Paul Cobb (Leiden: Brill, 2012), 61–84.

[19] See Raoul Vaneigem, *The Movement of the Free Spirit* (New York: Zone Books, 1994); see also Norman Cohn, *The Pursuit of the Millennium* (Oxford: Oxford University Press, 1970), chaps. 8–13.

[20] Hans-Jürgen Goertz, *The Anabaptists* (London: Routledge, 1980).

[21] Geoff Kennedy, *Diggers, Levellers, and Agrarian Capitalism* (Lanham: Lexington Books, 2008).

[22] See McKinley, *Illegitimate Children of the Enlightenment*, esp. 58–65.

[23] See Warren Breckman, *Marx, the Young Hegelians, and the Origins of Radical Social Theory* (Cambridge: Cambridge University Press, 1999).

[24] See Martin, *Men Against the State*.

[25] See Alexandre Skirda, *Facing the Enemy: A History of Anarchist Organization from Proudhon to May 1968*, trans. Paul Sharkey (Oakland: AK Press, 2002), esp. chaps. 8, 10, and 12.

[26] See James Fisher, *The Catholic Counterculture in America, 1933-1962* (Durham: University of North Carolina Press, 1989).

[27] See René Viénet, *Enragés and Situationists in the Occupation Movement, France, May '68*, trans. R. Perry & H. Potter (New York: Autonomedia, 1992).

[28] See Greil Marcus, *Lipstick Traces: A Secret History of the Twentieth Century* (Cambridge: Harvard University Press, 1990).

inequality. To this extent, anarchistic thought is every bit as conceivable under feudalism as it is under capitalism. Nor is it necessary for anarchistic thinkers to specifically identify as "anarchists." (Even Schmidt and Van der Walt admit something like this when they include the avowed Marxists Daniel De Leon and James Connolly in the historical anarchist movement).

In the penultimate section of this essay, I want to provide three examples of how ostensibly "non-anarchist" thinkers (namely, Spinoza, Sartre, and Lévinas) can be read "anarchically." In doing so, I want to demonstrate a way of thinking about anarchism as a philosophical or theoretical trope which recurs transhistorically, although we can understand many general political-theoretical constructions in this way. For example, what might be called the "socialist trope" appears in Greco-Roman historical contexts, late-antique/medieval contexts, and modern contexts. In such instances, a distinction must be made between the 19th-century socialist movement, which is obviously a product of capitalism and the industrial revolution, and the concept of socialism more generally, which is not bound to particular schemes of production or property relations. In the case of anarchism, the point is to show that the anarchist trope can surface in philosophical contexts quite divorced from the historical anarchist movement of the 19th century.

This sort of endeavor will be familiar to anyone who has studied "postanarchist" writers like Newman, May, and Call and their respective anarchist "readings" of Lacan, Deleuze, Foucault, Lyotard, Baudrillard. Although these readings have tended to serve purposes very specific to the postanarchist milieu—e.g., to critically explore the extent to which postmodernist and post-structuralist thought improves upon the theoretical and practical insights of classical anarchism when read anarchistically—I believe the methodology can be generalized in a way that serves anarchist studies more broadly. Relying inordinately on thinkers within the historical anarchist tradition tends to produce a theoretical echo chamber that places unhelpful limits on how we think about anarchism. In seeking to demonstrate the "anar-chistic" potential of thinkers we don't normally think of as anarchist—including many who lack any obvious relation to the historical tradition—my goal is not to show that these thinkers are "anarchists" in an absolute sense, but to discover mean-ingfully "anarchistic" (i.e., radically antiauthoritarian and egalitarian) attitudes, thoughts, and opinions in their writing. I think it is true that many "anarchistic" (but not explicitly

anarchist) thinkers[29] can offer extremely novel contributions to
conventional anarchist discourses surrounding, e.g., freedom,
intersubjectivity, the nature of moral responsibility, and so on.
Such contributions, in turn, provide new and more expansive
ways of thinking about the anarchist canon.

IV.

CASE #1: SPINOZA

Although Spinoza was "considered, during his lifetime and for a
century after his death, a man of appalling wickedness,"[30] he was
revered as a hero by the Romantics of the 19th century[31] and has
more recently been claimed as a champion of Enlightenment.[32] To
my mind, however, the most interesting recuperation of Spinoza
has been carried out by contemporary thinkers like Balibar,
Althusser, Negri, and Deleuze, for whom he stands as patriarch
over the family of ideas known as poststructuralist philosophy.[33]
Like the poststructuralists, Spinoza rejects the Cartesio-Kantian
subject and, by extension, the concept of an essentialized *human
nature*.[34] In this he departs not only from the liberal humanism of

---

[29] My choice of thinkers in this essay—which, as Ruth Kinna points out,
are conspicuously male and Western—is not intended to reflect any bias
on my part, but rather the specific and limited scope of my scholarly
expertise. As the previously cited works indicate, many examples of
female and non-Western "anarchistic" thinkers are available.

[30] Bertrand Russell, *A History of Western Philosophy* (New York: Simon &
Schuster, 1976), 569.

[31] Antonio Negri, "Spinoza's Anti-Modernity," *Les Temps Modernes* 46.539
(June 1991).

[32] Robert Alexander Duff, *Spinoza's Political and Ethical Philosophy* (New
York: Augustus M. Kelley, 1970); Lewis Samuel Feuer, *Spinoza and the
Rise of Modern Liberalism* (New Brunswick: Transaction Books, 1958). For
an opposing view, see S. Smith, *Spinoza, Liberalism, and the Question of
Jewish Identity* (New Haven: Yale University Press, 1997).

[33] See Louis Althusser, *Reading Capital* (Verso: London, 1997); Etienne
Balibar, *Spinoza and Politics* (New York: Verso, 1978); Gilles Deleuze,
Spinoza: Practical Philosophy (San Francisco: City Lights, 1988) and
Expressionism in Philosophy: Spinoza (New York: Zone, 1990); Antonio
Negri, *The Savage Anomaly: The Power of Spinoza's Metaphysics and
Politics*, trans. Michael Hardt (Minneapolis: University of Minnesota
Press, 1991). For a general overview of Spinoza's reception in modern
Contintental philosophy, see Warren Montag & Ted Stolze, *The New
Spinoza* (Minneapolis: University of Minnesota Press, 1998).

[34] Negri, *The Savage Anomaly*, 211, 237, 245, 266, 268; Deleuze, *Expressio-*

Hobbes, Locke, and Rousseau, but also from Marx and other thinkers of the early post-Hegelian Left.[35]

Deleuze in particular has made a convincing case for reading Spinoza as a kind of proto-structuralist at the level of ontology.[36] But this connection is not immediately obvious at the level of politics. Although Spinoza rejects the Cartesian humanism upon which much of the liberal tradition is founded, he nonetheless employs many of its key concepts, including natural right, the state of nature, and the social compact.[37] This fact, coupled with his ostensive endorsement of the liberal democratic state, places Spinoza immediately at odds with most thinkers on the post-Hegelian Left who tend to view social contractarianism as a bourgeois apology for class systems, the monopolization of force, etc.[38] It is thus far easier at first blush to read him as a liberal contractarian in the tradition of Hobbes or Rousseau than as a forebear of Hegel, Marx, and Nietzsche, let alone Deleuze and Foucault.[39]

On the basis of such considerations, a view of Spinoza emerges which resists any sort of convenient "genealogization." He is neither liberal nor radical, but rather a queer and perhaps confused amalgamation of both. To this extent, Spinoza's philosophy shares much in common with the anarchism of the 19th and early 20th centuries, which also blends classical liberal and post-Hegelian radical elements. Spinoza accepts a form of liberal contractarianism and rejects liberal humanism. For the anarchists, as for Sartre, "human nature" only exists to the extent that there is an aspect of human existence—namely, freedom—that is not reducible to causal forces that shape and determine non-human existence. On this limited score is their affinity with liberalism and humanism laid bare. It is simply a mistake, however, to

---

nism in Philosophy, esp. chap. 10.

[35] For more on Spinoza and Marx, see Althusser, *Reading Capital* and Balibar, *Spinoza and Politics*. See also Julie R. Klein, "Etienne Balibar's Marxist Spinoza," *Philosophy Today* 44 (2000): 41–50; Gordon Hull, "Marx's Anomalous Reading of Spinoza," *Interpretation* 28.1 (Fall 2000): 17–31; George L. Kline, "Spinoza East and West: Six Studies of Recent Studies in Spinozist Philosophy," *Journal of Philosophy* 58 (June 1961): 346–354.

[36] Deleuze, *Expressionism in Philosophy*, 1–11.

[37] See Deleuze, *Expressionism in Philosophy*, chap. 16.

[38] See for example Karl Marx, *Critique of Hegel's Doctrine of the State & Economic and Philosophical Manuscripts*, in Karl Marx, *Early Writings* (Harmondsworth: Penguin Books, 1992), 80.

[39] This is the reading of Duff (1970) and Feuer (1958); see note 32 above.

confuse such a belief in freedom with belief in an Augustinian soul, Cartesian subject, or Kantian transcendental ego. The anarchists are united with Spinoza in their rejection of such concepts.[40] Could they be united in more substantial ways?

In Spinoza's pan(en)theistic ontology, there is a single substance, *Deus sive Natura*, of which all things are finite and temporal modifications. It is this idea, more so than any other, which sets Spinoza so radically apart from his forebears, especially Descartes. For with the repudiation of any substantial distinction between God and man, creator and created, mind and body, the conventional dualism of Western metaphysics vanishes. Man becomes one of the infinite expressive modes of the attributes of God. What has heretofore been called mind, soul, or spirit is now identified with divine thought; the flesh, the body—indeed, matter itself—are in turn relegated to modes of the attribute of extension. Voluntarism gives way to parallelism, effectively abnegating the mind-body problem that has plagued philosophers since Descartes. With the rejection of dualism comes the rejection of free will, as well as all forms of teleological ethics that predicate a final cause (e.g., pleasure, *eudaimonia*, etc.) of human action. The traditional view of will as self-causing (hence irregular, non-predictable, and non-mechanistic) cause is impossible for Spinoza since: (a) all acts of will are reducible to cognitive acts by psycho-physical parallelism (b) and all acts, whether understood under the attribute of thought or extension, are determined by the same immutable laws which govern the one substance. To put it prosaically, there is no substantial difference between the causes of natural events (as when a boulder is impelled by gravity to roll down a hill) and the causes of "human events" (as when a man is impelled by hunger to eat a meal).

The *Tractatus Theologico-Politicus* presents Spinoza's political theory *vis-à-vis* the abovementioned concepts.[41] There he begins with the idea that Nature "has the sovereign right to do all that she can do; that is, Nature's right [*jus*] is co-extensive with her power [*potentia*]" (527). Moreover, since the universal power of Nature is nothing but the totality of all particular powers

---

[40] See Luc Bonet, "Spinoza: un philosophe 'bon à penser' pour l'anarchisme," *Le Monde Libertaire* 915 (1993), and Daniel Colson, "Lectures anarchiste de Spinoza," *Réfractions* 2 (2003).

[41] Baruch Spinoza, *Complete Works,* trans. S. Shirley, ed. M. Morgan (Indianapolis: Hackett, 2002); hereafter cited parenthetically by page number.

belonging to individual things, it follows that "each individual thing has the sovereign right to do all that it can do," that is, "to exist and to act as it is naturally determined" (527). Nature, therefore, prohibits nothing beyond what is undesired in practice or unattainable in principle. It disesteems neither "strife, nor hatred, nor anger, nor deceit, nor anything at all urged by appetite" (527). It is not bound by the laws of reason, which only seek mankind's survival and self-interest, but by innumerable other laws that govern being as a whole (528).

Human beings, in contrast, *are* governed by the laws of reason. Unlike the laws of appetite, which vary from person to person, the laws of reason are universal. This is because reason is directed toward the "proper and true utility" of all human beings *qua* modes[42]—that is, their common desire to persist, and to enjoy as many good affections and avoid as many bad affections as possible (528). Furthermore, because human beings' capacity to experience good affections and persist as modes is directly proportional to the amount of affective power they possess, reason is also directed toward the maximization of affective power.

In the state of nature, every individual has license to act on her particular appetites, even those that are injurious to others. The result, as Hobbes noted, is a "war of all against all" in which each individual's desires are in constant conflict with those of all others, thereby causing a net reduction in individual affective power. Since all human beings desire "to live in safety free from fear" and "to enjoy as a whole the rights which naturally belong to them as individuals," both of which are impossible in the state of nature, reason impels them to join together as one, forfeiting certain of their individual rights to the "common ownership" of the entire community (528). As a result, right is no longer "determined by the strength and appetite of the individual," but by the common will and shared power of all.[43] This common will, in turn, constitutes the sovereign power of the state.

The forfeiture of individual rights is only countenanced to the extent that human beings as a whole possess "more power and

---

[42] Deleuze, *Expressionism in Philosophy*, 263.

[43] Cf. Deleuze, *Expressionism in Philosophy*, 261: "Man in principle agrees in nature with man; man is absolutely or truly useful to man. Everyone, then, in seeking what is truly useful to him, also seeks what is useful to man. The effort to organize encounters is thus first of all the effort to form an association of men in relations that can be combined."

consequently more right over nature than each of them separately." (After all, any loss of right entails a corresponding forfeiture of power, and this is precisely what reason forefends). Although this is more likely to be true in a society than in the state of nature, it is not guaranteed to be so. Spinoza is sensible enough to realize that human beings, both within and without the state of nature, are not always guided by reason. The same irrational self-interest that engenders chaos in the state of nature can provoke tyranny and sedition in society.

For this reason, a contractual relationship between ruler(s) and ruled is necessary. On the one hand, sovereign power—whether invested in a monarchy, an oligarchy, or a democracy—is required to protect and promote "the public good and to conduct affairs under the guidance of reason" (530). On the other hand, citizens are required to honor the sovereign's authority by obeying it in all matters. In contrast to Hobbes, Locke, and Rousseau, for whom the underlying force of the social contract is reciprocal obligation (either explicit or implied), Spinoza's theory is practical rather than deontological. Citizens are impelled by reason to obey even objectionable commands, not because of duty or obligation, but because order is generally more conducive to their survival and well-being than chaos. Likewise, sovereign powers are impelled to promote the public good because failure to do so precipitates insurrection. As Spinoza points out, "The position has never been attained in which the state was not in greater danger from its citizens than from the external enemy, and where its rulers were not in greater fear of the former than the latter" (538). The relationship between ruler and ruled is thus symbiotic: the subject abdicates her natural right to the state in the interest of survival, and the sovereign pursues the common good in order to maintain its sovereignty.

This explains why human beings do not become slaves when they abandon the state of nature and submit themselves to the state. For Spinoza, a slave is one who obeys commands that are solely to the commander's advantage: "But in a sovereign state where the welfare of the whole people, not the rulers, is the supreme law, he who obeys the sovereign power in all things should be called a subject, not a slave who does not serve his own interest" (531). When a state is governed by reason alone, its authority is absolute—that is, its right extends as far as its power. Such a state—which Spinoza identifies with democracy—has no interest beyond promoting the public good, protecting its subjects from harm, and enabling them to pursue their chosen ends. As a result, it both deserves and receives their obedience. Yet even in a successful democracy, "no one transfers his natural right so absolutely that he has no further voice in affairs; he only hands it over to the majority of society, whereof he is a unit. Thus all men remain, as they were in a state of nature, equals" (531). Certain fundamental rights and powers, including the right to free thought and expression, remain unimpeachable (590).

In theory at least, the rational state regards the individual as sacrosanct and his rights as inviolable. The sovereign may use violence and force to curb the irrational appetites of its subjects, but such a use of force is limited by reason. Any state of affairs in which the ruled are more rational than the sovereign is guaranteed by psycho-physical parallelism to culminate in revolution. In this way, the transition from state of nature to rational state proceeds in a mechanistic and almost dialectic fashion. (This is how Spinoza both explains and advocates the rise of democracy, which he views as an ideally rational form of government [538]).

Interestingly, it is precisely this mechanistic and quasi-dialectical aspect of Spinoza's theory that distinguishes it from conventional liberal theories and reinforces the anti-humanism stressed by Deleuze and others. In denying freedom and Cartesian subjectivity (i.e., the confluence of soul and body as the locus of the "self"), Spinoza departs significantly from Hobbes, Locke, and others within the liberal tradition. Determinism leaves neither room for rational choice, nor any kind of choice for that matter. Parallelism, in turn, relegates the "self" to a network of desires determined by and expressive of bodily relations. There are no such things as autonomous, atomized, individual selves in the Cartesio-Kantian and liberal-humanistic sense. In all this Spinoza exhibits a pronounced affinity with Nietzsche, Foucault, Deleuze, and others for whom "freedom" and "the self" are fictions, mere expressions of an all-encompassing immanence (variously understood as desires, drives, power, etc.).

Spinoza is also united with Hegel and the post-Hegelian left (including the anarchists) in his emphasis on the social nature of ontology and ethics. Against liberal individualism, his ethico-political theory stresses larger and progressively more complicated relations, as well as the role such relations play in constituting both self and community. Like Hegel, his understanding of ego and alterity is trans-personal, immanent, and intersubjective rather than atomized and transcendental.

These distinctions reveal another radical aspect of Spinoza's philosophy—viz., his belief that the conventional methods of State and Church (traditional enemies of both Marxists and anarchists) enslave rather than liberate human beings. This is because obedience to the dictates of State and Church is more often than not motivated by passive affections (e.g., fear of punishment, hope for a better life in this world or the next) rather than reason. The highest ethical goal for Spinoza is a condition of perfection that is co-extensive with both knowledge and the intellectual love of God. To the extent that the state or any coercive institution is justified at all, it is only by means of helping human beings attain this condition through the cultivation of enlightenment and reason.

Despite these ostensibly radical features, however, Spinoza's theory would nonetheless appear to support the existence of a state. The question, however, is whether such a state needs to exercise *coercive authority* in order to fulfill its role within Spinoza's system. If not, then the ground is provisionally cleared for a more comprehensive anarchist reading of Spinoza. As we noted above, Spinoza endorses an extremely robust determinism that denies human beings any freedom apart from natural necessity. Anarchist theories, in contrast, generally hold to libertarian conceptions of freedom that are at least as robust as Spinoza's determinism, if not more so. (I forewent detailed discussion of such conceptions in this section because there are as many anarchist theories of freedom as there are anarchist theorists. Suffice it to say, however, that the issue of freedom opens at least one chasm between Spinoza and the anarchists that is absolutely unbridgeable. The question is: are there any others?)

Our discussion of anarchism as a philosophical orientation revealed that anarchism is founded in part on moral opposition to unjustifiable authority. Strictly speaking there are no moral or normative principles in Spinoza's system since, to put it simply, there is no freedom. Thus Spinoza's political theory does not oppose authority in the sense of prescribing against it. But this is not to say that unjustifiable authority has no place in the theory. On the contrary, this is roughly what Spinoza has in mind when he talks about the power of the sovereign exceeding its right—in other words, when it fails to act according to reason and in the interest of the public good.

Recall, however, that for Spinoza subjects are required to obey even objectionable commands. Does this mean that they must obey the sovereign even when it fails to act according to reason? I think not. What Spinoza has in mind here isn't a judgment of *reason* but a judgment of *appetite*. In other words, a subject may find a law or command "objectionable" in the sense of not liking it or recognizing that it causes her displeasure, but this is different from judging it to be invalid or non-binding. For example, even though I may find paying taxes objectionable, in the sense that I don't like paying them, I can still believe that a tax system is a good thing (*ceteris paribus*) and so pay my taxes accordingly. Reasonable subjects don't have to *like* commands in order to recognize them as reasonable.

The only circumstance under which the sovereign is permitted to compel compliance by force is when a subject is being irrational—i.e., refusing to obey a reasonable command. In such cases, however, it acts not against her will, but against her irrational desires or appetites. This is because the will for Spinoza is merely a reflection of reason, which universally demands obedience to all reasonable commands. A command is only unreasonable if it requires a citizen to do something that is not to her rational advantage. And if commands are unreasonable they will *necessarily* be recognized as such by all fully rational subjects and met with open disobedience and possibly even revolution. Thus for Spinoza "domination" or "coercive authority" is better defined as "power to compel the compliance of another when such compliance is not in her rational interest."

Understood in this way, coercive authority doesn't *need* to be opposed in Spinoza's system, because any such authority will necessarily be destroyed and replaced with reasonable authority. This follows from the nature of reason. But this raises an important question: why should there be any authority at all? That is, why do human beings have to bind themselves to a sovereign power that possesses more power and right than any of them do individually?

As far as I can tell, they do not. Spinoza is right to suggest that individual human beings have more power and right living in community than they do in the state of nature. But once they are in that state—a state in which the power of one is the power of all—there is no need to reify that collective power as a separate institution or apparatus (e.g., a monarch, parliamentary system, etc.) with its own idiosyncratic interests (e.g., in retaining its rule). For once such an institution exists, it will mimic human beings in all respects, including their tendency to act on selfish desire and irrational appetites. After all, whether it contains one king or a hundred senators, the sovereign power is still comprised of human beings. But if this is the case, there will always be revolutions as long as there are states.

The only way to stop this cycle, it seems, is to completely eliminate the distinction between the actual collection of human beings in a society and the political power of that society—in other words, to adopt a one-man-one-vote direct democracy wherein all decisions are made by consensus. In such a situation, each individual's right and power is truly coextensive with the right and power of society as whole, since there is no intermediate between her will and the general will. Every man "rules" himself and all others equally, thus there is no desire to "retain rule" and no fear of revolution. There is no distinction between sovereign and subject, thus no division of interests. All will participate in debate and voting for the exact same reason—namely, to come into their power and maximize their experience of good affections. I am not suggesting that human beings *would* move directly from the state of nature to radical democracy, just that they *will* move there eventually given the quasi-dialectical operation of reason. In other words, anarchy will not be *chosen*, but will *obtain* precisely at that moment when perfect rationality prevails within human community.

CASE #2: JEAN-PAUL SARTRE

One of the more puzzling and frequently overlooked aspects of Sartre's 1968-1975 period is revealed in the following claim, made to an interviewer shortly after the uprisings: "If one rereads all my books, one will realize that I have not changed profoundly and that I have always remained an *anarchist*."[44] When asked about this same quote seven years later, Sartre replied:

> That remains very true. . . . Still, I have changed in the sense that I was an anarchist without knowing it when I wrote *Nausea*. I did not realize that what I was writing could have an anarchist interpretation; I saw only the relation with the metaphysical idea of "nausea," the metaphysical idea of existence. Then, by way of philosophy, I discovered the anarchist in me. But when I discovered it I did not call it that, because today's anarchy no longer has anything to do with the anarchy of 1890. (24)[45]

---

[44] Jean-Paul Sartre, "Self-Portrait at Seventy," in *Life/Situations: Essays Written and Spoken*, trans. Paul Auster and Lydia Davis (New York: Pantheon, 1977), 24, emphasis mine; hereafter cited parenthetically by page number
[45] He reiterates the claim yet again in Alexandre Astruc's and Michel Contant's film documentary *Sartre By Himself* (1976).

What is odd, of course, is that prior to giving these interviews, Sartre had never once described his philosophy as anarchistic, nor referred to himself as an anarchist, nor associated with any self-identified anarchist movement (unlike Camus, whose libertarian politics he disdained). So what exactly is he talking about here?

Unfortunately, Sartre does not bother to explain in detail what he means by the word "anarchist," and although he distinguishes his "anarchism" ("the anarchy of today") from the "anarchy of 1890," he defines neither. Elsewhere in the same interview, however, he does say: "I never allowed anyone to hold power over me, and I have always thought that anarchy—which is to say, a society without powers—must be brought about" (24–25). Based on this definition of "anarchy," therefore, we can safely assume that an anarchist is, at minimum, one who believes that "a society without powers . . . must be brought about." But what exactly is a society without powers? Other reflections in the interview of Sartre's on May 1968 may provide a clue:

> For me, the movement in May was the first large-scale social movement which temporarily brought about some-thing akin to freedom and which then tried to conceive of what freedom in action is. And this movement produced people—including me—who decided that now they had to try to describe positively what freedom is when it is conceived as a political end. What were the people really demanding from the barricades in May 1968? Nothing, or at least nothing specific that power could have given them. In other words, they were asking for everything: freedom. They weren't asking for power and they didn't try to take it. For them, and for us today, it is the social structure itself that must be abolished, since it permits the exercise of power. (52)

The French *résurgence anarchiste* of 1968-1975 can be seen as a low point in Sartre's long and illustrious career. Although at the time he remained France's most important living intellectual, his longstanding authority as a philosopher had been weakened throughout the 1950s and 1960s by the rise of structuralists, poststructuralists, and various others who shared a common fondness for Sartre-bashing. (Foucault, for example, once described the *Critique of Dialectical Reason* as "the effort of a 19th-century man to imagine the 20th century.")[46] Even some of

---

[46] For a long time the structuralists dismissed Sartre as a "'courageous

the *Enragés* were dismissive of Sartre, both before and after 1968.[47] According to one famous story, when Sartre was invited to a meeting of students and professors to plan protests against the government, he was handed a piece of paper that read "Sartre, be brief."[48]

In another sense however, 1968 represented an unquestionably positive moment for Sartre, as evidenced by his unequivocal and enthusiastic support for the Paris Spring both in word and deed:

> Sartre involved himself wholeheartedly from the first days onwards, doing all he could to encourage the students and win support for them. Now in his sixties, Sartre spent a night at the barricades, spoke before a tumultuous packed house at the Sorbonne, declared his old colleague Raymond Aron unfit to teach because of his attack on the students, and humbly interviewed the student leader, Daniel Cohn-Bendit.[49]

---

and generous' man of an earlier era, animated by a spirit that had passed from the intellectual scene." This trend persisted well into 1968, by which time structuralism had mostly (though not completely) replaced existentialism as the dominant mode of French philosophy; Foucault, for example, publicly dismissed existentialism as an "enterprise of totalization" just two months before the uprisings. Interestingly, Foucault eventually reconciled with Sartre after 1968 and even collaborated with him. See Mark Poster, *Foucault, Marxism, and History* (Cambridge: Polity Press, 1984), 5. For more on structuralism and 1968, see Luc Ferry and Alain Renaut, *La Pensée 68: Essai sur l'anti-humanisme contemporaine* (Paris: Gallimard, 1988), and François Dosse, *The Sign Sets: 1967-Present*, vol. 2 of *History of Structuralism*, trans. Deborah Glassman (Minneapolis: University of Minnesota Press, 1997), especially part II, "May 1968 and Structuralism; or, The Misunderstanding."

[47] Especially the Situationists, who tended to regard Sartre as an establishment figure. See the English edition of the 1965 Situationist pamphlet *On the Poverty of Student Life* (Detroit: Black and Red, 1983).

[48] Jean-Paul Sartre et al., "On a raison de se révolter," *Telos* 22 (Winter 1974-75) : 65–66.

[49] Ronald Aronson, *Jean-Paul Sartre: Philosophy in the World* (London: Verso, 1980), 312. For Sartre's interview with Cohn-Bendit, see "'L'Imagination au pouvoir': Entretien de Jean-Paul Sartre avec Daniel Cohn-Bendit," *Le Nouvel Observateur*, special supplement, May 20, 1968. For an English translation, see Hervé Bourges and Daniel Cohn-Bendit, *The French Student Revolt: The Leaders Speak*, trans. B.R. Brewster (New York: Hill & Wang, 1968).

This period also marked his final break with both the PCF ("which is not a revolutionary party") and the Soviet Union ("which is not a socialist regime")[50] and ushered in his affiliation with the ultra-left Maoists, whom he regarded as "the only revolutionary force capable of adapting to new forms of the class struggle in a period of organized capitalism."[51] After that time, he cared little about his status as a celebrity, having refashioned himself as a "leftist intellectual" who "forsakes his privileges, or tries to, in actions."[52]

When Sartre talks about a "society without power," he seems to be suggesting that power is the *negation* of freedom. Since freedom is neither given by power, nor taken from it, freedom must come from the abolition of power itself through whatever social forms permit its exercise. As such, the power Sartre has in mind here is obviously some kind of *repressive* power—i.e., power which prevents rather than allows, disables rather than enables, limits rather than expands, constrains rather than mobilizes, closes possibilities rather than opens them, etc. Therefore, anarchy is a "society without *repressive* powers," and an anarchist, by extension, is one who believes that such a society must be brought about.

We know that Sartre considered himself part of the *Enragés* movement, which is undoubtedly what he has in mind when he calls himself an anarchist (indeed, a *lifelong anarchist*) in 1968 and again in 1975. Furthermore, we know that anarchy for Sartre is a "society without repressive powers" and that he, as an anarchist, strongly supports the creation of such a society. All of this suggests that Sartre's description of anarchism in the interviews is a *reading* or *interpretation* of the movement that he encountered and endorsed in 1968. Sartre's definition of anarchy as a

---

[50] Sartre et al., "On a raison de se révolter," 347, 42. Elsewhere Sartre says of the Soviet Union, "The machine cannot be repaired; the peoples of Eastern Europe must seize hold of it and destroy it"; see Jean-Paul Sartre, "Czechoslovakia: The Socialism that Came in from the Cold," in Jean-Paul Sartre, *Between Existentialism and Marxism*, trans. John Matthews (London: Verso, 1974), 117.

[51] "The Maoists in France," in Sartre, *Life/Situations*, 171. Sartre also says of the Maoists, "I am with you because at least apparently you want to prepare a society which will not be founded on the auto-domestication of man, but on his sovereignty" (Sartre et al., "On a raison de se révolter," 141). Cf. Aronson, *Jean-Paul Sartre*, 315.

[52] "Sartre Accuses the Intellectuals of Bad Faith" [interview by J. Gerassi], *The New York Times Magazine*, October 17, 1971, 118.

"society without repressive powers" is more or less consistent
with that of earlier anarchists such as Bakunin and Kropotkin,
but what are we to make of his claim to have *always* been an
anarchist?

Sartre's ideas about anarchy and anarchists seem to have been
shaped by his experiences with the *Enragés* of 1968. There is some
disagreement, however, about whether and to what extent the
Enragés ought to be considered "anarchists" in the first place.
There is no question that they were opposed to all forms of
coercive authority, including the state. (Cohn-Bendit claims, for
example, that, "only by overthrowing all governments and every
representative of authority, by destroying all political, economic
and authoritarian lies wherever they are found, and by destroying
the state, can we advance towards socialism.")[53] What set the
Enragés apart from their predecessors was their recognition of
new forms of authority over and above the traditional "somber
trinity." As Richard Gombin notes:

> [For them] the bureaucratic system of industrial society
> has considerably increased the sum total of the exploita-
> tion and repression of man in comparison with competi-
> tive capitalism and the liberal 19th-century state. The
> tremendous development of science and technology has
> led to the individual being completely taken over by the
> system; the individual is no more than a commodity, a
> reified object, placed on show, and manipulated by the
> specialists in cultural repression: artists, psychiatrists,
> psychologists, psychoanalysts, sociologists and 'experts' of
> all kinds. To fight against a 'spectacular' society, in which
> everything is treated as a commodity and in which
> creative energy spends itself in the fabrication of pseudo-
> needs, one must attack on all fronts simultaneously; not
> only on the economic and social fronts but also (and above
> all) on the cultural one: the virulent attacks on professors,
> on the system of education, and on university admin-
> istration, at Nanterre in 1967-68 sprang from this way of
> thinking.[54]

---

[53] Daniel Cohn-Bendit, *Obsolete Communism: The Left Wing Alternative*
(New York: McGraw-Hill, 1968), 222.
[54] Richard Gombin, "The Ideology and Practice of Contestation Seen
Through Recent Events in France," in David E. Apter & James Joll, eds.,
Anarchism Today (London: Macmillan, 1971).

The unprecedented oppression engendered by the late capitalist "society of spectacle" required new forms of resistance within heretofore untapped domains. For this reason, the *Enragés* emphasized the importance of self-management—not merely in the sphere of labor, but in the sphere of "everyday life."[55] This is made especially clear in their efforts during the uprisings of May 1968, some of which we have already mentioned. To offer another example: "Action committees instantaneously sprung up in neighborhoods made up of all the spectrum of society: the students, the workers, the peasants, the housewives. In the atmosphere of complete solidarity between everyone, students helped farmers to produce food for the city, while the housewives took care of delivery to the local shops."[56]

As noted above, Sartre defines anarchism as a society without repressive powers. Before attempting to analyze what he means by this, a few points are worth mentioning. First, like the anarchists, Sartre seems to acknowledge multiple sources of authority and exploitation. One obvious indication of this is that in the original French version of the interview mentioned above[57], he specifically refers to a society "*sans puissances*" (without powers) as opposed to "*sans puissance*" (without power). The use of the plural here seems telling. Another indication, as Ian Birchall notes, is the fact that "for Sartre racism, and the associated phenomena of fascism, colonialism and imperialism, were a central concern from his very earliest works to the very end of his life."[58] Unlike the PCF, which "reduced all questions of oppression to a mechanical model of class,"[59] Sartre recognized that repressive power manifests itself in a variety of local forms, ranging from sexism to homophobia.

Sartre also seems to advocate *active* opposition to authority (another important feature of anarchism) when he says "*une société sans puissances doit être provoquée*" ("a society without powers *must* be brought about"—emphasis mine). This conviction is especially evident in the post-1968 period, at which time Sartre began to redefine the responsibilities of intellectuals in terms of action:

---

[55] Roger Navarri, "Les dadaistes, les surrealistes et la revolution d'octobre," *Europe* 461/462 (September-October 1967).

[56] Decker, 411.

[57] Originally published in *Le Nouvel Observateur* in 1975.

[58] Ian H. Burchall, *Sartre Against Stalinism* (London: Berghahn, 2004), 129.

[59] Burchall, *Sartre Against Stalinism*, 207.

It is [his responsibility] to put his status at the service of
the oppressed directly. Just as the German intellectual who
told Hitler and talked about his anti-Nazism while he
earned money writing scripts for Hollywood was as
responsible for Hitler as the German who closed his eyes,
just as the American intellectual who only denounces the
Vietnam war and the fate of your political prisoners but
continues to teach in a university that carries out war
research and insists on law and order (which is a
euphemism for letting the courts and police repress active
dissenters) is as responsible for the murders and repression as is the Government and its institutions, so too, here
in France, the intellectual who does not put his body as
well as his mind on the line against the system is
fundamentally supporting the system and should be
judged accordingly.[60]

Such ideas are conspicuously reflected in Sartre's many political
activities both during and after May 1968, some of which we
noted earlier. We know, then, that Sartre is kin to the anarchists
in his commitment to direct action and his recognition of the
plural nature of oppression. The question is whether his endorsement of a "society without powers" is anarchistic in the sense
outlined previously (i.e., as opposed to all forms of closed,
coercive authority). I think it is. For evidence, we need only look
to a few examples from Sartre's post-1968 writings, most of
which are replete with anarchistic and anti-authoritarian senti-
ments. First, in "Elections: A Trap for Fools," Sartre very clearly
rejects electioneering in favor of direct action:

To vote or not vote is all the same. To abstain is in effect to
confirm the new majority, whatever it may be. Whatever
we may do about it, we will have done nothing if we do
not fight at the same time—and that means starting
today—against the system of indirect democracy that
reduces us to powerlessness. We must try, each according
to his own resources, to organize the vast anti-hierarchic
movement which fights institutions everywhere.[61]

---

[60] "Sartre Accuses the Intellectuals of Bad Faith," 119.
[61] Jean-Paul Sartre, "Elections: A Trap For Fools," in *Life/Situations*, 210.
See also Bill Martin, *The Radical Project: Sartrean Investigations* (Lanham:
Rowman & Littlefield, 2000), 79–90.

Second, in conjunction with his final and unequivocal repudiation of Soviet communism and his concomitant flirtation with Maoism, Sartre disavowed the concept of the vanguard party as well as the centralized, bureaucratized "worker's state" ruled by party dictator-ship ("Self-Portrait at Seventy," 60–61).[62] Third, he came to advocate workers' self-management, direct democracy, and the integration of *gauchiste* social movements into a proletarian "revolution from below."[63] Likewise, he believed that "political ideas and tactics should not be brought to the masses from the outside, as Lenin's *What Is To Be Done?* had implied, but that revolutionaries should learn from the masses."[64] Fourth, and finally, Sartre exhibited an "understanding of conventional authority as based on power alienated from its subjects, [a] rejection of bourgeois propriety, [an] acceptance of violence and illegality, and [an] unending willingness to contest and redirect himself."[65] Taken together, these examples strongly suggest that Sartre's post-1968 politics are indeed anarchistic, especially in the eclectic, and non-ideological manner of the *Enragés*.

At the same time, however, Sartre's claims to have been a *lifelong* anarchist are difficult to understand at first blush. At the height of the Cold War (1952-1956) Sartre was a firm supporter of Stalinism. In *The Communists and Peace*,[66] for example, "he deployed extended economic, social and historical arguments in an attempt to establish the Communists, especially in their negative traits, as the necessary and exact political expression of the proletariat."[67] Even after his break with Stalinism in the aftermath of the 1956 Soviet intervention in Hungary, Sartre remained for many years a loyal and steadfast supporter of both the Soviet Union and the Soviet-backed PCF. This ambivalence is reflected in most of Sartre's political works between 1956 and 1968, even those that are critical of Soviet policies. For example, although Sartre was profoundly disillusioned by the Hungarian intervention and ostensibly sought to condemn it in *The Spectre of*

---

[62] Cf. Martin, *The Radical Project*, chaps. 1 and 2.

[63] See D. Kellner's review of *On a raison de se révolter* in *Telos* 22 (Winter 1974-75).

[64] Sartre et al., "On a raison de se révolter," 147–160.

[65] Aronson, *Jean-Paul Sartre*, 314.

[66] Jean-Paul Sartre, "Les Communistes et la paix," in Jean-Paul Sartre, *Situations*, Vol. VI (Paris: Gallimard, 1964), and *The Communists and Peace: With an Answer to Claude Lefort*, trans. Irene Clephane (London: Hamish Hamilton, 1969).

[67] Aronson, *Jean-Paul Sartre*, 218.

Stalin,[68] his attitude throughout the book is seldom indignant or outraged. Instead, he addresses the Soviets patiently and empathically as well-meaning "comrades."[69]

Sartre's often obsequious attitude toward the Soviets during this period may be related to his sincere hope for a reformed U.S.S.R—a hope he never fully abandoned until 1968 ("Self-Portrait at Seventy," 18–20). It may also have been a political survival tactic:

> Before 1968 the communist movement seemed to represent the entire left, and to break with the party was to push oneself into a kind of exile. When you were cut off from the left, you either moved to the right, as many former socialists did, or stayed in a kind of limbo where the only thing you could do was to go as far as you could in thinking what the communists did not want you to think. ("Self-Portrait at Seventy," 18)

Whatever the case, by the late 1950s this attitude had given way to the much more openly and unapologetically anti-Soviet perspective of the *Critique of Dialectical Reason,* which Sartre describes as "a Marxist work against the communists" ("Self-Portrait at Seventy," 18).[70] It is here that we find the first explicit and unqualified expression of an idea that heretofore had merely lurked under the surface—namely, that "true Marxism had been completely twisted and falsified by the communists."[71] Although certain moves recall the apologetic of *The Communists and Peace* (as, for example, the claim that the centralization and bureaucratization of socialist revolutions follows necessarily from scarcity[72]), the *Critique* is the first systematic articulation of ideas that would prove crucial to Sartre's later anarchist turn. His rejection of vanguardism and Stalinist bureaucracy can be traced back to other works of the late 1950s, including *The Spectre of Stalin*; the same is true of various anti-racist and anti-colonialist works, including "On Genocide,"[73] "La Pensée politique de Patrice

[68] Jean-Paul Sartre, *The Spectre of Stalin,* trans. I. Glephane (London: Hamish Hamilton, 1969).
[69] Aronson, *Jean-Paul Sartre,* 313.
[70] Jean-Paul Sartre, *Critique of Dialectical Reason,* Vol. 1, trans. Alan Sheridan-Smith (London: Verso, 2004).
[71] Sartre, *Critique of Dialectical Reason.*
[72] Sartre, *Critique of Dialectical Reason,* 660–663.
[73] Jean-Paul Sartre, "Le Génocide," in *Situations,* Vol. VIII; trans. "On Genocide," in *Against the Crime of Silence: Proceedings of the Russell*

Lumumba,"[74] etc.

A case can be made that the whole of Sartre's existentialist philosophy, with its rejection of an essentialized human nature and avowal of freedom as the for-itself, provides a promising framework within which to develop anarchistic ideas. As Herbert Read noted in 1949, "Anarchism is the only political theory that combines an essentially revolutionary and contingent attitude with a philosophy of freedom. It is the only militant libertarian doctrine left in the world, and on its diffusion depends the progressive evolution of human consciousness and of humanity itself."[75] In the end existentialism may offer what anarchist theories have too often lacked—namely, an ontological and ethical foundation, an explanation of what freedom is, how we can create it for ourselves and others, and why we are obliged to do so. But we shall leave this question open for another time.

CASE #3: EMMANUEL LEVINAS

Emmanuel Levinas belongs to a tradition of philosophers all of whom offer sustained and radical critiques of traditional Western metaphysics. Unlike Nietzsche, Heidegger, and Derrida, however, Levinas grounds his critique of metaphysics in an extremely novel conception of ethics. Whereas traditional ethics is taken to follow upon ontology (or, in the case of Deleuze, to be immanent to ontology), Levinasian ethics is *prior* to ontology. With this prioritization comes a systematic critique of the privilege of Being and, by extension, the corresponding model of epistemology that posits subjects of consciousness before objects of knowledge. For Levinas, consciousness is produced through a face-to-face encounter with an Other to whom we have infinite ethical responsibility.

Despite Levinas' profound influence in metaphysics, ethics, and theology, very little attention has been paid to the political

---

International War Crimes Tribunal, ed. John Duffet (New York: Simon and Schuster, 1968).

[74] Jean-Paul Sartre, "La Pensée politique de Patrice Lumumba," in *Situations*, Vol. V; trans. Helen R. Lane, "Introduction" in *Lumumba Speaks: The Speeches and Writings of Patrice Lumumba, 1958-1961* (Boston: Little and Brown, 1972).

[75] Herbert Read, "Existentialism, Marxism, and Anarchism," in *The Essential Works of Anarchism*, ed. Marshall Shatz (New York: Quadrangle, 1972), 538.

ramifications of his philosophy.[76] One reason for this is that Levinas seldom wrote about politics in anything but occasional writings; indeed, none of his major works discuss the subject at length. As Howard Caygill notes, however:

> Of all the twentieth-century philosophers Levinas was the most directly touched by the violent events of the century's political history . . . . Such proximity to the convulsions of twentieth-century political history made reflection on politics and the exercise of political judgment a predicament rather than a choice for Levinas, and had an enormous, if unappreciated, impact on his formulation of an ethics of alterity.[77]

Caygill, of course, is one of many younger scholars who have begun to focus attention on the "enormous, if unappreciated" political dimension of Levinas' work. My goal in what follows is similar but a bit less ambitious. Instead of attempting to "construct" a genuine Levinasian politics, I will briefly explore how Levinas' conception of ethical responsibility can support a tactical, local, anti-teleological anarchistic political philosophy.

Taking his cue from Rosenzweig, Levinas founds his philosophy upon a radical critique of totality—i.e., a universal synthesis or globalizing perspective that tries to reduce all

---

[76] Some notable exceptions include Don Awerkamp, *Emmanuel Levinas: Ethics and Politics* (New York: Revisionist Press, 1997); Roger Burggraeve, *Emmanuel Levinas: The Ethical Basis for a Humane Society,* trans. C. Vanhove-Romanik (Leuven: The Centre for Metaphysics and Philosophy of God, 1981), 5–57; Roger Burggraeve, *From Self-Development to Solidarity: An Ethical Reading of Human Desire in its Socio-Political Relevance according to Emmanuel Levinas,* trans. C. Vanhove-Romanik (Leuven: The Centre for Metaphysics and Philosophy of God, 1985); Howard Caygill, *Levinas and the Political* (London: Routledge, 2002); Leorino Garcia, "Infinite Responsibility for the Other: The Ethical Basis of a Humane Society According to Emmanuel Levinas," in *Philippines after 1972: A Multidisciplinary Perspective,* ed. Ramon C. Reyes (Quezon City, Philippines: Ateneo de Manila University, 1985), 148–165; Noreen O'Connor, "The Person is Political: Discursive Practice of the Face-to-Face," in *The Provocation of Levinas: Rethinking the Other,* eds. Robert Bernasconi and David Wood (London: Routledge, 1988), 57–69; George Salemohamed, "Levinas: From Ethics to Political Theology," *Economy and Society* 21.2 (1992): 192–206.
[77] Howard Caygill, "Levinas' Political Judgment: The Esprit Articles," *Radical Philosophy* 104 (November-December 2000): 6–15.

experience.[78] Here Levinas is calling attention to Hegel in particular, who attempts to reduce both phenomena and our consciousness of them to the operations of a universal Mind. Against Hegel, Levinas argues that being is more than synthesis and reduction; it is rather "in the face to face of humans, in sociality, in its moral signification" (77). The self-other relationship cannot be synthesized or reduced; the Other always goes beyond my consciousness of it in a face to face encounter. Hence Levinas claims "first philosophy is an ethics" (77).

The face of the Other is not a thing in the world so much as a process or action—a "facing." As such it has no phenomenology; it does not appear or represent itself so much as speak, or rather command, and its commandment—"thou shalt not kill"—is ethical in content (85). When the face speaks, it does more than reflect back on the self in order to create Hegelian self-consciousness; rather it opens up a portal to infinite responsibility (88). This infinite responsibility to the Other is not an object of knowledge but a form of desire that cannot be satisfied; to this extent it "is like thought, which thinks more than it thinks, or more than what it thinks" (92).

For Levinas infinite ethical responsibility is "the essential, primary, and fundamental structure of subjectivity" (95). By comprehending my responsibility to the Other, I come to have an awareness of myself: "subjectivity is not for itself; it is, once again, initially for another" (96). Even before my comprehension of it, however, this responsibility is "imposed" upon me by the look of the Other; it precedes even my responsibility for myself (96). With comprehension comes the realization that I am responsible not only for the Other's life but for the Other's responsibility and the Other's death as well (99).

Responsibility for the Other is infinite in two senses. First, it is infinite because it can never be "discharged" through any particular action. I am always and already responsible for the Other, more so than I am even for myself: "We are all responsible of all and for all men before all, and I more than the others" (99). Second, responsibility is infinite because it holds irrespective of reciprocity; that is, I remain responsible for the Other even if the Other is somehow remiss in his/her responsibility for me. Indeed,

---

[78] Emmanuel Levinas, *Ethics and Infinity*, trans. Richard A. Cohen (Detroit: Duquesne University Press, 1985), 77; hereafter cited parenthetically by page number.

I am responsible for the whole world: "The I always has one responsibility *more* than all the others" (99).

As we noted above, the ethics of infinite responsibility "is not merely different from thinking . . . it cuts across ontology, it is radically and irreducibly 'otherwise than being or beyond essence'" (8). For this reason it is very difficult, if not impossible, to define ethics, as doing so "collapses the 'what ought to be' of ethics into the 'what is' of ontology" (8). At the very least, we know that Levinas' conception of ethics is very different from more traditional conceptions, all of which derive their prescriptive and and/or axiological content from ontological descriptions of the world. For Levinas, in contrast, prescription or commandment *precedes* being, and any attempt to describe the world is necessarily shaped and constituted by it.[79] At the same time, however, this pre-ontological ethics lacks the specific content we associate with traditional moral philosophy: it does not provide hard and fast principles of behavior nor systematic accounts of the good life. Unlike Kant, who claims that "ought implies can," Levinas begins with a "thou must which takes no account of a thou can." This becomes the precondition for the formulation of any second-order moral theory. Even before we develop a casuistry that tells us when it is acceptable and unacceptable to take the life of the other, we are "faced" with our own infinite responsibility for the Other's life and death.

For Levinas, then, responsibility is the structure of ethics, and responsibility is always understood in terms of "the two." Politics emerges only with the addition of "the third," and responsibility for "the third" is what Levinas means by *justice*. Regrettably, Levinas has precious little to say about what justice entails. One notable exception occurs in his essay "Politics After," where Levinas suggests that the just state is one that establishes and safeguards the conditions of possibility for acting on one's ethical responsibility. At the same time, Levinas is quick to acknowledge the capacity of real-world political entities to become unjust and even genocidal. For this reason, I think, the "state" is not so much a political entity for Levinas as it is an *ethical* entity; the state emerges wherever ethical responsibility is promoted and protected. But this is not an innate feature of the coercive appartuses which Deleuze calls "state-forms."

There is no hard and fast analogue to "oppression" (or Deleuzean repressive "force") in Levinas. This may be due in part

---

[79] In this he echoes Marx's thesis on Feuerbach: "The philosophers have merely attempted to understand the world; the point is to change it."

to the fact that Levinas is coming out of the phenomenological tradition of Heidegger and Husserl rather than the genealogical tradition of Nietzsche; that is, Levinas remains fundamentally concerned with the question of how things appear to us rather than the conditions of possibility for those appearances. As we have seen, moreover, how things appear to us for Levinas is primordially and inexorably linked to ethical responsibility, which strictly speaking lacks any conditions of possibility. Put another way, Levinas would deny that ethical responsibility is "produced" by something else (e.g., "force"). This does not mean, however, that there is no room for an account of force—especially oppressive force—in Levinas' theory. On the contrary, oppressive force (especially in egregious cases like genocide) seems to be the principal antithesis of Levinasian justice; it is what prevents ethical responsibility from being pursued and protected in the political context of the three. We will return to this point below.

As we have seen, one of the salient features of ethical respon-sibility for Levinas is that it is *infinite*—in other words, it cannot be discharged or otherwise done away with. To this extent, the justice that comes about from protecting and promoting ethical responsibility is always deferred, always "to come" (to use Derrida's and Blanchot's locution). Just as for anarchists respite from oppressive power (read: justice) cannot be obtained by "abolishing" force *tout court*, justice for Levinas cannot be obtained by a permanent "discharging" of ethical responsibility— say, through the establishment of a utopian republic. Justice, then, is a *practice* for Levinas, not a state. Here he follows the anarchists in insisting that the program of resistance must be ongoing, fluid, and ever-vigilant.

So, too, Levinas would most likely deny that evil can be located at a unitary site any more than infinite ethical responsibility itself can. Wherever there is an encounter between the two there is a possibility of evil, and wherever there are encounters among the three there is a possibility of injustice. The converse holds as well—possibilities of evil always entail possibilities of righteousness, but as we saw above that possibility can never be known ahead of time. (This calls attention to the "messianic" quality of Levinas' philosophy, a quality that had a great influence on Derrida's later political writings.) To this extent, Levinas would stringently deny—with Deleuze and many anarchists—that justice can be vouchsafed through *destruction* or any other reactive practices. Rather, justice must be *created* through the pursuit of possibility.

By way of summary: Levinas is very anti-Manichean in

insisting that evil and injustice are *effects*—perhaps inevitable effects—of infinite ethical responsibility. Injustice is not arbitrarily imposed (though he often speaks of injustice being "instantiated"). Political liberation, for Levinas, would indeed be a consequence of the collapse and dissolution of oppressive structures, but any such liberation is produced by infinite ethical responsibility itself. Put another way, ethics undoes the same injustices to which it occasionally gives rise. In this sense Levinas is very much of a piece with Deleuze, for whom desire always contains both revolutionary and fascist inclinations that manifest themselves variously.

Levinas further insists that "the infinite within the finite," like Deleuzean desire, is not a thing in the world so much as a "process" or "event" which gives rise to or produces subjectivity. To this extent it is both ubiquitous and constitutive; it cannot be "done away with" or discharged in favor of something else. This is not to say, however, that oppression is invincible or that it cannot be resisted when it occurs. Though he is by no means clear on this score, Levinas does seem to think that there is a transgressive, liberatory operation of ethical responsibility that can in some sense be "channeled" at the level of practice—in anarchist terms, insurrection (in Deleuzean terms, deterritorialization or escape along lines of flight) *is* a possibility, and the actualization of this possibility is not necessarily a product of mere chance or coincidence.

Again, Levinas would deny that oppression emerges at a unitary locus (e.g., capitalism, patriarchy, etc.) that can be identified and combated. There is no "macrofascism" to which all "microfascisms" can be reduced; rather, oppressive structures are identified solely in terms of their attempts to limit the pursuit of ethical responsibility or else to actively undermine that responsibility, and this can and does happen within multiple sites. As with Deleuze, this necessitates a praxis that is always and already *local* in orientation; the emancipatory collapse of an oppressive structure ("a Nazi Germany") at one site quickly gives rise to the generation of a new structure (an "Israel") at another site. Political praxis must be dynamic, fluid, and eternally vigilant lest the new structure become oppressive.

Lastly, Levinas' political philosophy spurns teleological or utopian discourses as a foundation for praxis, as any such discourses inevitably reproduce the structures they aim to oppose. It is this insight, more so than any other, which underlies occasional essays such as "Politics After." For Levinas, the revolution necessarily lacks a *telos* or *eschaton* and so must be in some sense *eternal.* Ethical responsibility cannot be discharged; justice and love are always (a la Derrida) "to come." Freedom is not a goal so much as a practice or process that is immanent to the struggle against un-freedom. Anarchism emerges as the condition of possibility for engaging in this open-ended and free-floating "practice of freedom" which does not, and need not, culminate in a utopian "end of history." All of this is by way of saying that Levinas' philosophy does evince a meaningful political content—one that is decidedly anarchistic in orientation.

V.

In this essay I have tried to articulate a distinction between two expressions of anarchism—viz., as a historical movement and as a philosophical or theoretical orientation. Although these expressions frequently overlap with one another, they are not identical. This means that the study of anarchist history can and should proceed along two distinct but related trajectories, the first of which seeks to understand and analyze the movement, the second of which seeks to understand and analyze the philosophy. Both forms of inquiry are capable of making important contributions to the anarchist canon but, as I have suggested, the canon itself is best understood as a repository of anarchistic ideas that can be consulted and marshaled in the service of contemporary struggles.

Anarchist history in the second sense amounts to the history of anarchist ideas. Its principal methodology involves what I have called "reading anarchically"—the hermeneutic practice of discovering anarchistic attitudes, ideas, and thoughts in literature, philosophy, and other venues. Whether or not Schmidt and Van der Walt's *Black Flame* succeeds as a work of history in the first sense, it fails because it neglects this second sense of doing history. The authors would loudly disclaim Spinoza, Sartre, and Levinas as anarchists, and I would agree with them—they are not "anarchists" in the sense of belonging to a historical anarchist movement or self-identifying as "communist anarchists." But these individuals (and many others besides) can be read as "anarchistic" thinkers whose ideas should be seen as important and worthwhile to anarchists. For this reason alone, they are worthy candidates for "canonization."

At the same time I am sympathetic to Schmidt and Van der Walt's fear of making everyone and everything an anarchist. I want to maintain a real distinction between a historical anarchist political tradition (including the philosophical ideas that emerge from within that tradition) and other political traditions. I believe, however, that anarchist ideas can emerge, and have emerged, in contexts other than the historical anarchist political tradition. I take it for granted that ideas from the former can and often will be in tension with ideas from the latter— perhaps we could call it a tension between anarchism and the anarchic, or something like that— but I think this tension is healthy. Our understanding of classical anarchist ideas can inform our understanding of "anarchistic" ideas just as much as the other way round.

In closing, I would emphasize that "reading anarchically" does not commit one to the view that there are no better or worse anarchist thinkers. Even within a broad and diverse canon it is still possible to recognize and appreciate "The Greats" using commonsensical criteria of judgment. Nor does "reading anarchically" entail a relativistic attitude toward competing anarchist theories. It leaves open the possibility that that anarcho-syndicalism, for example, is superior to insurrectionism as a strategic philosophy. This, however, is a position that must be argued on political-theoretical, rather than strictly historical grounds. "Reading anarchically" does not permit the mass excommunication of entire anarchist traditions simply because of their minoritarian status within the broader historical movement. Lastly, "reading anarchically" does not commit one to the view that everyone who thinks anarchistically is an "anarchist" in the same way that, for example, Bakunin, Kropotkin, or Goldman were anarchists—i.e., not just anarchistic thinkers, but important members of the historical anarchist movement. It simply acknowledges that the condition of possibility for any great movement is a great idea, and that ideas can and do take on lives of their own.

Anarchist Developments in Cultural Studies
ISSN: 1923-5615
2013.1: Blasting the Canon

Would the Real Max Stirner Please Stand Up?

Elmo Feiten*

ABSTRACT
This paper criticizes a range of recent positions on Max Stirner's
relationship to the anarchist canon. A recent rise in academic attention
to Stirner offers a possibility for new analyses to clear away the
misconceptions of the past, however some old mistakes are still
consistently repeated, not all important insights find their way into the
present discussion, and some new readings of Stirner even introduce
new inadequacies. Addressing specifically the controversial definition of
the anarchist canon in *Black Flame* and the debate surrounding the
concept of postanarchism, I show the theoretical and argumentative
problems present in different texts, both those that identify Stirner as
part of the anarchist canon and those that exclude him from it. Present
difficulties in situating Stirner's thought are traced back to his original
canonization as an anarchist, by Marxists on the one hand and
individualist anarchists on the other.

KEYWORDS
Black Flame, Friedrich Engels, Marxism, Max Stirner, post-anarchism,
post-structuralism, Saul Newman

When Max Stirner published his only book, *The Ego and Its Own*,
in 1844, hardly anyone called themselves an anarchist, apart from
Proudhon and Moses Hess, an early German socialist (cf. Zenker
2010: 132). Despite the fact that Stirner never adopted the label,

---

*Elmo Feiten has studied English, Cognitive Science, and Cultural
Studies at the University of Freiburg, Germany, and is currently investi-
gating the significance of Max Stirner's thought as an instance of radical
Enlightenment in relationship to anarchism and poststructuralism.

his work features prominently in important scholarly investigations of anarchism, from the influential study by Paul Eltzbacher first published in 1900 and still in print today, to works like Daniel Guérin's of 1965. However, the most important anarchists never dealt with Stirner in depth; Bakunin never mentioned him at all, and Kropotkin only dealt with him in passing and only after a resurgence in interest had made Stirner impossible to ignore (cf. Laska 1996: 27, 45). Even Proudhon, whom Stirner had criticized directly, never responded or commented on Stirner's work (cf. Laska 1996: 45). Stirner was first identified as an anarchist in Friedrich Engels' *Ludwig Feuerbach and the End of Classical German Philosophy*, a classification that was adopted by the earliest scholarly studies of anarchism, E.V. Zenker's of 1895, Paul Eltzbacher's of 1900, and Ettore Zoccoli's of 1907. Most anarchists who include Stirner as one of their main influences have been labelled as individualist anarchists; this is related to the fact that Stirner's work, after having been almost forgotten, experienced a kind of renaissance in the wake of Nietzsche's success since the 1890s, as many considered Stirner a forerunner of Nietzsche (cf. Laska 1996: 33–41).

In the last two decades, Stirner's thought has been brought into discussions of anarchism in connection with post-structuralism, in the context of debates around the possibility of post-anarchism, and more recently as a reaction against the very narrow definition of anarchism undertaken in *Black Flame: The Revolutionary Class Politics of Anarchism and Syndicalism*. Throughout the history of his reception Stirner's thought has been misinterpreted and mislabelled, both consciously and accidentally, with malignant intentions or through wishful obfuscation. The recent debates afford the opportunity of clearing away the misconceptions of the past; however, some old mistakes are still consistently repeated, not all important insights find their way into the present discussion, and some new readings of Stirner even introduce new inadequacies. This paper will explain a set of different misconceptions that have played a role in contemporary debates about the relationship between Stirner and anarchism and trace their connections to the history of Stirner's canonization as an anarchist.

* * *

Michael Schmidt and Lucien van der Walt argue in *Black Flame* that common conceptions of anarchism include many thinkers who were not actually anarchists, and they trace this phenomenon to Eltzbacher's seminal study of anarchism in which he identified the "seven sages": Godwin, Stirner, Proudhon, Bakunin, Kropotkin, Tucker, and Tolstoy (Schmidt and van der Walt 2009: 35, 39). After briefly describing each of these thinkers and their "radically different ideas", Schmidt and van der Walt assert: "Faced with such a diverse group of thinkers . . . , Eltzbacher was in a quandary" (2009: 39). However, one could argue that Eltzbacher's position was not as dire as the authors of Black Flame present it: their account of Stirner is significantly different from that of Eltzbacher's with the result that his "group of thinkers" is far less "diverse" than theirs.

Schmidt and van der Walt characterize Stirner's position as a "misanthropic bourgeois individualism" (2009: 48). In contrast to this, Eltzbacher cites Stirner as saying, "I too love men, not merely individuals, but every one. But I love them with the consciousness of egoism; I love them because love makes me happy, I love because love is natural to me, because it pleases me. I know no 'commandment of love'" (2011: 97). Where Schmidt and van der Walt assert that Stirner "did not actually advocate the abolition of the state" (2009: 36), Eltzbacher cites Stirner as saying: "I am the mortal enemy of the State" (2011: 102). In fact, the very paragraph that Schmidt and van der Walt cite in order to question Stirner's anti-statism also contains strong support for it. They quote: "My object is not the overthrow of an established order but my elevation above it" (2009: 36), but they leave out what this entails for Stirner: "If I leave the existing order, it is dead and passes into decay" (qtd. in Eltzbacher 2011: 110). Quoting selectively, Schmidt and van der Walt distort the meaning of their citations: "my purpose and deed are not . . . political or social" (2009: 36) sounds very different when read in a paragraph that advocates insurrection instead of revolution: "The Revolution aimed at new arrangements: the Insurrection leads to no longer having ourselves arranged but arranging ourselves" (qtd. in Eltzbacher 2011: 110). The overall impression of Stirner's attitude towards the state, the nature of his egoism, and the role of the individual that results from Eltzbacher's account is quite different from the picture drawn by Schmidt and van der Walt's highly selective and cursory summary: The notion of a 'union of egoists' is not even mentioned in Black Flame. Schmidt and van der Walt's refusal to award the label 'anarchist' to "such a diverse group of thinkers" might stem from the fact that their attempt at tracing Eltzbacher's analysis does not recreate (or apparently even register) the individual analyses of his seven sages but instead proceeds at least in the case of Stirner from a facile distortion of his thought; their different verdict is hardly surprising as it is not even based on the same preconditions (2009: 39).

Against Eltzbacher's conception, Schmidt and van der Walt outline what they argue is the only correct version of the anarchist canon, accepting of his seven sages only Bakunin and Kropotkin as anarchists: "An outline of figures like Godwin, Proudhon, Stirner, Bakunin, Tucker, Kropotkin, and Tolstoy demonstrates clearly that they cannot be taken as representative of a single doctrine, unless that doctrine is defined at a general level that obscures the radical differences between these thinkers" (2009: 41). Further, they write that, "One problem with such an approach is that it fails to provide an effective definition" (2009: 41). Effective for what? "A good definition is one that highlights the distinguishing features of a given category, does so in a coherent fashion, and is able to differentiate that category from others, thereby organising knowledge as well as enabling effective analysis and research" (Schmidt and van der Walt 2009: 43). The problem here is that a "good definition" in this case is something that can only be applied to very specific phenomena, those with clearly defined boundaries and internal coherence:

> We suggest that the apparently ahistorical and incoherent character of anarchism is an artefact of the way in which anarchism has been studied, rather than inherent in anarchism itself. Using a deductive method, but taking more care in our selection of the representatives of anarchism, we can develop a different, more accurate, and more useful understanding of anarchism. (Schmidt and van der Walt 2009: 44)

The problem is that an appeal to "anarchism itself" identifies anarchism as a historical phenomenon, but the idea that a more coherent and monolithic account of anarchism is also "more accurate" is a methodological *trompe l'oeil*. The crucial difference here is between a term that has a history entangled in the history of the phenomenon it denotes and an analytical category that is applied in hindsight to a certain pattern in a set of data. In demanding that anarchism have a clear definition, the coherence of the object of analysis is guaranteed simply by pruning the object until it fits the demand. As Eltzbacher notes, "How can one take any of them as Anarchistic teachings for a starting-point, without applying that very concept of Anarchism which he has yet to determine?" (2011: 6).

The method already implies the result, because it is chosen precisely for the sake of producing this result, and previous definitions of anarchism are rejected because their results are deemed undesirable: "If the anarchists include figures as different as the seven sages, . . . then anarchism *must* seem incoherent and therefore cannot be subjected to a rigorous theoretical interrogation" (Schmidt and van der Walt 2009: 43). The solution to this problem is to find the biggest possible subset of these thinkers that still presents a coherent object for theoretical analysis. This is a laudable endeavour, but the problem remains: there is no analytical reason to call this subset anarchism. For the theoretical analysis of a doctrine, it matters what texts and people are included in its canon, but not whether that canon is called anarchism or, for example, class struggle anarchism or anarcho-syndicalism.

The reason for calling it anarchism is one of political identification, a matter of the language used in building a political movement and a sense of belonging. The argumentative impetus of *Black Flame* seems to be that a historical analysis of anarchism shows that it has more theoretical and historical coherence than previously attributed to it, that anarchism is, to invert the criticism of the seven sages approach, a movement with a single doctrine. However, the platformist implications of this argument are the inevitable result of the theoretical demands from which it proceeds, which one might provocatively describe as a platformist methodology. Gabriel Kuhn, in his lucid commentary on the issue, has pointed out that, "Schmidt and van der Walt have *reasons* for choosing the definition of anarchism they chose," but he chooses not to speculate on what they might be (Kuhn 2011). To me, it seems likely that the reasons are relatively clear: a platformist organization that unites all anarchists under a commonly endorsed theoretical framework makes most sense if the common ground between different anarchist approaches is as big as possible, and this can either be achieved by convincing every anarchist to adopt a similar position—which might prove difficult since most anarchists in a historical study are already dead—or by arguing anyone who strays too far from the ideological mainline central to a platformist organization is not an anarchist. In accordance with Eltzbacher's methodological considerations, we can record here that *Black Flame* does not so much "develop a different . . . understanding of anarchism" but more precisely charts the history of what is considered anarchism according to a notion thereof that precedes the writing of this history (Schmidt and van der Walt 2009: 44).

Despite the fact that Schmidt and van der Walt only deal with Stirner's thought cursorily, because they don't consider him an anarchist, they are adamant about his opposition to anarchism. According to Schmidt and van der Walt, Stirner "invoked egoism against socialism" in a debate with Moses Hess and Wilhelm Weitling (2009: 67). The problem with this is that the socialism Stirner argued against is a very specific, and very early, form of socialism with the result that his criticism cannot immediately be assumed to apply to all possible forms of socialism (cf. Adler 2000: 27–29). Indeed, in his own reply to his critics, Stirner makes clear that he is only opposed to any fixed vision of the future that turns into an obligation and a duty for individuals, rather than a tool for realizing their interests: "Egoism, as Stirner uses it, is not opposed to love nor to thought; it is no enemy of the sweet life of love, nor of devotion and sacrifice; it is no enemy of intimate warmth, but it is also no enemy of critique, nor of socialism, nor, in short, of any *actual interest* . . . , not against socialists, but against sacred socialists" (Stirner 1845). The contrast that Schmidt and van der Walt draw when they advocate "cooperation rather than Stirnerite individualism" might be correct for specific individualist misreadings of Stirner, but only appears tenable if one completely ignores the union of egoists, Stirner's form of voluntary association (2009: 38).

Stirner's egoism is not an appeal for individuals to be less altruistic, but only to become aware of the fact that seemingly altruistic behaviour can be separated into that which is motivated by a personal interest in, or love for, the other, or by a sense of duty, of holy obligation. Stirner agitates only against the latter motivation for behaviour, showing that duty relates to an abstract conception of universal good, or universal interest, which exists only as a spook. Far from denying cooperation, Stirner animates the individual to associate freely in whatever constellation is capable of advancing his or her own interest. One common misconception is that Stirner's individual is an abstraction as well (Plechanov 2001: 50). However, Stirner focuses on the individual made from flesh and blood and its interests, showing on the contrary that concepts like class or society cannot have interests because they are just concepts. However, Stirner recognizes very well the common interests of individuals in similar economic circumstances, advocating not competition but cooperation:

> Abolishing competition is not equivalent to favouring the guild. The difference is this: In the guild baking, etc., is the affair of the guild-brothers; in competition, the affair of chance competitors; in the union, of those who require baked goods, and therefore my affair, yours, the affair of neither the guildic nor the concessionary baker, but the affair of the united. (Stirner, 1907)

Plechanov, despite being critical of Stirner, actually praised his achievement in attacking bourgeois reformers and utopian socialists who thought the proletariat could be emancipated by the virtuous acts of the propertied class. In arguing that those who suffer from the current relations should abolish them in their own interest, Stirner, according to Plechanov, is "preaching class-struggle" (Plechanov, 2001: 50).

Schmidt and van der Walt do not question what Stirner means when he says "egoism," but they also describe Stirner's thought in terms he rejects, like "virtue" and "right" (Schmidt and van der Walt 2009: 36, 52). However, from their descriptions of Bakunin and Kropotkin, it seems that there might be certain points of contact between Stirner and their "broad anarchist tradition." Stirner's union of egoists can fittingly be described in Bakunin's words as "the free federation of common interests, aspirations and tendencies" (qtd. in Schmidt and van der Walt 2009: 48). Likewise, there is no contradiction between Stirner's thought and Bakunin's call for "*equality and collective labour*—obligatory not by law, but by the force of realities." Those points where Stirner seems to differ most obviously include the relationship between individual and society and the role of morality.

According to Schmidt and van der Walt, the "basic premise of all of the anarchist arguments was a deep and fundamental commitment to individual freedom. For the anarchists, however, freedom could only exist, and be exercised, in society" (2009: 47). There is a subtle, but crucial, difference here to Ruth Kinna's claim that "Kropotkin argues that the proper method of social inquiry is to start 'from a free individual to reach a free society'" (1995: 267). The question of whether a free society is made by free individuals or the other way around may seem to some degree an almost irrelevant question about chicken and eggs. However, this could also be conceived as the question of which word is stressed in libertarian socialism. For Stirner, any voluntary association entails that the individual is free at any time to leave the union, thus forfeiting any rights and obligations that might have been agreed upon in the terms of the association. This right to secession is also mentioned by Schmidt and van der Walt, but the possibility appears very marginal when compared to e.g. Guérin's account of Bakunin, and it seems less of an option because it is related to an "anarchist society" that always appears in the singular, completely omitting the possibility of joining or founding a different anarchist society (Schmidt and van der Walt 2009: 70; cf. Guérin 1967: 33–35).

Schmidt and van der Walt argue that "if individual freedom was defined as freedom from every restriction, anarchists were not in favour of individual freedom", which is not at odds with Stirner, who saw absolute freedom not only as a pipe dream and a physical impossibility, but also conceded that any association with others would impose certain limits on individual freedom, which would be more than made up for by the greater fulfilment of interests (Schmidt and van der Walt 2009: 70). However, there seems to be a theoretical problem with the emphasis that Schmidt and van der Walt place on "legitimate coercive power", which is mentioned five times, as opposed to the possibility of leaving any particular anarchist society, mentioned only once (Schmidt and van der Walt 2009: 33, 48, 67, 70, 204). The problem is that the moment any individual is coerced, this basically constitutes the end of "free agreement and free cooperation, without sacrificing the autonomy of the individual", as Schmidt and van der Walt cite Kropotkin (qtd. in Schmidt and van der Walt 2009: 65). Of course, there needs to be a tool for preventing abusive elements from endangering the functioning of society, but the only way of doing this that does not formally end the status as a voluntary association is the expulsion of these elements from the associ-ation. If someone who infringes upon the agreements of an association accepts a certain punishment in exchange for the possibility of remaining part of that association, this would leave them with the free choice to remain part of the society or not, but it would also be distinct from coercive force applied on a member of the association. Stirner, however, would not use the term 'society' here: "the union exists for you and by you, society contrariwise claims you for itself and exists even without you; in short, society is sacred, the union is your own; society uses you up, you use up the union" (qtd. in Eltzbacher 2011: 105).

The problem of morals is intricately bound up with a general problem of Stirner's reception: Often what appears to be an opposition to Stirner's thought is actually just a reaction against specific readings of Stirner, most of which are referred to as 'individualist,' and most of which are expounded by people who are also strongly influenced by Nietzsche. The result is that it is entirely unclear in how far Kropotkin's "misanthropic bourgeois individualism" actually contains a valid critique of Stirner (qtd. in Schmidt and van der Walt 2009: 242). Schmidt and van der Walt claim "Kropotkin also found it increasingly necessary to defend anarchism against Stirnerite and Nietzschean ideas, which he believed provided a recipe for 'the slavery and oppression of the masses'" (2009: 242). The source they are citing is Ruth Kinna's article on Kropotkin's mutual aid, which however does not mention Stirner; the passage referenced deals with Nietzschean individualism and in fact quotes Kropotkin's claim: "whatever a man's actions and line of conduct may be, he does what he does in obedience to a craving of his nature . . . . Let him act as he may, the individual acts as he does because he finds a pleasure in it, or avoids . . . a pain" (qtd. in Kinna 1995: 269). Kinna explains that Kropotkin aligns this claim that "individuals are psychological egoists" with his ideas about society by arguing that "what gives pleasure to the individual is the community and what gives pain is harming it" (1995: 269).

Kropotkin and Stirner did not share the same views about what precisely gives humans pleasure and pain, but Kropotkin's position is exactly the position that Stirner occupies. The point where Stirner diverges from Kropotkin is that he rejects any statements about human nature in general because they are bound to distort the natural behaviour of the individual who is obliged to live up to some 'human potential' defined by whomever happens to be accepted as an authority on human nature. Stirner writes that even the duty of living according to one's nature is meaningless because that is what happens anyway in the absence of duties. Stirner's differentiation here is very close to the later distinction made in psychoanalysis: Stirner rejects any notions of good and evil that the individual internalizes through societal pressure—which correspond to the super-ego—because they prevent the fulfilment of desires and interests: the id. Stirner concedes that the individual can sometimes suppress particular urges and interests, but only if they endanger the fulfilment of other interests, as the result of a rational consideration—an achievement of the ego—and not because they infringe on some irrationally internalized principle such as religion or morality.

It is entirely possible that the individualist currents Kropotkin was worried about cite both Nietzsche and Stirner as their intellectual inspirations, a common combination. However, for an analysis of Stirner's thought alongside anarchism it is very important to not only recognize the often joint reception of Stirner and Nietzsche but also to tease out the differences in their actual writings. It might be argued that the fact that the revival of interest in Stirner in the 1890s coincided with the growing popularity of Nietzsche's writings contributed to an understanding that is more individualist than Stirner's work alone warrants; the possible connections between Stirner's work and non-individualist forms of anarchism get obscured by the immediate association with Nietzschean individualists. Saul Newman points towards the difference between Nietzsche and Stirner in his reply to Benjamin Franks. His argument also invalidates the idea that Stirner's thought entails a "'disguised return' of 'privileged minorities'" (Schmidt and van der Walt 2009: 47):

> While this social dimension of egoism is perhaps insufficiently elaborated and developed—Stirner makes certain references to the possibility of a "union of egoists"—it is by no means ruled out in his account. Nor is there an implied hierarchy in Stirner's thinking, between the liberated ego and others, as Franks suggests. For Stirner, the possibilities of radical freedom offered by egoism and "ownness" can be grasped by anyone; there is no Nietzschean sentimentality here for aristocracy. (Newman 2011a: 160)

The fact that Stirner does not have a positive social vision beyond the idea of voluntary association is inextricably tied up with his entire critical position: The question of how exactly self-aware egoists will cooperate cannot be answered in advance if it is to be the result and expression of the interests of the unique individuals engaged in it. This is the case because according to Stirner any general account of human interests, or of good and evil, will prevent individuals from following their own particular interests and lead them instead to aspire to some ideal, a criticism that also includes any specific form of social organisation that is deemed optimal. If there is such a thing as a general human nature, it would also find its expression in the development of every individual's particular nature, but they would not need to have access to any linguistic representation of it. On the contrary, any idea of human nature that the individual respects enough to sacrifice its own interest would actually prevent the fulfilment of its natural interests.

In summary, my objection to the way *Black Flame* depicts Stirner is not that he is not considered an anarchist and consequently not dealt with in a book about anarchism, but on the contrary, that even though he is not considered an anarchist and his thought is not dealt with at any length, his exclusion from anarchism is stated emphatically, and this exclusion is based on a small number of misconceptions which are easily refuted and which appear to be at least partly second-hand. It seems that contrary to the verdict of Schmidt and van der Walt, there are potential points of contact between Stirner's work and that of the more classical anarchists— regardless of whether Stirner himself is considered an anarchist or not. These points of contact have of course only been hinted at here. Given the persistently problematic and contradictory accounts of Stirner's thought in general, it is entirely plausible not to label Stirner as an anarchist, simply because the political implications of his critique are not clear enough to compare them to the politics of anarchists. In order to create an anarchist canon that is functional as a political philosophy, *Black Flame* cannot identify Stirner as an anarchist without recourse to detailed studies showing that his work is indeed compatible with anarchism—which arguably do not exist at the moment. However, there is a wide gap between either refusing to positively identify Stirner as an anarchist because of the difficult state of his reception or definitively situating him outside the anarchist canon while re-inscribing old prejudices and misreading into the is assessment of Stirner's thought.

However, any investigation into the relationship between Max Stirner and anarchism is not only hampered by the spread of the faulty understanding that some of his opponents have of him, but also by the readings of his work that are undertaken by his most vocal advocates. Saul Newman has been writing about the potential utility of Stirner's thought for radical political philosophy for more than ten years, but the way he reads Stirner is at times problematic. The explanation lies in the overall impetus of his project: He seeks to overcome the limitations he identifies in classical anarchism by applying the theories of Stirner and assorted French post-structuralists, among which he includes Foucault, Derrida, Deleuze, and Lacan. The problem here is that he deals with Stirner not as an anarchist, but as a forerunner of post-structuralism, and thus the theoretical combination of Stirner and post-structuralism he devises is neither clearly connected to any anarchist thinker, nor are they clearly anti-statist. Newman's description of Stirner has undergone a process of revision, his current view being that there are some parallels between Stirner and anarchism, notably in the treatment of anti-statism and voluntary association, but that Stirner does not fit into the "anarchist tradition". Consequently, "some kind of anarchist politics and ethics" derived from Stirner would be "a post-foundational anarchism or, . . . *postanarchism*" (Newman 2011b: 205–206). This suggests an alternative origin of the prefix 'post-', which seems to imply a move away both from the earlier emphasis on post-structuralism and from the meaning of postanarchism as 'after anarchism,' the meaning that has until now been contested the most in critical debate and is at least chronologically problematic if derived primarily from Stirner's thought.

More problematic than the general status of Newman's post-anarchism, however, are specific aspects of Stirner's reception that distort and at times contradict Stirner's writings. This is not meant to denigrate Newman's achievement in bringing Stirner back into debates about radical political philosophy, but merely to share some important critical observations. Stirner is still not very widely read, much less understood, making it especially important to point out mistakes in the views of those few who do publish their ideas about him, because most readers are unlikely to be sufficiently familiar with Stirner to recognize them unaided. In his account of Stirner's thought, Newman often uses the vocabulary of post-structuralism, which is a dangerous under-taking: Stirner's work is already a conscious rebellion against the opaque style of Hegelian philosophy and written in a much clearer language than the works of his peers, notwithstanding a number of words that he uses in an idiosyncratic fashion, such as egoism, the ego or unique one, and the inhuman or un-man. It is this last term that marks Newman's first misreading of Stirner: Newman identifies Stirner's critique of the abstract ideals at the heart of philosophical and political accounts of the subject with Althusser's theory of interpellation and the ideological deter-mination of the subject.

By seeing themselves as just one instance of the concept of man, or of the citizen, individuals are enthralled to the ideological content of these concepts already in their conceptions of them-selves. Where Newman goes wrong is when he identifies Stirner's solution to this problem as the un-man, the opposite of the concept of man, as "an extra-ideological standpoint from which ideology may be resisted" (Newman 2001a: 309). On the contrary, Stirner clearly states that the un-man is merely that particular which is condemned while the universal essence of man is exalted. In his critique of Bruno Bauer's philosophy, Stirner points out that since every individual is unique, and thus particular rather than universal, every human is actually an un-man, but this is only in order to show the internal inconsistency of the philosophy he is criticizing. His solution is simply to abandon the universal category of man as an ideal, and along with it the term un-man, and instead refer to the individual as the unique (also translated as "ego"). Newman still pits the concept of un-man against that of man, only reversing the hierarchy, but Stirner abolishes the entire dichotomy.

This misreading is logically connected to Newman's contention that "We live in a symbolic and linguistic universe, and to speculate about an original condition of authenticity and immediacy, or to imagine that an authentic presence is attainable behind the veils of the symbolic order or beyond the grasp of language, is futile. There is no getting outside language and the symbolic" (Newman 2011a: 156). This world-view makes it impossible to integrate Stirner's radical critique of philosophy in it, which consists precisely in leaving linguistic representation. Rather than going beyond language, Stirner reduces its relation to the individual from a definition to a mere pointing at what exists prior to representation, rather than describing and thus interpellating it. In arguing that the actual individual can only be talked about by saying nothing of it, by not describing it, Stirner demonstrates how his critique of language creates what could be called zero-degrees of interpellation: "You—unique! What thought content is here, what sentence content? None!" (Stirner 1845). Like Althusser, Stirner analyzes the creation of a liberal humanist subject in the form of linguistic concepts, an analysis which anticipates the theoretical link between the linguistic and political concepts of representation and subject. In sharp distinction to Althusser, and in stark contrast to the Lacanian perspective of the subject that Newman subscribes to, Stirner believes that it is possible for the individual simply to stop relating to themselves in terms of linguistic representation. His 'unique' is only a reference to the individual, it points neither to a signified not other signifiers, but to the individual as it exists independent of language, in the flesh. By being hailed as a human, or a citizen, the individual is identified as part of an ideological system of representation. In contrast to this, Stirner invents the phrase of the unique precisely to point out that any actually existing person cannot be represented in philosophy. The unique is in the last phrase, because it does not carry any thought content which could be related to other phrases. "There is no conceptual development of the unique, one cannot build a philosophical system with it" (Stirner 1845).

Similar points can be made about Newman's later reading of Stirner which he makes alongside Foucault's work on ethics, but they would not add to our present concern: just like the individualist proponents of Stirner's thought in the 1890s, Newman is in danger of distorting Stirner at the very same time as spreading knowledge of and interest in him. John Henry Mackay did much to popularize Stirner, but his reception of Stirner's thought has been subject to criticism. Gustav Landauer regretted that Stirner became associated with Mackay so closely, because Mackay's individualism obscured Stirner's emphasis on socialization based on the individuals' interests (Wolf 2003: 4). Similarly, Bernd Laska argues that Mackay reduces Stirner's thought to a form of "ultra-liberalism," and observes that Stirner's re-discovery towards the end of the 19th century "under the patronage of Nietzsche" led to a "banalisation" of Stirner as a "radical individualist" (Laska 1996: 59, 41). Although individualist anarchists helped popularize Stirner's thought, they simultaneously also influenced readers towards a sometimes problematic Nietzshean individualist reading of Stirner, a pattern which Newman's recent popularization of Stirner might repeat with respect to post-structuralism. This is especially dangerous since Newman also gives correct summaries and assessments of some aspects of Stirner's thought, making it very hard to tell the faithful renditions from the distortions and misreadings. Like individualist anarchism before it, post-anarchism seems to have the potential to both reveal new connections between Stirner's thought and anarchism and to create new obstacles for any investigation by identifying Stirner with one particular part of anarchism, the properties of which might then distort the reception of Stirner.

The debate around post-anarchism has prompted many to criticize texts in which anarchism's supposed shortcomings are rectified by post-anarchism. In this context, the way Stirner is used to negotiate the meaning of anarchism is also at times problematic. In his criticism of the reductive account post-anarchists like Todd May and Saul Newman have given of classical anarchism, Allan Antliff cites Emma Goldman, Kropotkin, and Bakunin in order to show that anarchism is neither limited to essentialist humanism nor to a view of power as entirely negative and separate from the subject (Antliff 2007). The main focus of his argument, however, is the thought of Stirner and his reception by some Russian anarchists from the time of the revolution of 1917, such as Lev Chernyi and the brothers Gordin. The crucial role that Stirner plays as an anarchist here is problematic for two separate reasons: Argumentatively, using Stirner as an exemplary anarchist is problematic because neither May nor Newman use him as such. May does not deal with Stirner at length, and Newman treats Stirner as separate from anarchism—one chapter each is devoted to anarchism and Stirner in *From Bakunin to Lacan*, and Stirner is used as a proto-poststructuralist, "at least as relevant to poststructuralism as Nietzsche," in order to criticize anarchism (Newman 2001b: 9; cf. Choat, 2010: 53). Basically, Antliff's reply to May and Newman is not very strong unless one accepts Stirner as a prototypical anarchist, but even scholars like Eltzbacher or Guérin, who call Stirner an anarchist, highlight his difference from other anarchists, which makes it problematic to use him as a stand-in for anarchism in general. Incidentally, this problem is also present to a lesser extent in Simon Choat's criticism of a lack of postanarchist interest in Marxism: his discussion of the relation between post-structuralists and "classical anarchist thinkers" is limited to comments by Deleuze and Derrida on Stirner— disregarding the fact that Stirner is not treated as a classical anarchist by the post-anarchists he is replying to, the problem being a tendency among thinkers to be unreliable when describing their own relationship to Stirner (Choat 2010: 60–61).

Antliff's argument only holds sway against the post-anarchist view of classical anarchism insofar as it shows that Stirner was a classical anarchist as well. This however is not explicitly argued, but rather assumed from the outset, and Stirner's warm reception in Russian anarchist circles does not automatically make Stirner an anarchist: Paul Avrich's account does not connect the writings of the Gordins to Stirner; Antliff's juxtaposition of quotes makes them seem compatible, but not necessarily genealogically related (cf. Avrich 1967: 176–179). Avrich and Antliff agree that Lev Chernyi's "associational anarchism" is strongly influenced by Stirner, but unlike Antliff, Avrich always talks of "Stirner and Nietzsche," when referring to the individualists of 1917 (Avrich 1967: 180, 172). This might be a sign that this specific connection exists only between individualist anarchism and a certain individualist reading of Stirner, again raising the question of the precise relation between Stirner's and Nietzsche's thought.

Probably more problematic than the particularity of the link that is constructed between Stirner and the Russian anarchists is the way Antliff uses Marxist sources to establish Stirner as an anarchist from the outset. The paper is opened with a quotation from Engels' *Ludwig Feuerbach and the End of Classical German Philosophy*: "Finally came Stirner, the prophet of contemporary anarchism" (qtd. in Antliff 2007: 56). Later on, Antliff refers to Marx and Engels' "polemics against the anarchists of their day—notably Bakunin and Max Stirner" and a footnote further qualifies this: "The anarchist theory of the individual is critiqued at length in chapter three of . . . *The German Ideology*" (Antliff 2007: 59, 65). With these references we arrive at the beginning of Stirner's identification as an anarchist and also at the origin of a considerable portion of the misreading of Stirner that have proved especially persistent.

The citation that forms the preface to Antliff's article is taken from Engels' description of the philosophical developments of Young Hegelianism in the late 1830's and 1840's in Germany. In Engels' text, the identification of Stirner as an anarchist is directly followed with, "—Bakunin has taken a great deal from him," and this claim is repeated later: "Stirner remained a curiosity, even after Bakunin blended him with Proudhon and labelled the blend 'anarchism'" (Engels 1888). The crucial problem with citing Engels as an authority is that the entire text of *Ludwig Feuerbach and the End of Classical German Philosophy* is filled with ideological distortions that were tailored to fulfil specific propagandistic purposes (cf. Arvon 1975). A lucid analysis of this aspect of the text has been provided by Henry Arvon who points out specific inaccuracies of the time line and explains the reasons Engels had in the 1880's to use the term 'dialectical materialism' where at most a historical materialism existed, but most of these details are not pertinent here.

What is central is that Engels deliberately obscures the role Stirner played in Marx's turn away from Feuerbach's humanism (cf. Arvon 2012). Engels' first mention of Stirner in the text is followed by a paragraph that summarizes his description of the Young Hegelian movement up to Stirner with an emphasis on their idealism: "the idea, is here the primary, nature the derivative, which only exists at all by the condescension of the idea" (Engels 1888). This already stands in blatant contradiction to Stirner's thought, but Engels goes on: "Then came Feuerbach's Essence of Christianity. With one blow it pulverised the contradiction, in that without circumlocutions it placed materialism on the throne again" (Engels 1888). This is wrong. Feuerbach's *Essence of Christianity* appeared before Stirner's *The Ego and Its Own*, in which Stirner heavily criticized Feuerbach's humanism. This is what drove Marx and Engels to turn away from Feuerbach and towards the development of their historical materialism, and this influence of Stirner is what Engels is trying to obscure by painting a completely distorted picture of the past (cf. Arvon 2012).

This knowledge about the nature of the text of course provides strong reasons to be sceptical about Engels' identification of Stirner as the "prophet of contemporary anarchism" and his claim that he exercised a strong influence on Bakunin (which has been interpreted to damn both writers by their mutual association) (Engels 1888; cf. Laska 1996: 39; cf. Arvon 2012: 196). In order to open a productive debate about Stirner and his possible relationship to anarchism, it is surely important that the sources available are assessed critically. Relying on the judgement of Engels, especially in this particular text, is problematic for anyone who is interested in such a project and not in propaganda. Engels was probably the first to identify Stirner as an anarchist, at the very least his claim was very influential in popularizing this identification. The question of whether Stirner can be considered part of the anarchist canon was thus guided by interest extraneous and even hostile both to the thought of Stirner and to anarchism when it was first discussed.

Referring to the chapter on Stirner in *The German Ideology* as a critique of "[t]he anarchist theory of the individual" is also proble-matic (Antliff 2007: 65). Not only is this chronologically imprecise as regards Stirner who was not yet considered an anarchist when *The German Ideology* was written, but the use of the definite article makes it sound as if Stirner's work is not just anarchist, but in fact the only anarchist theory of the individual. This, together with the reference to Marx and Engels polemicizing against "the anarchists of their day—notably Bakunin and Max Stirner," creates an impression of Stirner and Bakunin as equally anarchist, with a common opposition to Marx and Engels. The result is similar to the claims made by Engels and equally devoid of an argumentative basis. Identifying Stirner as an anarchist, particularly in the context of *The German Ideology* in a misleading manner, can be observed equally in the writings of

Paul Thomas who comments on Marx' polemics against 'the
anarchists' from a Marxist perspective.

Thomas published a study on Marx's relationship to Stirner,
Proudhon, and Bakunin in 1980, and an article of his about
Stirner and Marx has recently been published in Newman's *Max
Stirner*. Thomas identifies Stirner as an anarchist without any
explicit argument, despite the fact that many of the general
characteristics of anarchism that Thomas outlines do not fit
Stirner at all: Thomas' description of the anarchist understanding
of individual-society relations goes against Stirner's whole body
of ideas. His contention that Marx wrote against the anarchists
because "the emergent revolutionary movement needed to be
shielded against rival revolutionary creeds" makes no sense at all
with respect to Stirner (Thomas 1980: 9, 15). Not only was there
no such situation when *The German Ideology* was written, but the
fact that Marx never had the work published invalidates this
reason for writing it and also reveals the following statement as
either wishful thinking or a telling lapse:

> While Marx's attack on Feuerbach in the first section of
> *The German Ideology* has been contrasted, quite rightly,
> with his earlier near adulation of Feuerbach, it has rarely
> been recognized that it was none other than Stirner who
> impelled Marx into taking this new position as publicly
> and dramatically as he did. (Thomas, 1980: 140)

The fact remains that Marx never publicly commented on
Stirner or responded to the criticism of his work that Stirner had
included in his book, a detail that does not inhibit Thomas from
referring to Marx' private ranting and publicly enduring silence
as "throwing down the gauntlet" (Thomas 2011: 138). Thomas
defends the position adopted by Marx in *The German Ideology*
even today, parroting criticisms of Stirner that the latter had
refuted entirely in his reply to his critics of 1845. Thomas asserts
that "the ego of Stirner's is not a 'corporeal individual' but 'a
category constructed on the Hegelian method'" (Thomas 2011:
128), a charge to which Stirner had replied at length:

> What Stirner says is a word, a thought, a concept; what he
> means is neither a word, nor a thought, nor a concept.
> What he says is not the meaning, and what he means
> cannot be said. . . . Since you are the content of the unique
> [this, there is no more to think about a specific content of

the unique, i.e., a conceptual content. . . . Only when nothing is said about you and you are merely named, are you recognized as you. As soon as something is said about you, you are only recognized as that thing (human, spirit, christian, etc.). But the unique doesn't say anything because it is merely a name: it says only that you are you and nothing but you, that you are a unique you, or rather your self. . . . You—unique! What thought content is here, what sentence content? None! Whoever wants to deduce a precise thought-content of the Unique as if it were a concept, whoever thinks that with "unique" one has said about you what you are, would show that they believe in phrases, because they don't recognize phrases as phrases, and would also show that they seek specific content in phrases. (Stirner 1845)

Stirner's critique of philosophy cannot be explained here in detail, but he seeks to turn language back into a tool, rather than something which prescribes goals and duties for the individual, and he does so by rejecting terms that carry a conceptual content in favour of an empty term that has only a referential function, thus pointing at the individual of flesh and blood without making any claims or statements about it. At least it seems that any investigation into the possible points of contact between Stirner and anarchism can only be fruitful if every existing verdict of Stirner is critically compared to his actual writings, and if the distinction between Stirner and his reception is at all times clear.

Schmidt and van der Walt are free to entertain their own understanding of what anarchism really means, and if they exclude Stirner from the "broad anarchist tradition" that is not unjustified (2009: 9). However, it is entirely unhelpful to refuse any engagement with Stirner's thought, but at the same time assert his incompatibility with the theory of anarchism. Any such claim is bound to be detrimental to a serious comparison of Stirner and thinkers like Bakunin and Kropotkin if it proceeds from a view of Stirner's thought that is both uninformed and uninterested. The persistence of prejudice and misconceptions about Stirner can at least partly be related to his appropriation by individualist since the 1890's and the mixing or conflation of Stirner's thought with Nietzsche's that seems to have gone along with this. In contrast to *Black Flame*, Saul Newman's reception of Stirner has a rather uncertain position with regard to his potential anarchism. On the one hand, of the thinkers Newman uses to construct his post-anarchism, Stirner is the most anarchist by far; on the other, Stirner is explicitly contrasted with the supposed essentialist humanism of classical anarchism, which he is said to overcome. In addition, Stirner's thought is expressed in a structuralist world-view that directly contradicts his central criticism of political philosophy. Critics of Newman's approach, however, use Stirner as a classical anarchist without taking into account that Newman does not. Not only does this cause their argument to miss the target, but their depictions of Stirner's work as a classic in the anarchist canon are based on Marxist texts which sacrifice factual accuracy to political needs and tactical deliberations. Generally, current debates contain many different positions on Stirner's relationship to anarchism, but they are all prone to misreading Stirner or relying on dubious sources. The question of whether Stirner can be considered part of the anarchist canon, or what specific effect a definite inclusion or exclusion would have, cannot even be addressed on this basis, but will have to proceed from investigations that are yet to take place.

REFERENCES

Adler, Max (2000). "Max Stirner: Ein Beitrag zur Feststellung des Verhältnisses von Socialismus und Individualismus." *Der Einzige: Vierteljahresschrift des Max-Stirner-Archivs Leipzig* 3.11: 26–34.
Antliff, Allan (2007). "Anarchy, Power, and Poststructuralism." *Substance: A Review of Theory & Literary Criticism* 36.2: 56–66.
Arvon, Henri (1975). "Engels' Feuerbach kritisch beleuchtet." In *Atheismus in der Diskussion: Kontroversen um Ludwig Feuerbach*, eds. H. Lübbe and H.M. Sass. Munich/Mainz: Chr. Kaiser/ Matthias Grünewald.
Avron, Henri (2012). *Max Stirner: An den Quellen des Existenzialismus*, trans. G.H. Müller. Rangsdorf, Germany: Basilisken-Presse.
Avrich, Paul (1967). "The Russian Anarchists—Paul Avrich." LibCom: http://libcom.org/history/russian-anarchists-paul-avrich.
Choat, Simon (2010). "Postanarchism from a Marxist Perspective." *Anarchist Developments in Cultural Studies* 1: 51–71.
Eltzbacher, Paul (2011). *Anarchism*, trans. Steven T. Byington. *Project Gutenberg*: http://www.gutenberg.org/files/36690/36690-h/36690-h.htm.
Engels, Friedrich (1888). *Ludwig Feuerbach and the End of Classical German Philosophy*. *World Socialist Website*: http://www.wsws.org/IML/ludwigfeuerbach/index.shtml.
Foucault, Michel. (1997). "The Ethics of the Concern for Self as a

Practice of Freedom." In *Essential Works of Michel Foucault, 1954–1984; Volume 1, Ethics: Subjectivity and Truth*, ed. Paul Rabinow, trans. Robert Hurley, 281–301. New York: The New Press.

Guérin, Daniel (1967). *Anarchismus: Begriff und Praxis*, trans. H.H. Hildebrandt and E. Demski, Trans. Frankfurt am Main: Suhrkamp.

Kinna, Ruth (1995). "Kropotkin's Theory of Mutual Aid in Historical Context," *International Review of Social History* 40: 259–283.

Kuhn, Gabriel. (2011) "The Meaning of Anarchism: *Black Flame*, Definitions, and Struggles over Identity." *Institute for Anarchist Studies*: http://www.anarchiststudies.org/node/529.

Laska, Bernd A. (1996). *Ein dauerhafter Dissident*. Nürnberg: LSR-Verlag.

Laska, Bernard (2000). *Von Stirner zu Kant: Gerhard Lehmann. L.S.R.* [website]: http://www.lsr-projekt.de/lehmann.html.

Newman, Saul (2001a). "Spectres of Stirner: a Contemporary Critique of Ideology." *Journal of Political Ideologies* 6.3: 309–330.

Newman, Saul (2001b). *From Bakunin to Lacan: Anti-Authoritarianism and the Dislocation of Power*. Lanham: Lexington Books.

Newman, Saul (2011a). *The Politics of Postanarchism*. Edinburgh: Edinburgh University Press.

Newman, Saul (2011b). *Max Stirner: Critical Explorations in Contemporary Political Thought*. Houndsmills, UK: Pallgrave Macmillan.

Plechanov, Georg (2001). "Anarchismus und Sozialismus." In *Texte (1892-1894): Heft 3*, ed. K. Fleming, 47–52. Leipzig: Max-Stirner-Archiv.

Schmidt, Michael & van der Walt, Lucien (2009). *Black Flame: The Revolutionary Class Politics of Anarchism and Syndicalism*. Oakland: AK Press.

Stirner, Max (1845). "Stirner's Critics," *Vagabond Theorist*: https://sites.google.com/site/vagabondtheorist/stirner/stirner-s-critics/stirner-s-critics-1.

Stirner, Max (1907). *The Ego and Its Own*, ed. B. Tucker, trans. S. Byington. *L.S.R.* [website]: http://www.lsr-projekt.de/poly/enee.html.

Thomas, Paul (1980). *Karl Marx and the Anarchists*. London: Routledge.

Thomas, Paul (2011). "Max Stirner and Karl Marx: An Overlooked Contretemps." In *Max Stirner: Critical Explorations in Contemporary Political Thought*, ed. Saul Newman, 113–142. Houndsmills, Basingstoke: Palgrave Macmillan.

Zenker, Ernst Viktor (2010). *Anarchism: A Criticism and History of the Anarchist Theory*. Project Gutenberg: http://www.gutenberg.org/files/31903/31903-h/31903-h.htm.

Anarchist Developments in Cultural Studies
ISSN: 1923-5615
2013.1: Blasting the Canon

Bakunin Brand Vodka
An Exploration into Anarchist-punk and Punk-anarchism

Jim Donaghey*

ABSTRACT
Punk and anarchism are inextricably linked. The connection between
them is expressed in the anarchistic rhetoric, ethics, and practices of
punk, and in the huge numbers of activist anarchists who were first
politicised by punk. To be sure, this relationship is not straightforward,
riven as it is with tensions and antagonisms—but its existence is
irrefutable. This article looks back to 'early punk' (arbitrarily taken as
1976-1980), to identify the emergence of the anarchistic threads that run
right through punk's (ever advancing) history. However, it must be
stressed that any claim to being 'definitive' or 'complete' is rejected here.
Punk, like anarchism, is a hugely diverse and multifarious entity. Too
often, authors leaning on the crutch of determinism reduce punk to a
simple linear narrative, to be weaved through some fanciful dialectic. In
opposition to this, Proudhon's concept of antimony is employed to help
contextualise punk's beguiling amorphousness.

KEYWORDS
Punk, hardcore, anarchism, anarcho-punk, DIY, subculture, counter-
culture

INTRODUCTION
    I am an anarchist.[1]

*Jim Donaghey has been a self-confessed punk for more than 10 years,
and there's little hope of redemption now. As well as making noisy noise
with bands you've never heard of, Jim is a walking cliché (vegan-
anarchist-bike-punk . . . ?), has pitched in with local activist groups

Anarchism and punk have been closely associated since the latter's first intrusion into the public sphere in late 1976. Punk's roots and nascence can be traced much further back,[2] but it was the Sex Pistols' profanity-laden[3] television interview with Bill Grundy[4] that saw 'punk' splashed across the front pages in the UK. Less than a week previously the Sex Pistols had released their first single, 'Anarchy in the U.K.' with its opening lines, 'I am an antichrist, I am an anarchist.' Whatever Johnny Rotten's[5] inspiration for the lyric, this utterance placed 'anarchy' firmly into the popular conception of punk. Even as the Sex Pistols were revealed as a short-lived profiteering publicity stunt rather than a voice of revolution, the anarchy/punk association endured and developed to produce numerous politically coherent, activist, and effective manifestations. It would seem, then, that there is a good deal more to this association than just a (half-)rhyme for a pop-song.

Penny Rimbaud of Crass, a band often identified as the progenitors of the anarcho-punk movement,[6] has remarked that:

---

around Europe, and is toiling towards a PhD at Loughborough University, UK, scrutinising the relationships between anarchism and punk in contemporary contexts. He is currently involved with Leicestershire Solidarity Group, FC Kolektivo Victoria, and making an irreverent racket with fellow punks, Die Wrecked.

[1] Sex Pistols, 'Anarchy in the U.K.' The single was released November 26, 1976 (EMI), and subsequently released on the album *Never Mind the Bollocks* on October 27, 1977 (Virgin).
[2] The term 'punk' *had* been used in a generic or descriptive sense by music critics in the US to refer to 'unregenerate rock-and-rollers with an aggressively lower-class style,' as far back as 1964: Dave Laing, *One Chord Wonders: Power and Meaning in Punk Rock* (Milton Keynes: Open University Press, 1985), 11–12; citing Greil Marcus, ed., *Stranded: Rock and Roll for a Desert Island* (New York: Knopf, 1979), 72.
[3] The Sex Pistols said 'shit' twice during the interview, which had previously only been said twice in the entire history of British TV. Other words used such as 'rotter' have lost much of their ability to offend over the last 36 years, but attitudes of contemporary 1970's audiences must be borne in mind, as will be discussed later.
[4] *Today Show* (Granada), December 1, 1976, only actually broadcast in London, but with much wider impact because of press reporting.
[5] Johnny Rotten, a.k.a. John Lydon, former singer of the Sex Pistols, a contestant on reality TV gameshow *I'm A Celebrity Get Me Out Of Here!* in 2004, featured in TV advertisements for Country Life butter in 2008, and currently singing with a reformed Public Image Limited.
[6] It should be stressed that the term 'anarcho-punk' does not apply to all

had anyone mentioned Bakunin, we would probably have assumed it was some kind of vodka.[7]

Curiously, these self-professed anarchists adopted the terminology, imagery, and philosophy of anarchism but were initially ignorant of its canon of 'key thinkers'—so their deployment of anarchism must have stemmed from elsewhere.

This article will explore some of the complex relationships between punk and anarchism, dealing particularly with an intuitive anarchism identifiable in early punk—i.e., an anarchism developed *in absence of the anarchist political canon*. If such a thing as a 'punk-anarchism' can be said to exist,[8] its form and later development are evident in microcosm from the very beginnings of punk as an identifiable movement. Anarchistic rhetoric and practice in early punk appear in the following ways:

- Shock tactic: a posture of 'anarchy' to project an image of danger and allure.
- Hippie hangover: influences from hippie and avant-garde movements and a continuation of 1960's counter-culture and the anarchistic threads therein.
- Reactive anarchism: opposition to hierarchical, state, and societal repression.
- Practical necessity: the DIY (do-it-yourself) organising principle as taking over the means of production for

---

anarchist punk bands, but rather refers to a specific (though diverse) punk sub-genre including bands such as Conflict, Subhumans, AntiSect, Stalag 17, Toxic Waste, Zounds, Icons of Filth, The Mob, Poison Girls, Rudimentary Peni, Amebix, Cress, The Ex, Flux of Pink Indians, Rubella Ballet, etc. Participants in this scene did not generally accept the 'anarcho-punk' tag willingly, since being labelled as *anything* was anathema to their motivating principles. As Ian Glasper points out, the 'whole idea behind, sort-of, anarchic punk was that it didn't want to be tagged, pigeon-holed, . . . and controlled in that manner': Glasper, interviewed in *The Day the Country Died: A History of Anarcho Punk*, dir. Roy Wallace (2007); available at: http://fuckcopyright.blogspot.com/2009/04/day-country-died-2007.html.

[7] Penny Rimbaud (aka J.J. Ratter), *Shibboleth: My Revolting Life* (Edinburgh: AK Press, 1998), 109.

[8] The notion of a 'punk-anarchism' is, of course, completely self-defeating (just like the term 'anarcho-punk')—but in this instance the term will be used selectively to highlight those aspects of anarchism within punk that may be considered as distinct from other strains of anarchism.

workers' self-control, owing to a lack of mainstream industry assistance (or interference).

- Intuitive anarchistic politics: disavowal of (capital 'P') Politics.

From the outset, it is necessary to stress the amorphousness of punk and highlight difficulties in defining it. In common with anarchism, punk is a *popularly conceived* movement, not founded on any doctrine or programme. Despite the oft-claimed influence of a handful of leading figures,[9] punk is formed from a myriad of influences and is constantly evolving along the tensions between these antagonistic strains. Each individual's experience of, and perspective on, punk is unique—for every claim that punk '*is*' something, there is likely another to counter that it '*is not.*' This multiplicity of apparent contradictions appeals to those employing Marist-Hegelian dialectics,[10] but such attempts at synthesis are unconvincing. Smoothing over punk's inherent contradictions and wilfully ignoring those aspects which refuse to fit with the imposed ideology reduces complexity to a simple narrative (which, rather cynically, aligns neatly with Marxist socio-economic dogma). This refusal of synthesis means an embrace of contradiction and of *antimony*. As Proudhon put it, the 'plurality of elements, the struggle of elements, the opposition of contraries,'[11] are the conditions from which free society can emerge, as

---

[9] Such as Richard Hell, Malcolm McLaren, Johnny Rotten, Jimmy Pursey, or Joe Strummer

[10] For example, see: Dick Hebdige, *Subculture: The Meaning of Style*, (London: Routledge, 1979); Stacy Thompson, *Punk Productions: Unfinished Business* (Albany: State University of New York Press, 2004); Sean Albiez, 'Know history!: John Lydon, Cultural Capital and the Prog/Punk Dialectic,' in *Popular* Music, Vol. 22/3 (Cambridge University Press, 2003), 357–374; and Kieran James, '"This is England": Punk Rock's Realist/Idealist Dialectic and its Implications for Critical Accounting Education,' *Science Direct: Accounting Forum 33* (2009): 127–145. Stephen Taylor takes a slightly different tack on the dialectical approach, saying: '[m]y effort at synthesis, then, consists in the kind of post-Hegelian negativity described by Julia Kristeva . . . an "affirmative negativity" or "productive dissolution" of fetishism': Steven Taylor, *False Prophet: Fieldnotes from the Punk Underground* (Middletown: Wesleyan University Press, 2003), 80.

[11] Pierre-Joseph Proudhon, *Théorie de la propriété*; cited and translated in Diane Morgan, 'Saint-Simon, Fourier, and Proudhon: "Utopian" French Socialism,' in *History of Continental Philosophy*, Vol. I (1780-1840), ed. Tom Nenon (Acumen Press, 2010), 302 [265–304].

well as being the conditions that a free society engenders. As Diane Morgan writes of Proudhon, '[o]ut of these antimonies, their conflicts and precarious equilibrium, comes growth and development; any fusional resolution or the elimination of one of the terms would be the equivalent of death.'[12] In punk's refusal to have its contradictions synthesised into convenient narratives, the essence of antimony is embodied.[13]

This article does not claim to be 'definitive' or 'complete'[14]— any such presentation of punk is pointless, misguided, and worst, *misguiding*. Terry Perlin's comment that, 'there are as many anarchisms as there are anarchists,'[15] readily applies to punk as well. Rather, it is the overlap and interaction between punk and anarchism, inherently ill-defined as they are, that is of interest here. By examining the numerous issues that arise from the relationships between anarchism and punk, insight into both movements can be garnered and a contribution can be made to the multifarious and ever-shifting mosaics that make up our understanding of these complicated and contradictory entities.

'Early punk' will be taken here as 1976-1980 (or so), though

---

[12] Proudhon, *Théorie de la propriété*; in Morgan, 'Saint-Simon, Fourier, and Proudhon,' 301. In Proudhon's words: 'What particular proposition . . . can be called *truth*? None; opposition, antagonism and antimony burst out everywhere. The real truth is: (1) in equilibrium, a thing which our reason excellently conceives . . . but which is only a relation; (2) in the whole, which we can never possibly embrace': P.J. Proudhon, *Théorie de l'impôt*, in *The Works of P.J. Proudhon*, ed. Benjamin Tucker, Vol. XV (1868), 226-227; cited by Henri De Lubac, in *The Un-Marxian Socialist* (London: Sheed and Ward, 1948), 146. This conceptualisation of 'truth' seems to foreshadow post-structuralist epistemology, despite Proudhon's own position within positivist enlightenment thought.

[13] Indeed, punk's antimonous traits have contributed to its remarkable longevity.

[14] Unlike, for example, Alex Ogg's *No More Heroes: A Complete History of UK Punk from 1977 to 1980* (London: Cherry Red, 2006), or Ian Glasper's *Burning Britain: The History of UK Punk, 1980-1984* (London: Cherry Red, 2004), which describes itself on the back cover as 'the definitive overview of this previously overlooked era,' or Glasper's *Trapped in a Scene: UK Hardcore, 1985-1989* (London: Cherry Red, 2009), which describes itself as 'the definitive document of UK Hardcore' (back cover). These are probably just lazy adjectives to encourage book sales, and in fact Glasper's books otherwise avoid this kind of hyperbole, but the assertions of 'completeness' or being 'definitive' sit entirely at odds with the understanding of punk in this article.

[15] Terry M. Perlin, "Preface," in Terry M. Perlin, ed., *Contemporary Anarchism* (New Brunswick: Transaction Books, 1979).

this interval is largely arbitrary. Peaks and troughs of punk activity may be identifiable across its history, but the inter-relatedness of these scenes is lost in the frequent assertion of distinct or separate 'waves.' The 1976-1980 dating commonly pops up in oral histories and outsider considerations of punk,[16] roughly correlating to the mainstream media's attention span for punk, with the added romance of regime change in the UK in 1979 and the US in 1981. As an illustration of this, the combined coverage for punk and associated topics and bands in the mainstream music magazines *NME, Melody Maker, Sounds, Zig Zag*, and *Trouser Press* was: 22 articles in 1976, 77 articles in 1977, 88 articles in 1978, 39 articles in 1979, 22 articles in 1980, and 3 artciles in 1981.[17]

But! The number of active punks and punk bands did not diminish in concert with this decline in mainstream media interest. Rather, the profitability of early punk had been depleted, so the mainstream media's gaze was turned to the commercial potential of the New Romantics, and the more marketable 'New Wave.' For this article, the 1976-1980 interval might perhaps be justified in that it runs up to the emergence of anarcho-punk as an identifiable movement—but even this supposed division is highly porous, and the main reasoning behind this particular interval is to focus the discussion down to a level that is manageable in a few thousand words, while also challenging some accepted conceptions of 'early punk.'

The five sub-headings that follow (shock tactic, hippie hangover, reactive anarchism, practical necessity, and intuitive anarchistic politics) identify the various ways in which 'anarchy' and anarchism appear in early punk, *without a canon.* These threads are interrelated, so some crossover between them should be expected. To repeat, these five strands are offered as hangers to provide a sketch of early punk, not a complete picture; numerous conflicting elements co-exist with them, and although

---

[16] For example, Alex Ogg's *No More Heroes* contains this interval in its title, Legs McNeil and Gillian McCain's *Please Kill Me: The Uncensored Oral History of Punk* (New York: Grove Press, 2006) contains everything from 1980 onwards as an Epilogue, and John Robb's *Punk Rock: An Oral History* (London: Random House, 2010) covers a wider spectrum of dates, although 1980-1984 are lumped together, while 1976-1979 have indivi-dual chapters or even several sub-chapters each.

[17] Prior to 1976, some of these publications make use of the word 'punk' but as an adjective to describe a raw rock 'n' roll sound. The articles are stored at www.rocksbackpages.com, though they are not complete to the point of including advertisements that might be aimed at punk readers.

space limitations mean that these antagonisms are not fleshed out in detail here, the point is to embrace them.

Some cases of explicit anarchism are evident in early punk. Craig O'Hara, Dave Laing, and Brian Cogan all particularly identify Crass as 'one of the few communal organisations dedicated to consistency and a clear ideological focus'[18] in the early punk milieu, even though Crass themselves cast doubt on this point. Black Flag's name was adopted 'in symbolic reference to the Black Flag of Anarchy,'[19] 'a threatening thing.'[20] Raymond Pettibon, who devised the Black Flag name and logo, describes himself as a 'card-carrying anarchist'[21] in the late 1970's. But even though a degree of explicit anarchism was evident at the earliest stages of punk's development, this was a minority strand, and as O'Hara points out, '[i]t would be a lie . . . to say that these original Punks had well-developed social and political theories.'[22]

SHOCK TACTIC: A POSTURE OF 'ANARCHY' TO PROJECT AN IMAGE OF DANGER AND ALLURE

As suggested in the opening paragraph, the anarchy professed by early 'punk idols' was often little more than rhetorical posturing and lacked political substance. Revolutionary language did not preclude collaboration with major corporate labels, and numerous sell-outs, so 'anarchy' must have carried a different meaning for these bands. Understanding this meaning is not straightforward, since in the 1970's, as today, 'anarchy' was used pejoratively by the mainstream media, implying chaos and disorder. As George Katsiaficas puts it, 'the propensity for quick fixes on fragmentary factoids often leads the media to use (erroneously) the term "anarchist".'[23] The emotive power of the term 'anarchy'[24] also

---

[18] Brian Cogan, '"Do They Owe Us a Living? Of Course They Do!" Crass, Throbbing Gristle, and Anarchy and Radicalism in Early English Punk Rock,' *Journal for the Study of Radicalism* 1.2 (2007): 83 [77–90].

[19] Stevie Chick, *Spray Paint the Walls: The Story of Black Flag* (London: Omnibus Press, 2009), 62.

[20] Gary McDaniel (aka Chuck Dukowski), bassist in Black Flag, quoted in Chick, *Spray Paint the Walls*, 62.

[21] Raymond Pettibon, quoted in Steven Blush, *American Hardcore: A Tribal History*, 2nd edn. (Port Townsend: Feral House, 2010), 52; also quoted in Chick, *Spray Paint the Walls*, 62.

[22] Craig O'Hara, *The Philosophy of Punk: More than Noise!*, 2nd edn. (Edinburgh: AK Press, 1999), 27.

[23] George Katsiaficas, discussing media reports on the autonomen of Germany in the late 1980's/early 1990's, *The Subversion of Politics:*

appealed to early punk bands that were attracted to the mythology that surrounded 'anarchism' in its popular (mis)understanding. In ignorance of the anarchist canon, they developed a form of oppositional politics, initially rooted in shock, that can be described as anarchistic. Several themes of shock and offence were prevalent (sexual explicitness and deviance,[25] violence,[26] drug use,[27] disgust or worthlessness[28]), but profanity and World War Two/Nazi imagery are particularly revealing in regard to the appearance of 'anarchy' in punk.

Late-1970's social attitudes were comparatively more conservative than today and popular punk-profanities such as 'rotter,' 'bugger,' or 'wanker' have lost much of their offensive-ness.[29]

European Autonomous Social Movements and the Decolonisation of Everyday Life (Atlantic Highlands: Humanities Press, 1997), 197.

[24] This is also the reason Proudhon adopted the term in the first instance.

[25] For example: 'Sex Boy' (Germs), 'Sit On My Face Stevie Nix' (Rotters), 'Fuck and Suck' (Mad Virgins), 'Bondage Boy' (Sick Things), 'Orgasm Addict' (Buzzcocks), 'Killer Queers' (Controllers), 'I Like Boys' (Snifters), 'Homo Safari' (Xtc), 'Disease' (UK Subs), 'We Are All Prostitutes' (Pop Group), 'Psycle Sluts' (John Cooper-Clarke), 'Slut' (Vomit Pigs), 'Loner with a Boner' (Black Randy and the Metrosquad), 'Pornography' (Revenge), and also band names such as Buzzcocks, Tits, Sex Pistols, Mad Virgins, Snatch, Buttocks, Slits, Throbbing Gristle, Vibrators, Crabs, and Stinky Toys.

[26] For example: 'Get Raped' (Eater), and also the band names Raped and The Stranglers.

[27] For example: euphemisms such as 'Lady Esquire' (UK Subs), and more explicitly, 'Now I Wanna Sniff Some Glue' (Ramones), 'Cocaine Smile' (Slaughter and the Dogs), or 'Daddy Is My Pusher' (Tits).

[28] For example, on the theme of disgust: 'Gobbing On Life' (Alberto Y Los Trios Paranoias), and also band names such as Acme Sewage Company, Fatal Microbes, Germs, Open Sore, Vomit Pigs, Urinals, and Celia and the Mutations. On the theme of stupidity: 'Brainless' (Deadbeats), 'No Brains' (Eater), and the band names Bad Brains and Crass (and their singer's stage name 'Steve Ignorant'), and also the stage personas of the Ramones. On the themes of rottenness and worthlessness: 'Rot and Roll' and 'Teen Slime' (Dogs), 'Gutter Kids' (Dyaks), 'Born To Lose' (Heartbreakers), 'Ugly' (Stranglers), 'Freak' (V2), and also the band names Proles, Viletones, Pigs, Pigz, Riff Raff, Sick Things, Yobs, and Rotters.

[29] As a marker of changing attitudes to profanity, it is now acceptable to use the word 'shit' on television in the US as an adjective or in an exclamatory sense (though, inexplicably, not to denote feces). This law change was mercilessly exploited by the subversive TV cartoon series *South Park*, which managed to accumulate a total of 162 'shits' in one 25-minute episode, 'It Hits the Fan,' Series 5, Episode 1, first aired on June 20, 2001.

Christian moral crusader Mary Whitehouse brought the last successful prosecution for blasphemous libel in the UK against *Gay News* in 1977,[30] but a similar problem of moral pique arose for Crass when they had to exclude the song 'Reality Asylum' from their 1978 debut album *Feeding of the 5000* because an Irish pressing plant objected to its blasphemous content.[31] Aside from religious 'swearing,' some early punk song titles that used profanity include 'Fuck You' (Alberto Y Los Trios Paranoias), 'You Bastard' (Alternative TV), 'Oh Shit!' (Buzzcocks), and 'The Bitch' (Slaughter and the Dogs), with the lyrics to many more songs peppered with similar language. In other instances, profanity is used covertly, as in the Sex Pistols' 'Pretty Vacant,' in which the last syllable of vacant is deliberately mispronounced to sound like 'cunt.'[32] Racially-based profanity was also frequently used by early punk bands, such as the song title 'Rock and Roll Nigger' (Patti Smith), the band name NY Niggers, and in the lyrics to 'White Punks on Hope' (Crass), 'White Noise' (Stiff Little Fingers), and 'Holiday in Cambodia' (Dead Kennedys).[33] Crass's line, 'we're all just niggers to the rulers of this land,'[34] echoes

---

[30] For publishing James Kirkup, 'The Love That Dares to Speak Its Name,' in 1976; available at *Annoy.com*: http://annoy.com/history/doc.html?Document ID=100045. The offending content was homosexual necrophilia between a Roman centurion and Jesus Christ's crucified corpse: 'in each wound, his side, his back, his mouth—I came and came and came.' In 2008, the Criminal Justice and Immigration Act (section 79) abolished the crime of blasphemy in the UK (excepting Northern Ireland!).

[31] The track was replaced with roughly 2 minutes of silence entitled 'The Sound of Free Speech.' 'Reality Asylum' was released as a single in 1978 on Small Wonder Records. The second pressing of the *Feeding of the 5000* album (*The Second Sitting*), released in 1980 (Crass Records), did include a version of 'Reality Asylum,' though it is titled simply 'Asylum.'

[32] Strangely, this song was played during the London 2012 Olympics opening ceremony, with 'vaCUNT' heard by an estimated 900 million people viewing globally (see: http://in.reuters.com/article/2012/08/07/oly-ratings-day-idINL6E8J78H620120807). In this case, either the profane association was missed, or its potential ambiguity was used somewhat subversively.

[33] Black Flag's 'White Minority' and the Clash's 'White Riot' both clumsily employ themes of racial segregation, even if that was not their intention. Crass criticised what they saw as the Clash's unwelcome interference with their song 'White Punks on Hope': 'Black man's got his problems and his way to deal with it, so don't kid yourself you're helping with your white liberal shit.'

[34] Crass, 'White Punks on Hope,' *Stations of the Cross* (Crass Records,

with Patti Smith's 'Rock and Roll Nigger,' the liner notes of which say, 'any man [sic] who extends beyond the classic form is a nigger.'[35] Stiff Little Fingers, from Belfast, launch into a racist tirade in 'White Noise,' using words such as 'nigger,' 'golly gob,' 'monkey,' 'paki,' 'curry coffee queer,' and 'yid,' which is only revealed as parody in the final verse, moving from 'black wogs' and 'brown wogs' to 'green wogs'—i.e., 'the Irish' as perceived by 'the Brits.'[36] In these instances, punks *identify with* oppressed black communities, but use powerfully offensive and racist words to make their point.[37] These were not *intended* as racist songs, whatever their ambiguity, but crucially, the use of highly offensive racist language imbued them with shock value. This would have been tempered, since racist language would have provoked less shock-value in the 1970's than today (inversely to attitudes concerning profanity and sexual 'deviance'). For instance, the BBC (and ITV) comedy TV protagonist Alf Garnett regularly used words such as 'coon,' 'wog,' and 'paki' from 1965 to 1992.[38] These words were taboo-stretching comedy fodder as we were invited to laugh *at* the ageing bigot, but many must have been laughing *with* the character instead. These highly charged words were broadcast on state television to mainstream audiences, making them commonplace and therefore appear acceptable.

Punk's frequent use of WWII and Nazi imagery carried poignant shock value in the 1970's, since many people that had been personally affected were still alive. Examples include songs titles like 'Adolph You Beauty!' (Chosen Few), 'Nazi Training Camp' (D.O.A.), 'California Über Alles' (Dead Kennedys), 'The Gasman Cometh' (Crass), 'Fascist Pigs' (Nosebleeds), 'Decadent Jew' (Nuns), 'Just Like Dresden' (NY Niggers), 'Swastikas on Parade' (Residents), 'Belsen Was A Gas' (Sex Pistols), 'Mein

---

1979).
[35] Patti Smith, liner notes to *Easter* (Arista Records, 1978); quoted in Stephen Duncombe and Maxwell Tremblay, eds., *White Riot: Punk Rock and the Politics of Race* (London: Verso, 2011), 37.
[36] 'Paddy is a moron. Spud thick Mick. Breeds like a rabbit. Thinks with his prick. Anything floors him if he can't fight or drink it. Round them up in Ulster. Tow it out and sink it': Stiff Little Fingers, 'White Noise,' *Inflammable Material* (Rough Trade, 1979).
[37] Unsurprisingly, this ambiguity led to the National Front and the British Movement taking a particular interest, with some early punk participants becoming involved with these racist groups.
[38] In the sitcoms created by Johnny Speight, *Till Death Us Do Part* (BBC, 1965-1968, 1970, 1972-1975), *Till Death . . .* (ITV, 1981), and *In Sickness and In Health* (BBC, 1985-1992).

Kampf' (Spitfire Boys), 'Hiroshima Mon Amor' (Ultravox), 'Swastika Girl' (Viletones), and band names such as Chosen Few, London SS,[39] Stormtrooper,[40] and Martin and the Brownshirts. The swastika was one of the most prominent examples of this shock-tactic. Jamie Reid used it in his Sex Pistols artwork, as did Arturo Vega associated with the Ramones, and many punks wore armbands or t-shirts featuring the insignia. Roger Sabin identifies several possible shock connotations within the swastika:

> two-fingers to the 'peace and love' ethic of the hippies; the same to parents, who were of an age to have experienced the war; a nod to the 'camp' S & M aesthetic . . . ; an ironic symbol of living 'in a fascist regime'; or simply a nice bit of hip (anti-) fashion. But it could also very possibly mean some degree of sympathy with fascist aims . . . .[41]

Sabin's final point is the most controversial of these (as he intends it); however, Laing writes that '*Sniffin' Glue*[42] made clear, and other evidence suggests, that punks who wore [Nazi] armbands were not doing so because they endorsed fascism. Their purpose was *to shock.*'[43] The World Wars had been beatified by the state, with numerous remembrance days, ceremonies, and symbols to reinforce a feeling of patriotism and worthy sacrifice within the populace. To defile memories of 'the fallen' was sacrilege, so punks using the swastika wielded considerable shock value.

As much as the political spectre of Nazism was raised for its shock value, it is with similar motivation that 'anarchy' was used. As noted above, anarchy was not popularly understood in a political/philosophical sense, rather, it represented the hell-on-earth that would assumedly ensue if the constraints provided by social norms and government control were to disappear. This theme chimed with the media-fuelled fears of impending crisis for the economy and society.[44] Political groups on the left and

---

[39] London SS are more accurately described as a 'proto-punk' band, albeit one that never actually played a gig.

[40] Stormtrooper was Crass's original name.

[41] Roger Sabin, "'I Won't Let that Dago By": Rethinking Punk and Racism,' in Roger Sabin, ed., *Punk Rock: So What?* (London: Routledge, 1999), 209 [199–218].

[42] Early punk fanzine.

[43] Laing, *One Chord Wonders*, 96 (emphasis added).

[44] Many analyses take the economic situation preceding punk's nascence as a key factor in its early development. Jon Savage in particular goes in-

right were able to motivate increased support, with several industrial disputes ongoing, and electoral success for the neo-fascist National Front, who were also active in street-level racist attacks. It must be recalled that the dominant form of extra-parliamentary 'leftism' at this time was orthodox Marxism, or the Trotskyism of the Socialist Workers Party (SWP). The Soviet Union was *still* being reified by many as the only viable alternative to capitalism, and despite the beginnings of change brought by 1968 and the birth of the 'new left,' debate and action was still bogged down in old-fashioned hierarchical unions, and dogmatic groups like Militant[45] and the SWP. As such, the political philosophy of anarchism was not afforded space for serious consideration. Against the backdrop of the Cold War, the UK found itself with a weak government, a crippled economy, an army of unemployed people, the rising popularity of fascist thugs and totalitarian communists, and civil war in Northern Ireland. The mainstream media, in its unending thirst for hyperbole, could only be expected to prophesise impending 'anarchy' in the UK. But if 'anarchy' was generally understood by early punks in *this* sense, then much of the 'anarchy' professed is essentially inseparable from its political opposite, the Nazi swastika. The use of 'anarchy' as shock tactic in this context is certainly in the absence of any anarchist political canon.

HIPPIE HANGOVER: INFLUENCES FROM HIPPIE AND AVANT-GARDE MOVEMENTS AND A CONTINUATION OF 1960'S COUNTER-CULTURE AND THE ANARCHISTIC THREADS THEREIN

While much of the 'anarchy' posited by early punk bands was mere wordplay, this is not to say that ignorance of the anarchist canon was its essentially defining feature. Influences include anarchic threads from hippie and 1960's counter-culture[46] that

---

depth in explaining the bleak situation for workers, and the austerity measures being enforced in the UK by the International Monetary Fund: see Jon Savage, *England's Dreaming: Anarchy, Sex Pistols, Punk Rock, and Beyond*, rev. edn. (New York: St. Martin's Press, 2002). Essentially though, discussion of the economy focuses on rapidly rising unemployment figures, 'doubl[ing] in the period 1975-77 from 700,000 to 1.4 million': Rimbaud, *Shibboleth*, 110.
[45] A far-left branch of the Labour party in the UK.
[46] George McKay also argues that hippie and punk are in some sense reunited in the 1980's, because the 'quarter-organised chaos of free festivals offer[ed] an easy homological fit': George McKay, *Senseless Acts of Beauty: Cultures of Resistance Since the Sixties* (London: Verso, 1996),

indirectly weave punk into a lineage that stretches back deep into anarchism's history.

As an example, Crass adopted anarchist language and imagery, but this did not stem from a prior knowledge of classical philosophers or activists, nor from involvement in explicitly anarchist political groups. Members had been involved in hippie and avant-garde cultures, which would have inevitably had at least some degree of engagement with anarchist ideas. This exposure helped shape Crass's response to the problems they identified in the music industry and society at large. As Rimbaud states, '[i]n all honesty, I wasn't aware of anarchism until about one year into Crass. I knew what it meant in the loose term of the word before, but in terms of a label, it was more default.'[47] However, this influence was not easily accepted into early punk's 'anti-hippie politics.'[48] As Rimbaud puts it, 'that particular form of hope was a dream,' and 'we abandoned the flowers for the black rags of another movement . . . if we weren't to be allowed to play our game of life, we'd have to fight for the right to do so.'[49] Rimbaud's case is particularly telling, since the anti-hippie statements above are directed at his immediate lived experience —the personal disavowal of a movement to which he had belonged illuminates the perceived rupture from hippie.[50] There was also a feeling that the movements of the 1960's had failed to achieve *anything*—'the idea of "we can change the world" became "what good did it do anyway,"'[51] and 'the promises of the British sixties . . . [were] a con game people ran on themselves.'[52] This

25.

[47] Penny Rimbaud, quoted in George Berger, *The Story of Crass* (London: Omnibus Press, 2008), 128.

[48] Roger Sabin, "Introduction," in Sabin, ed., *Punk Rock*, 4.

[49] Rimbaud, *Shibboleth*, 215, 324.

[50] He recounts emerging from the utopian idyll of their countryside commune, Dial House, 'back into the "real" world,' 'the horrific reality of the nuclear age' (Rimbaud, *Shibboleth*, 68, 156).

[51] Andrew Boyd, 'Irony, Meme Warfare, and the Extreme Costume Ball,' in *From Act Up to the WTO: Urban Protest and Community Building in the Era of Globalisation*, eds. Benjamin Shepard and Ronald Hayduk (New York: Verso, 2002), 248; cited in Ben Holtzman, Craig Hughes, and Kevin Van Meter, 'Do it Yourself . . . and the Movement Beyond Capitalism,' in *Constituent Imagination: Militant Investigations // Collective Theorization*, eds. Erika Biddle, Stevphen Shukaitis, and David Graeber (Edinburgh: AK Press, 2007), 44.

[52] Greil Marcus, 'Johnny Rotten and Margaret Drabble,' *Rolling Stone*, March 9, 1978; cited in Greil Marcus, *In The Fascist Bathroom: Writings on*

sense of defeat and betrayal goes a long way in explaining early punk's reputed disdain for their sub-cultural forebears.[53] For those who had become disillusioned with hippie, and for younger people who felt let down that hippie no longer offered an alternative, the reaction was to reject it wholesale—captured in the punk motto, 'don't be such a fucking hippy.'[54] Perhaps though, it was the significant common ground between early punk and hippie that necessitated such rhetorical rancour.

Sabin has argued that punk was 'the last gasp of the 1960's counterculture,' particularly in a continued anti-'establishment' posture and in 'tactics for subverting mainstream culture, and its DIY ethic.'[55] Rimbaud, who was 'at the core both of the hippie and of the punk movement in Britain,'[56] describes hippie as 'a rejection of systems that govern with fear, control by force, and that in the name of the Father have slaughtered millions upon millions of innocent victims.'[57] This anti-religion/anti-state position draws an overt anarchistic thread between hippie and punk, though this connection is most clearly expressed as a shared sense of non-conformity, anti-consumerism, anti-materialism, and anti-capitalism. Expressed in Phil 'Wally' Hope's ebullient language, hippies were:

> the new warrior class, the children of tomorrow, here to avenge the theft of the rainbow, to paint colours on the face of grey conformism, to move the moribund curtains of bourgeois mediocrity, to reclaim the sun.[58]

Punk, 1977-1992 (London: Penguin, 1993), 17.

[53] 'Never trust a hippie' was a line in the Sex Pistols' 'Who Killed Bambi' (*The Great Rock 'n' Roll Swindle*, 1979), and NOFX's 'Always Hate Hippies' was released on the *Fuck the* Kids EP (Fat Wreck, 1996)—NOFX also released the *Never Trust a Hippy* EP in 2006. The Casualties 'Kill the Hippies' was recorded in the early 1990's, but released on *The Early Years, 1990-1995* (Punk Core, 2001).

[54] Mark Sinker, 'Concrete, So As to Self-Destruct: The Etiquette of Punk, its Habits, Rules, Values and Dilemmas,' in Sabin, ed., *Punk Rock*, 123 [120–139].

[55] Sabin, 'Introduction,' *Punk Rock*, 4.

[56] Rimbaud, *Shibboleth*, back cover.

[57] Rimbaud, *Shibboleth*, 153.

[58] Phil 'Wally' Hope, quoted in Rimbaud, *Shibboleth*, 65. Hope was a central organiser of numerous hippie festivals across Britain, including the first three Stonehenge festivals. Incidentally, the 101ers fronted by Joe Strummer (later of the Clash) played the third Stonehenge festival, providing another personal link between hippie and punk.

While early punks rejected such ethereal imagery, the underlying opposition to repressive society was shared. Lucy O'Brien understands this challenge to society's norms (particularly chauvinism and sexism) as an 'unpicking that started with celebratory abandon on the underground 60s freakscene [and] became a giant unravelling with punk.'[59] There are, then, some elements of punk that can be considered to have been inherited directly from the hippie movement, despite its expressed anti-hippie mentality. As Rimbaud says, 'I've never seen any sort of difference between bohemian, beatnik, hippie, punk. They're all one and the same to me.'[60] While methods of expressing this anti-'establishment' mentality are different—punk's confrontation versus hippie's escapism—their dissatisfactions with mainstream society are extremely similar.

Avant-garde and Situationism have often been applied to punk in an effort to place it within the tradition of 'bohemia and radical art.'[61] The 'conventional view,' according to Laing, is that punk was 'heavily influenced by Situationism,'[62] a view shared by Greil Marcus, though disputed by many others. Several members of Crass were previously involved in avant-garde music projects, namely Exit and Ceres Confusion, and Bill Osgerby describes early punk as 'a piece of radical theatre, a calculated attempt to enflame and outrage establishment sensibilities,'[63] while Kieran James identifies a (tenuous) link between the Clash and the Situationist International (S.I.), and Laing makes a comparison between the shock-tactics employed by dada and punk, as does O'Hara when he addresses:

> unusual fashions, the blurring of boundaries between art and everyday life, juxtapositions of seemingly disparate objects and behaviours, intentional provocation of the

---

[59] Lucy O'Brien, 'The Woman Punk Made Me,' in Sabin, ed., *Punk Rock*, 187 [186–198].

[60] Penny Rimbaud, interviewed in *Crass: There is No Authority But Yourself*, dir. Alexander Oey (Submarine Channel, 2006); available at: http://www.minimovies.org/documentaires/view/crass.

[61] Bill Osgerby, '"Chewing Out a Rhythm On My Bubble-gum": The Teenage Aesthetic and Genealogies of American Punk,' in Sabin, ed., *Punk Rock*, 166 [154–169].

[62] Sabin, 'Introduction,' *Punk Rock*, 4.

[63] Bill Osgerby, *Youth in Britain Since 1945* (Oxford: Blackwell, 1998); cited in Paul Cobley, 'Leave the Capitol,' in Sabin, ed., *Punk Rock*, 172 [170–185].

audience, use of untrained performers, and drastic reor-
ganisation (or disorganisation) of accepted performance
styles and procedures.[64]

It has been suggested that Malcolm McLaren (Sex Pistols'
manager) and Jamie Reid (Sex Pistols' artist) represent a link with
Situationism. Both of these individuals had been exposed to the
S.I. through King Mob,[65] and Laing suggests that this exposure
led McLaren and Reid to use 'Situationism to radicalise rock.'[66]
Dave and Stuart Wise, writing in 1978, contest that Jamie Reid's
album covers for 'Pretty Vacant' and 'Holidays in the Sun' were
'lifted straight from' existing Situationist literature.[67] However,
this link is limited to those participants who were old enough to
have actually been involved in preceding cultural scenes. The
identification of McLaren as puppet-master of the entire early
punk era is dubious, particularly when even his ability to influence the band he managed cannot be accepted unequivocally. His
supposed introduction of Situationism into punk is dismissed by
John Lydon as '"bollocks"—an erroneous fantasy contrived for
coffee-table revolutionaries.'[68] This is backed by Stewart Home
who also disputes that there was any 'serious or significant sense
in which punk was a product of Situationist ideas.'[69] In fact, many
of the links drawn between avant-garde and punk are based on
comparison alone. The observed similarities are taken as evidence

---

[64] James, '"This is England",' 132; Laing, *One Chord* Wonders, 76; O'Hara, *The Philosophy of Punk*, 32–34.
[65] Bob Black, 'The Realisation and Suppression of Situationism,' in *What is Situationsim? A Reader*, ed. Stewart Home (Edinburgh: AK Press, 1996), 147.
[66] Laing, *One Chord Wonders*, 126.
[67] Dave and Stuart Wise, 'The End of Music,' in Home, ed., *What is Situationsim?*, 63. Originally published as a pamphlet by 'Calderwood 15' (1978). Patti Smith also used the Andre Breton dada motto, 'beauty will be convulsive or not at all,' on the front of her *Radio Ethiopia* LP (Arista Records, 1976).
[68] John Lydon (with Keith and Kent Zimmerman), *Rotten: No Irish, No Blacks, No Dogs* (New York: St. Martin's Press, 1994), 4; cited in Osgerby, 'Chewing Out a Rhythm on My Bubble-gum,' in Sabin, ed., *Punk Rock*, 155.
[69] David Huxley, '"Ever Get the Feeling You've Been Cheated?": Anarchy and Control in *The Great Rock 'n' Roll Swindle*,' in Sabin, ed., *Punk Rock*, 86 [81–99]. Home has written books on both punk and Situationism: see *The Assault on Culture: Utopian Currents from Lettrisme to Class War* (London: Aporia Press, 1988) and *Cranked Up Really High: Genre Theory and Punk Rock* (London: Codex, 1996).

that punk was *directly inspired* by Situationism, but this is too strong an assertion. O'Hara qualifies his claims by stating that early punks were probably 'quite unknowing'[70] of similarities with the avant-garde, *yet still* goes onto assert that punks were influenced by these movements, rather than intuitively approaching similar problems with similar tactics. Another key objection is that 'avant-garde' connotes vanguardism,[71] which sits at odds with punk's populist grounding. So, while outward comparisons may be drawn between punk and avant-garde movements, and a few individuals can be placed within both movements, their underlying motivations and approaches are essentially different and it is an overstatement to suggest that punk represents an expression of the avant-garde art philosophy.

So, even as early punk's rhetoric emphasised a break from the past, the anti-'establishment' tradition of hippie and avant-garde can be identified. These influences are largely indirect, and are felt in a negative sense as much as positive—i.e., some rhetoric and practices are carried through, but equally the failures of previous movements are learned-from (or rejected) in an effort to present a more resilient form of rebellion. This tradition of rebellion, freedom, and equality is (crudely) anarchistic.

REACTIVE ANARCHISM: IN OPPOSITION TO HIERARCHICAL/STATE REPRESSION AND THE REACTION AGAINST EARLY PUNK

Murray Bookchin argued that contemporary anarchism developed from 'initially inchoate but popular attempts to resist hierarchical domination.'[72] This idea of an anarchic reaction to repression can be identified in the case of early punk, the development of which was largely shaped in reaction to the repression weighed upon the emergent movement. Ian Glasper identifies the 'rebellion inherent in punk from Day One.'[73] Further, 'Punk was almost unanimously denounced by clergymen, politicians, parents, and pundits for its "degeneration of the

---

[70] O'Hara, *The Philosophy of Punk*, 32–33.
[71] This may appear startlingly obvious, but words that are used to name or signify a particular entity or movement frequently lose the impact of their original meanings.
[72] An interpretation he claims to share with Peter Kropotkin. See Murray Bookchin, 'The Ghost of Anarcho-Syndicalism,' *Anarchist Studies* 1 (1993): 3-24; available at: http://dwardmac.pitzer.edu/Anarchist_Archives/bookchin/ghost2.html.
[73] Ian Glasper, *The Day the Country Died: A History of Anarcho Punk, 1980-1984* (London: Cherry Red Books, 2006), back cover.

youth" and its potential to cause an upheaval of British culture and politics.'[74] The hysterical language used against punk was in terms of moral depravity—to paraphrase Bernard Brooke Partridge,[75] punk is 'disgusting, degrading, ghastly, sleazy, prurient, voyeuristic and generally nauseating . . . vastly improved by sudden death . . . the antithesis of humankind.'[76] Aside from Tory rantings, the mainstream media also demonised punk as 'a national menace.'[77] Papers such as *The Sun, Daily Mirror,* and *Lancashire Evening Post* peddled adjectives like 'sick and filthy,' 'outrageous and depraved.'[78] Robin Eggar of the *Daily Mirror* attacked the Crass single 'How Does it Feel to be the Mother of a Thousand Dead'[79] as 'the most revolting and unnecessary record I have ever heard.'[80] Holtzman, Hughes, and van Meter note that '[t]he media both created and reinforced fears,'[81] in what Cobley describes as 'a peculiar ideological battleground whose landscape, made up of manifest disgust at abjection, betrayed latent fears of a more *explicitly political nature.*'[82] However, punk's 'saleability' meant the newspapers could not afford to simply ignore it. Their reporting, negative or not, fuelled punk's hype.

The music industry was also repressive. Laing notes 'radio stations . . . intent on excluding it,' 'exceptional media hostility,' 'many acts of censorship and banning,' and 'sporadic refusals to stock [punk records] by chain stores infected by fits of general "immorality".'[83] Crass having to remove a track from their album, discussed above, is another example. As punk became increaseingly popular, major labels could no longer ignore potential

---

[74] Ben Holtzman, Craig Hughes, and Kevin Van Meter, 'Do it Yourself . . . and the Movement Beyond Capitalism,' in Biddle et al., eds., *Constituent Imagination*, 46.

[75] Conservative member of Greater London Council.

[76] Bernard Brooke Partridge, delivered to camera in *The Great Rock 'n' Roll Swindle,* dir. Julien Temple, 1980; quoted in Huxley, '"Ever Get the Feeling You've Been Cheated?",' in Sabin, ed., *Punk Rock,* 95.

[77] Cobley, 'Leave the Capitol,' in Sabin, ed., *Punk Rock,* 173.

[78] *Lancashire Evening Post* (1976): see Cobley, 'Leave the Capitol,' in Sabin, ed., *Punk Rock,* 174.

[79] Released on Crass Records and in reference to the death toll from the Falklands War of 1982—Thatcher being the 'Mother' in question.

[80] Rimbaud, *Shibboleth,* 241.

[81] Holtzman, Hughes, and Van Meter, 'Do it Yourself,' in Biddle et al., eds., *Constituent Imagination,* 46.

[82] Cobley, 'Leave the Capitol,' in Sabin, ed., *Punk Rock,* 175 (emphasis added).

[83] Laing, *One Chord Wonders,* 34, 37.

capital gains. Bands that did sign with major labels were duly exploited, but in the main, repression continued in some form throughout early punk. *Even* the Sex Pistols' 'God Save the Queen' was driven '"underground", so that it could only be obtained in certain smaller shops and could be heard only in private homes.'[84] Laing writes that this repression was then heavily reported by the mainstream media, who 'frothed over the "treasonable" nature of the song,' creating advertising for the record and helping sales, so that the media outlets 'were forced to re-admit it when its sales figures won it a place in their best-seller lists.'[85] So, repression from the music industry was not total since capital interests could outweigh any 'moral' concerns once a band exhibited a critical mass of popularity and profitability. Ironically, repression contributed to punk's public image as 'dangerous,' therefore making the bands more popular, and subsequently more attractive to the record labels as a profitable signing.

The most serious repression came from the state, carrying the threat of incarceration. Crass 'attracted almost constant State harassment.'[86] For example, '[t]he release of 'Reality Asylum' led to a visit from Scotland Yard's Vice Squad' and 'a threat of prosecution for "criminal blasphemy",' Further, Tory MP Tim Eggar (brother of Robin Eggar of the *Daily Mirror*) 'wrote to the Attorney General requesting that Crass be prosecuted under the Obscene Publications Act,' local police used to regularly intimidate inhabitants and search visitors to Dial House (Crass's residence), and MI5 reputedly tapped their phone line to record their conversations.[87] When Crass were brought to trial for breach of the Obscene Publications Act, the judge ruled that Crass's music 'might have a tendency to deprave and corrupt people likely to come into contact with them.'[88] State repression was not confined to Crass. For many punk gigs 'the local State . . .

---

[84] Laing, *One Chord Wonders*, 38. It seems rather strong to describe anything the Sex Pistols were involved with as 'underground.'

[85] Laing, *One Chord Wonders*, 38.

[86] Rimbaud, *Shibboleth*, 255.

[87] Rimbaud, *Shibboleth*, 112, 241, 121.

[88] Rimbaud, *Shibboleth*, 256–257. Even Crass's lawyer for the case took the perceived threat extremely seriously, as Rimbaud recalls: 'Outside the courtroom, our lawyer offered his commiserations. "Don't worry," I responded, "the bomb's fused to go off in precisely four minutes." For a moment he froze, then he turned as white as a sheet, and then he took to his heels' (Rimbaud, *Shibboleth*, 257).

refused access to public halls,[89] and Tad Kepley, a punk and anarchist activist in the US, remembers 'worrying about the cops coming in, fucking kicking your ass.'[90] Prior to the Clash's 1977 gig in Munich, according to Paul Simonon, 'the police came and dragged us out from the hotel.'[91] Wider society also presented problems for punks. O'Brien notes, 'there was actually a lot of painful stuff going on around it. You were seen as deviant.'[92] Greg Gaffin of Bad Religion recalls 'how frightening it was to live in a world where people were violently opposed to you . . . people wanted to kill us for the way we looked,' and Kevin Seconds of 7 Seconds remembers 'being chased down the street with baseball bats.'[93]

This repression from so many sectors points to punk being perceived as a very real threat, and a determined effort to repress it. However, '[d]espite straight society's studious efforts to ignore its new radicals, and the media's determination to discredit them,' writes Rimbaud, 'punk had become a household word.'[94] In fact, as suggested above, this hysterical 'moral panic'[95] contributed to punk's hype and its attraction as something forbidden: 'infectious . . . incredibly underground, dangerous.'[96] Rimbaud suggests the revolutionary impetus in punk:

I saw it as a job, a battle, a kick-back at the archaic structures . . . . I was one of the new fifth columnists, resistance fighters, counter-culturists, self-confrontationists. . . . Yes, this time it was our turn.[97]

And even more explicitly:

I consider punk to have been essentially a revolutionary movement.[98]

---

[89] Laing, *One Chord Wonders*, xiii.
[90] Blush, *American Hardcore*, 352.
[91] Paul Simonon, interviewed in *Punk in London*, dir. Wolfgang Büld (Odeon Entertainment/Munich Film School/HFF München, 1978)
[92] O'Brien, 'The Woman Punk Made Me,' in Sabin, ed., *Punk Rock*, 193.
[93] Blush, *American Hardcore*, 352.
[94] Rimbaud, *Shibboleth*, 154.
[95] Term coined by Stanley Cohen, in *Folk Devils and Moral Panics: The Creation of the Mods and Rockers* (London: MacGibbon and Kee, 1972).
[96] Richie Birkenhead, quoted in *All Ages: Reflections on Straight Edge*, comp. Beth Lahickey (Huntington Beach: Revelation Books, 1997), 17.
[97] Rimbaud, *Shibboleth*, 73.
[98] Penny Rimbaud, in conversation with George McKay, "Subcultures &

Some of the 'inchoate' anarchic themes that emerged were lyrical attacks against establishment institutions, and popular targets were the government and the police. The band name Thought Criminals, and the songs 'The Prisoner' (D.O.A.) and 'Criminal Mind' (The Ruts) express feelings of criminalisation. Songs about the police include 'Police Oppression' (Angelic Upstarts), 'The Murder of Liddle Towers' (Angelic Upstarts), 'Fascist Pigs' (Nosebleeds), 'The Cops Are Comin'' (Outcasts), 'Secret Police' (Unwanted), 'Task Force (Undercover Cops)' (Razar), and 'C.I.D.' (UK Subs). The police are recognised as agents of state oppression, and are scorned and derided for their chosen form of servitude. Lyrics concerning government in early punk were more varied, from the gentle irony of 'Don't Worry About The Government' (Talking Heads), to more pointed sarcasm of 'Leaders of Men' (Joy Division), complaints of government harassment such as 'Government Official' (F-Word), 'Pay Your Rates' (Fall), 'Censorship' (Models), and 'Law And Order' (Stiff Little Fingers), up to totalitarian state imagery like 'Fascist Dictator' (Cortinas) and '1984' (Unwanted).[99] The religious establishment was another target, examples include Bad Religion's name and anti-Christian motif (a Christian cross contained within a red circle and bisecting line), Siouxsie and the Banshees' 'The Lord's Prayer' (a sex-fetishist parody), the Damned's 'Anti-Pope,' Suburban Studs' 'No Faith,' and Crass's 'Reality Asylum'. 'God Save the Queen' by the Sex Pistols provides one frequently cited anti-monarchist example, but so too does Drones' 'Corgi Crap,' with the line, 'Don't wanna be no blue-blood, it makes me ill to think of them!'[100] Numerous other facets of society's repression were targeted as well, and Mark Sinker sums up the oppositional position of punk:

All choices—what you ate, how you walked, when you

Lifestyles: Subcultures and Lifestyles in Russia and Eastern Europe" (conference), University of Salford, December 4-6, 2008.
[99] O'Hara argues that '[t]he Punk movement was originally formed in nations holding capitalist, pseudo-democratic policies. Because of this, capitalism and its problems became the first target of political Punks': O'Hara, *The Philosophy of Punk*, 74. While this fails to account for punk's popularity in Communist and non-Western states, the anti-capitalist rhetoric in early punk is typified in 'Money Talks' by Penetration and 'Let's Lynch the Landlord' by Dead Kennedys (which encourages an extremely direct approach to rent boycott).
[100] Drones, 'Corgi Crap,' *Further Temptations* (Valer, 1977).

slept, who you liked—were to be rated primarily against their likely immediate effect; what reaction had you provoked from who.[101]

It is readily conceded that early punk lacked a coherent political ideology, but its oppositional elements are clear. Punk was repressed as a threat to the establishment and as a result punk *identified itself* as a threat to the state, the government, the police, the church, the monarchy, capitalism, and mainstream mass culture. This resistance to hierarchical domination, as Bookchin suggests, looks very much like a nascent anarchism.

PRACTICAL NECESSITY: THE DIY (DO-IT-YOURSELF) ORGANISING PRINCIPLE AS TAKING OVER THE MEANS OF PRODUCTION FOR WORKERS' SELF-CONTROL, IN THE ABSENCE OF THE MAINSTREAM INDUSTRY

The repression discussed above, and the anarchistic reaction generated, are best observed in the sphere of production (cultural, musical, *and* material). Initially the mainstream music industry was extremely reticent to become involved with punk, but the lure of profit meant numerous early punk bands were unscrupulously exploited. Within a short time punk fell out of favour with the corporate labels with 'New Wave' as a safer, more easily managed investment. This combination of refusal and exploitation led to the adoption of a DIY ethic as a central organising practice in punk, both out of necessity (if major labels refused to work with them) and out of choice (since signing to a major label would usually mean meagre monetary return and loss of artistic freedom and integrity). This DIY ethic then, to some extent, represents direct worker/producer control over the means of production, and the dissemination and 'marketing' of that product. Another important effect of this was to decentralise the networks created by punk, in stark contrast to the highly centralised mainstream music industry.

Laing writes, 'Punk rock was unusually concerned with the "production apparatus",' and '[j]ust as the fanzines demystified the process of producing and publishing the written word, so the early punk labels demonstrated the simplicity with which anyone could become a recording artist,' thus 'represent[ing] the virtual dissolution of the barrier between performer and audience that

---

[101] Sinker, 'Concrete, So as to Self-Destruct," in Sabin, ed., *Punk Rock*, 125.

was part of the ethos of much punk activity.'[102] Rimbaud writes,
'[p]unk had originated as a statement, "do it yourself": your own
band, your own sounds, your own words, your own attitude and
your own future.'[103] Holtzman et al. describe DIY as 'anything
from music and magazines to education and protest [being]
created in a nonalienating, self-organised, and purposely
anticapitalist manner'—'the idea that you can do for yourself the
activities normally reserved for the realm of capitalist production,' 'a means of circumventing the powers-that-be.'[104] Holtzman
et. al's definition of DIY is markedly similar to an anarchist
understanding of direct action. Processes of production in music
were exposed and demystified by early punk, and in its circum-
vention of the 'big 6' record companies' dominance, DIY also
represents a direct and prefigurative approach—themes
inexorably linked with contemporary anarchism. The DIY
approach is a first step in creating alternative forms of production
that attempt to break away from the capital-motivated norm.
Punk's anti-capitalist position can be identified in various bands'
relationships with the mainstream music industry, and as Ian
MacKaye recalls, 'I was really struck by the fact that this was
completely non-commercial music.'[105] Gregg Ginn found that
'[h]ooking up with a major label was completely out of the
question at the time . . . . People from major labels were afraid to
go to Black Flag gigs throughout most of the band's existence.'[106]
Jake Burns from Stiff Little Fingers recalls major labels 'offering
us lots and lots of money, and we sort of realised, no, there's
actually more value in people understanding what you want to do
and respecting that.'[107] Glasper notes some of the key aspects of
DIY as it became entrenched as a central organising principle of

[102] Laing, *One Chord Wonders*, 127, 17, 78.

[103] Rimbaud, *Shibboleth*, 78.

[104] Holtzman, Hughes, and Van Meter, 'Do it Yourself,' in Biddle et al.,
eds., *Constituent Imagination*, 44.

[105] Ian MacKaye (interview), in Lahickey, comp., *All Ages*, 96. MacKaye
played with Teen Idles, Minor Threat, Fugazi and others in the
Washington, D.C. area, and he helped create the straight-edge hardcore
movement.

[106] Gregg Ginn, interview with Eric Olsen, *Blog Critics: Music* [website],
2003: http://blogcritics.org/archives/2003/11/21/183736.php; cited in Chick,
Spray Paint the Walls, 92. Ginn was a founder and member of south-
Californian hardcore progenitors, Black Flag.

[107] Jake Burns, interview with Alan Parker, Part 1 (conducted June 13,
2001), track 16 on Stiff Little Fingers, *Inflammable Material*, reissue (EMI,
2001).

the anarcho-punk movement of the early 1980's, both in what it
negated and what it strove to create:

> No more corporate companies . . . this was the birth of
> *genuinely* DIY labels. . . . No more big booking agents
> controlling punk shows . . . now fans of the music could
> communicate directly with the bands, and book them . . .
> the meagre door takings being ploughed back into
> worthwhile causes locally. No more glossy magazines . . .
> anyone who could string two words together and use a
> stapler was a potential fanzine editor. . . . the kids were
> taking back control and making a difference.[108]

Early punk DIY releases such as the Buzzcocks' *Spiral
Scratch*[109] and Scritti Politti's *4 A Sides*[110] included details such as
the number of each take or overdub, and the production costs for
the record. As such, the production process was demystified and
the common perception that a major label was required to release
a band's music was shattered. Mick McGee of Mayhem recalls the
empowerment of DIY: '[I]f you robbed three phone boxes you
could almost set up your own record company, and that was
what we were relying on. That gave access to upcoming bands to
actually get their records heard.'[111] Cogan notes that, 'Throbbing
Gristle realised that to take a truly radical and outsider posture in
punk rock, the first step must be to control the production and
distribution of their own work.'[112] Dave Harker notes that, 'Crass
ran themselves on a self-sufficient basis, organising their own
tours, records and distribution. Their sole concern was to make
enough money to live, not to have top 40 hits or play a large
stadium.'[113] Laing recognises the impact of this self-organisation,
and using independent systems of distribution meant that punks
could 'evade *to some degree* the insistence of the market values
and forces and increasingly to offer different definitions of music

---

[108] Glasper, *The Day the Country Died*, 8 (emphasis added).
[109] Self-released by the Buzzcocks under the label-name 'New Hormones'
in January 1977.
[110] Rough Trade, 1979. Rough Trade is an early example of a DIY label.
Sometimes the term 'indie' label is used, but in the contemporary context
this no longer has any relation to 'independence' of any kind, and such
labels are usually just imprints for one of the majors.
[111] Glasper, *Burning Britain*, 9.
[112] Cogan, '"Do They Owe Us a Living?",' 85.
[113] Dave Harker, quoted in the zine *Pop and Politics Do Mix!* (Lancashire,
April 1991); cited in O'Hara, *The Philosophy of Punk*, 160.

and different positions and roles for the listener.'[114] DIY gave early punk bands the freedom to create their own music, and to produce and distribute it in forms not motivated by capital. The difficulties in organising alternative systems of distribution were more than outweighed by the benefits of creative freedom and the enhanced sense of direct communication achieved.

DIY media also proliferated, and 'influenced enough people to begin a network of locally based fanzines that would soon connect a worldwide Punk network.'[115] Without multinational record labels to coordinate and distribute most punk music, alternative networks developed to fulfil this role, which pushed (and was pushed by) the decentralisation of punk. Even early on, punk was to be found in suburbs, rural areas, far-flung industrial towns, as well as in the cities. This decentralisation was supported by networks of cooperation and information exchange. Dave Laing notes the distribution of independent and DIY labels in the UK as listed by *Zig Zag* magazine in 1978: '120 companies with a repertoire of punk material, mostly with just a handful of titles and *nearly all based outside London.*' Labels such as Anonymous Records in Macclesfield, Duff Records of Bangor, Good Vibrations in Belfast, and Vole Records of Wolverhampton meant that the 'metropolitan monopoly of the record industry had been seriously challenged for the first time.'[116] This is not to say that punk existed in a uniform manner across its wide geographical spread. Paul Cobley was, as he describes it, 'a provincial punk,' which 'represented a considerable leap of faith,'[117] compared with the accessibility of punk in the major urban centres. In the US as well, the decentralised and widespread appeal of punk was recognised. Jello Biafra of the Dead Kennedys 'championed young bands in every city—when such interest by headliners was unheard of.'[118]

This nascent network of punk scenes enabled 'pioneering' punk bands to travel widely outside of the main cultural hubs. Crass's negative experiences with venues such as the Roxy in

---

[114] Laing, *One Chord Wonders*, 21 (emphasis added).

[115] O'Hara, *The Philosophy of Punk*, 64.

[116] Laing, *One Chord Wonders*, 14 (emphasis added). Ian Glasper's trilogy of analyses of punk in the 1980s divides the UK into separate areas, each burgeoning with punk bands—in his own words, he covers 'the country region by region' (Glasper, *Burning Britain*, back cover).

[117] Cobley, 'Leave the Capitol,' in Sabin, ed., *Punk Rock*, 171.

[118] Blush, *American Hardcore*, 117.

London led the group to 'seek out alternatives for our gigs.'[119] Rimbaud notes that this led Crass to 'play in an extraordinary range of venues in far-flung places in the British Isles where no band had ever played before. This act of de-centralisation was essential to our overall philosophy, and greatly contributed to the wide-spread effect that we were able to have.'[120] In North America, Black Flag, D.O.A., and the Dead Kennedys were having similar experiences and 'sought out like-minded artists, and aided unknown upstarts' in 'their zeal to establish a united scene.'[121] Biafra recalls the cooperation between bands: 'We were all sharing information. Whenever somebody cracked open a new town, the other two bands [Black Flag and D.O.A.] found out about it.'[122] Tim Kerr of Big Boys notes the influence of early punk bands arriving in towns that would otherwise be off the touring radar: 'When Black Flag came through and started hitting every little town . . . all these kids started picking up instruments and starting bands.'[123] These networks were essential for dissemination of underground and DIY music. The Sex Pistols' 1977 single 'God Save the Queen' would have been unlikely to reach the singles chart number one spot without the huge number of underground record shops willing to peddle the suppressed record.[124]

Separation from capital, particularly at punk's earliest stages, could not be complete: 'even in their prime [the punk rockers of 1976] were part of the capitalist system [even if] only marginally.'[125] DIY and independent networks could be relied upon for creation of music, recording, distribution, and media, but *not* for things like pressing vinyl, sourcing equipment,

---

[119] Rimbaud, *Shibboleth*, 125.

[120] Rimbaud, *Shibboleth*, 125. Crass's 'decentralisation' was largely confined to the UK, since they were reluctant to play abroad where they had less understanding of local political situations. Crass did play in New York in their very early days, as well as the Netherlands and Germany, and Iceland towards their demise, but these were fairly exceptional venues compared to their usual UK-based touring schedules.

[121] Blush, *American Hardcore*, 115.

[122] Quoted in Blush, *American Hardcore*, 322.

[123] Quoted in Blush, *American Hardcore*, 322.

[124] These networks continue to enable bands to tour relatively cheaply, so bands and promoters require less financial reimbursement to break even, making punk accessible and affordable.

[125] This inference is drawn from another article, referenced only as 'Emery, 2007 chapter VI,' which has been impossible to locate so its source cannot be verified: see James, '"This is England",' 137.

shipping records, or buying and fuelling tour vans. These tasks, within a capitalist framework, involve huge costs and are usually remunerated through large-scale production. These overheads necessitated having to pass costs on to the 'consumer,' in the form of commoditised products; however, any risk of greedy price-hiking by record stores was frequently eschewed with 'pay no more than' notices,[126] which also helped to negate any profit motive the bands themselves might succumb to. Later developments, such as recordable cassettes, mp3, cheaply available recording equipment, and punk-run pressing plants have helped to break down some of these impasses, making DIY and direct worker/producer self-control even more viable. The 'virtue' of DIY was discovered through necessity, but quickly became entrenched as a poignant manifestation of the intuitive anarchism inherent in early punk, and a continuing central tenet of punk cultures that exist outside of mainstream interference.

INTUITIVE ANARCHIST POLITICS: DISAVOWAL OF (CAPITAL 'P') POLITICS.

The four themes above make evident an evolution—rooted in punk's antimonies—from initial oppositionalism, through resistance of repression, to an embracing of DIY as part of a conscious self-identification as a 'real'[127] punk movement. These approaches could be readily mapped from the anarchist canon, but this was not the case for early punk. This is not to say that early punk operated apolitically or in ignorance of its own political significance. Early punk rejected dominant political discourses, frequently framed as opposition to 'Politics' in general, as in the songs 'Politics' (The Damned) and 'Modern Politics' (Panik). This was a refusal of 'either-or' options—Conservative or Labour within parliament, Socialist Workers Party (SWP) or National Front (NF) as 'radical' alternatives. The rejection of political parties is an obvious extension to the reactive anarchism discussed above, so the focus here will be on the rejection of extra-parliamentary political groups such as the SWP and NF. As

---

[126] Crass used these frequently: *Stations of the Crass*, for example, carries a 'pay no more than £5' notice. Record fairs and collectors tend to ignore these today—one copy of *Stations of the Crass* was recently seen for £12 at a record fair in Belfast, and the seller missed the irony when questioned on the 'pay no more than' notice . . . .

[127] 'Real punk' was a popular generic term in the very late 1970's and early 1980's.

Billy Idol[128] put it when asked about the political stance of Siousxie and the Banshees, 'we're not communists or fascists,'[129] —the notion of being 'Tory' or 'Labour' is not even countenanced.

The Pigs' song 'National Front' states how the NF have 'got it all wrong,'[130] going on to deride them as fascists—a description the NF were keen to play down, despite its accuracy. Many early punks were also at pains to explain the use of the swastika as shock tactic rather than an indication of Nazi sympathies, as discussed above. A traditional interpretation in much of the literature is that punk was essentially void of explicit political content, with various groups staking a claim, until the Rock Against Racism (RAR) concerts of 1978 when punk came down on the Left. Certainly, punk was well represented at the events with bands such as Stiff Little Fingers, Generation X, Tom Robinson Band, Elvis Costello, the Ruts, the Clash, X-Ray Spex, and the Buzzcocks all taking part. So an association between early punk and 'the left' in its broadest sense is generally fair, as far as a rejection of the NF is concerned (with some significant exceptions). However, many early punks and punk bands were conscious that RAR and the Anti-Nazi League (ANL) were front-organisations recruiting for the SWP. Sabin notes 'open hostility to RAR/the ANL' in early punk, and 'a distrust of being used (especially as a tool in a socialist revolution).'[131] Sabin puts this down to 'punk's broadly anti-authoritarian ethic—expressed both as an untheorised hatred of being told what to do and in more sophisticated *anarchist* terms.'[132] Lydon states, 'I'm not a revolutionary, socialist or any of that . . . . It's replacing the same old system with a different clothing.'[133] So, while the right-wing was widely rejected by early punk, so too was the left. Laing comments that 'many punk bands were eager to avoid anything that smacked of programmatic commitment,'[134] whether left or right. The rejection of the orthodox left-right dichotomy is particularly telling in the case of Crass. As a band that had

---

[128] Billy Idol also played with Chelsea and Generation X, before pursuing a solo pop career.

[129] Billy Idol speaking in a Siousxie and the Banshees interview; quoted in Laing, *One Chord Wonders*, 126.

[130] The Pigs, 'National Front', from the Youthanasia 7" (Bristol Records, 1977).

[131] Sabin, '"I Won't Let that Dago By",' in Sabin, ed., *Punk Rock*, 206, 207.

[132] Sabin, '"I Won't Let that Dago By",' in Sabin, ed., *Punk Rock*, 206 (emphasis added).

[133] Lydon, *Rotten*, 311; cited in Albiez, 'Know History!', 367.

[134] Laing, *One Chord Wonders*, 126.

attracted a great deal of attention while remaining outside of the major label circus, Crass were 'put under increasing pressure to clarify [their] political affinities.' As Rimbaud puts it, '[t]he Left, in the guise of middle class liberals, wanted us to support the workers, whereas the workers, mostly in the guise of skinheads, wanted us to support the Right.'[135] Crass's position was to reject these since 'both the right and left wing parties [use] power to control and coerce people,'[136] and as long as they could 'shrug off either camp, [they] were free to expose both to [their] message of anarchist self-determination.'[137] While Crass's refusal to be drawn to either the left or right was largely pragmatic and based on a budding anarchism, this same position was frequently being taken intuitively across the early punk milieu.

The class consciousness of early punk is understandable in relation to the class-based society from which it sprang, particularly in the UK. People were acutely aware of their social standing based on where they lived, what occupation their families had, their accent, their school, etc. However, punk broke down these barriers.[138] Albiez describes this as a dramatisation of 'social changes that were eroding deference, the British class system, high and popular cultural boundaries.'[139] The establishment conception of class was recognised but intentionally *not* re-expressed in early punk; if anything, early punk subverted these conceptions. However, the ideas and relations of class within punk did not equate with those of the Marxist orthodoxy either. Previous notions of class were eschewed, with punk creating a 'déclassé,' 'underclass' or 'outsider class' of its own[140] in what Daniel Traber describes as a tactic of 'self-marginalisation to articulate a politics of dissent.'[141] Early punk's

[135] Rimbaud, *Shibboleth*, 108.
[136] 'Crass,' *Flipside* 23 (March 1981); cited in O'Hara, *The Philosophy of Punk*, 83.
[137] Rimbaud, *Shibboleth*, 109.
[138] In the case of Crass, this created a 'heady mixture of [Ignorant's] working-class anger and [Rimbaud's] middle-class nihilism' (Rimbaud, *Shibboleth*, 94), and the Clash were identified as '[m]iddle-class in background, working-class in the themes of their songs': Greil Marcus, 'The Clash,' *New West*, September 25, 1978; cited in Marcus, *In The Fascist Bathroom*, 29.
[139] Albiez, 'Know History!', 366.
[140] 'Here I am among the dispossessed, all punks together': Linder, quoted in O'Brien, 'The Woman Punk Made Me,' in Sabin, ed., *Punk Rock*, 193.
[141] Daniel S. Traber, 'L.A.'s "White Minority": Punk and the Contra-

class-consciousness is evident in songs such as 'I Hate the Rich' (The Dils), 'I Don't Wanna be a Rich' (Guilty Razors), 'Eton Rifles' (The Jam),[142] 'Ghosts of Princes in Towers' (Rich Kids), and 'Class War' (The Dils), which all attack the privileged classes. Tricia Henry dutifully regurgitates the tired description of early punk as 'a movement consisting of underprivileged working-class white youths,' who were 'self-consciously proletarian,'[143] but Lydon recognises as much oppression *within* the working class as from without: 'When you grow up in a working-class environment, you're supposed to stay inside and follow the rules and regulations of that little system. I won't have any of that.'[144] Albiez agrees that early punk's idea of class 'was not launched from a position of socialist class solidarity,' but rather from a 'class-informed hyper-individualist stance,'[145] so certainly the assertion that punk was operating from an orthodox socialist perspective is dismissed. Early punk's 'class' was neither that of the establishment, nor of Marxism—the combination of individualism and class-consciousness *was anarchist*. Punk's concept of class is broader than narrow proletarianism, and the individual is understood to be a vital component of a wider 'we,' rather than being subsumed as a cog into the larger social machine. Of course, as has been stated many times here, early punk was amorphous and its politics were not yet coherently codified, but an anarchistic conception of class within punk is apparent.

An anarchistic concept of freedom was also prevalent in early punk, in songs like 'I Wanna Be Free' (Rings), 'Freedom' (Unwanted), 'Freedom (Is A Heady Wine)' (Yachts), 'Privilege (Set Me Free)' (Patti Smith), and the band name TSOL (True Sounds of Liberty). Marcus notes that punk was 'a new kind of free speech. It inaugurated a moment—a long moment, which still persists—when suddenly countless odd voices, voices no reasonable person could have expected to hear in public, were being heard all over

---

dictions of Self-Marginalisation,' *Cultural Critique* 48 (Spring 2001): 30.

[142] Ironically (and cringe-inducingly), former Etonian and current Conservative UK Prime Minister David Cameron has expressed a fondness for this particular song. More on this and Paul Weller of the Jam's reaction can be found in an article in John Harris, 'Hands Off Our Music!' *The Guardian*, March 18, 2008: http://www.guardian.co.uk/music/2008/mar/18/popandrock.politicsandthearts.

[143] Tricia Henry, *Break All Rules! Punk Rock and the Making of a Style* (Ann Arbor: UMI Research Press, 1989), 67, 8.

[144] Lydon, *Rotten*, 311.

[145] Albiez, 'Know History!', 366.

the place.'[146] Lesley Wood of the Au Pairs felt that, 'if you're going to have any kind of social change, personal relationships in society have got to change [...]. It is *really important to feel free.*'[147] James identifies an emphasis on 'mental freedom [as] an important type of liberation . . . freedom from false conscious-ness.'[148] Sinker iterates the individualist grounding of freedom within punk: 'no-one else's rules apply to you. You take full responsibility for the consequences of your own rules, your own beliefs. You choose to obey or disobey for your *own* reasons.'[149] This personal responsibility and self-direction are extremely important ideas relating to freedom in both early punk *and* anar-chism,[150] and essentially precludes the applicability of ideologies that fail to value freedom as a prime tenet.

Owing to the importance of freedom, a particular conception of class, and a populist/non-programmatic basis, it is extremely difficult to identify early punk's implicit politics as anything other than a crude, nascent, or inchoate anarchism. Combined with the previous four themes under discussion, the case for early punk as an instance of intuitive anarchistic practice is compelling.

CONCLUSION

So, even prior to the emergence of anarcho-punk and other punk scenes explicitly engaged with anarchism, anarchistic currents are apparent in early punk. Once again, this is not to say that

---

[146] Marcus, *In The Fascist Bathroom*, 2-3.

[147] Lynden Barber, 'Au Pairs: Sex Without Stress,' *Melody Maker*, June 12, 1982: http://www.rocksbackpages.com/article.html?ArticleID=15923&Search Text=Au+Pairs; cited by Lucy O'Brien, 'Can I Have a Taste of Your Ice Cream?' *Punk and Post-Punk* 1.1 (January 2012): 38.

[148] James, '"This is England,"' 137.

[149] Sinker, 'Concrete, So as to Self-Destruct,' in Sabin, ed., *Punk* Rock, 129 (emphasis in original).

[150] Of course, as Sabin points out, '[m]ost accounts assume that punk was "liberating" politically, and created a space for disenfranchised voices to be heard—notably women, gays and lesbians, and anti-racists' (Sabin, 'Introduction,' in Sabin, ed., *Punk Rock*, 4). So this picture cannot be presented universally—as with so many other aspects of punk. Lucy O'Brien writes that '[t]he punk scene . . . was not always one of halcyon acceptance. While there were men wrestling with questions of masculinity and feminism, there were just as many content to leave it unreconstructed' (O'Brien, 'The Woman Punk Made Me,' in Sabin, ed., *Punk Rock*, 194).

early punk was uniformly anarchist, but that even where early punk seems most removed from political anarchism and the anarchist canon, anarchistic practices and rhetoric can *still* be identified. From these beginnings a far more coherent and consistent anarchism emerges. The tag of 'punk-anarchism' is too simplistic, but the presence of anarchist rhetoric *and practice* in punk's earliest manifestations is clear.

The destructive reigns of Thatcher and Reagan in the 1980's enhanced punk's negative unity, crystallised its anarchist politics, and fomented punk's vitriol even further.[151] Anarchy in a positive sense was touched upon by the likes of Crass even at this early stage, as Rimbaud comments, '[w]e wanted to offer something that gave rather than took, something of value that would survive short-lived faddism.'[152] This was further developed towards the end of 'early punk,' and as Glasper writes, the end of the 1970's 'was a time when punk stopped being merely a radical fashion statement, and became a force for real social change; a *genuine revolutionary movement.*'[153]

However, this reinvigoration of political anarchism, in both cultural and material aspects, has often met with criticism from old-fashioned workerist and syndicalist anarchist sects. The antagonism between already-existing anarchists and the emergent punk-inspired anarchists of the 1980's is exemplified by Nick Heath, writing for the anarchist periodical *Black Flag*: 'This new wave [of punk-anarchism] was very much defined by lifestyle and ultimately a form of elitism that frowned upon the mass of the working class for its failure to act.'[154] However, such differences are extremely overstated and the similarities and overlaps between these supposedly distinct approaches is best exemplified in DIY as a form of workers-control and seizure of (some of) the means of production. Certainly a greater appreciation, or at least understanding, of the anarchism developed in punk can only benefit the wider anarchist movement—particularly in view of punk's role in politicising

---

[151] The same can be observed in punk's development within Communist Eastern-bloc countries in the 1980's, and in the 1990's under dictatorships such as Suharto's in Indonesia (both of which are case-studies in my forthcoming PhD thesis).

[152] Rimbaud, *Shibboleth*, 101.

[153] Glasper, *The Day the Country Died*, back cover.

[154] Nick Heath, 'The UK Anarchist Movement—Looking Back and Forward,' originally written for *Black Flag*; posted online November 15, 2006: http://www.libcom.org/library/the-uk-anarchist-movement-looking-back-and-forward.

thousands of individuals to an anarchist perspective.[155]

---

[155] Politicisation through punk and understanding of the mutual criticisms between 'punk anarchism' and other anarchist strands are key themes of my wider PhD thesis.

Anarchist Developments in Cultural Studies
ISSN: 1923-5615
2013.1: Blasting the Canon

Mikhail Bakunin's Post-Ideological Impulse
The Continuity Between Classical and New Anarchism

Ryan Knight*

ABSTRACT

This paper is lead by a particular question: does anarchist political theory present an unsolvable paradox? More specifically, is theory itself a constriction to the authentic social freedom which anarchism clearly supports? I explore these questions through a discussion of the thought of classical social anarchist Mikhail Bakunin. I use Bakunin's work to analyse the "new anarchist left," in an effort to understand the conscious attempt to distance anarchism from classical anarchism. I highlight the post-ideological character of Bakunin's work and anarchism's overarching skepticism of authority. Furthermore, I argue that contemporary activists can learn from the thought of Mikhail Bakunin, and that there is something to be said for recognizing the continuity of anarchist thought and activity.

*

Ryan Knight is a PhD candidate in Political Science, with a focus in political philosophy, at the University of Hawaii at Manoa, USA. He completed both his BA and MA in political science at San Francisco State University, USA. His interests include non-western political theory, anti-capitalist thought, cultural studies, and revolutionary theory, among many other things.

KEYWORDS
anarchism, post-ideology, left strategy, Mikhail Bakunin

In recent years we have seen the emergence of what many are calling a new anarchism. This new anarchism is seen to be post-ideological in that it is anti-sectarian, gathering its influence from a variety of traditions. It doesn't accept a particular ideology because it sees any overarching structure as an authoritarian threat to human spontaneity and freedom. A prime example is what developed in Seattle in opposition to the WTO or, even more recently, some of the anarchist currents that are found in Occupy Wall Street. In contrast, classical anarchism is argued to be different in that it is sectarian, dogmatic, and ideologically strict. In effect, classical anarchism is dismissed as anachronistic, outdated, and irrelevant to our modern times.

I would like to argue against this unfortunate dismissal of classical anarchism by briefly exploring the classical social anarchist Mikhail Bakunin's post-ideological theories, which highlight his relevance to the anarchist currents in today's social movement activity. However, I would first like to spell out what I mean by post-ideological. From there, I would like to delineate the supposed difference between new anarchism and classical anarchism before moving on to what I see as Bakunin's relevance to contemporary anarchist movements as understood in this post-ideological framework.

WHAT EXACTLY IS POST-IDEOLOGICAL ANARCHISM?

David Neal, in "Anarchism: Ideology or Methodology," makes a clear distinction between two tendencies in anarchist activity, helping us understand this post-ideological inclination. In this paper, Neal attempts to make a distinction between anarchism as an ideology and anarchism as a methodology. For Neal, an ideology consists of a "consistent set of ideas based on a core principle" (Neal 1997). In this sense, an ideological anarchist, whom Neal refers to as "big A anarchists," stresses the adherence to a strict set of principles which guide true anarchist action. He writes,

> The [big A] Anarchist stresses ideological confor-
> mity as the prerequisite for social revolution—in
> other words, you swallow A, B, and C doctrines
> and THEN you are an Anarchist. Their plan of
> action revolves around: 1) creating a central
> Anarchist organization; 2) educating (e.g., indoc-
> trinating) the working class as to the tenets of
> Anarchism; 3) thereby building a mass move-
> ment; 4) creating a social revolution. The Anar-
> chist is comfortable with the idea of a manifesto,
> platform, or other guiding doctrine as the means
> of "spreading the gospel"—their emphasis is unity
> in thought and action, and ideological conformity
> as the basis for effective organization." (Neal
> 1997)

For Neal, these "big A anarchists" threaten the anti-authoritarian and spontaneous elements of anarchism by basing their understanding of anarchism on a fixed set of standards. Rather than allowing anarchism to develop from voluntary association based upon common need and outside of over-arching authority, ideological anarchists promote an adherence to a particular abstract anarchist program, one that requires a certain amount of authority to maintain.

For Neal, "big A anarchism" differs from "little a anarchism" or what he calls methodological anarchism precisely because "little a anarchism" is carried out through voluntary associations based upon common needs. It doesn't adhere to fixed ideological structures or preconceptions about what anarchism is specifically, it is based upon a more open form of anarchism. In this sense, anarchism isn't a strict future theory to which we are to adhere, it is a way of embodying particular ideals of mutual aid, voluntary cooperation, and direct action. This means that we can use anarchism methodologically without even knowing or agreeing upon what anarchism really is. "Little a anarchism" rejects central anarchist organizations as instruments of authority that squash human freedom. It sees itself as a loose conglomeration of a variety of anarchist-inspired currents, actions, and ideas. "Little a anarchism" can be said to reject abstract ideological structures that shape and guide human behavior in a particular direction. It relies upon a free humanity, which acts voluntarily according to needs. Neal argues:

> My main objection to ideological anarchism is that it depends not on free-thinking and direct action, but on obedience, passivity, and conformity, to an externality—either a manifesto, a platform, or other mechanisms of control. Further, it focuses on a top-down, centralized organization as a means of bringing anarchism from the center outward. (Neal 1997)

For Neal, "little a anarchism" is an anarchism that rejects obedience to strict dogmatic social theory, and which instead develops itself through free, spontaneous action.

The difference in approach is reflected in different attitudes towards anarchist history and practice. "Big A anarchists" fear that the rejection of ideological commitment leads to a rejection of the history of anarchist thought, at least in terms of admitting its usefulness. The repercussions are division and the serious splintering of continuity in anarchist thought and action. "Little a anarchists" treat the lack of ideological commitment in the new generation of activists as beneficial and the formal commitment to anarchism's past as constraining. From this perspective, the rich history of anarchism has no strategic relevance to contemporary struggles.

WHERE ARE THE DIFFERENCES BETWEEN CLASSICAL AND NEW ANARCHISM?

"Little a anarchism" is a major component in the makeup of what is being called new anarchism. The claim is that it represents a shift away from the more dogmatic anarchism of the mid 20th century and anarchist currents within the old left. David Graeber explains this shift:

> At the moment, there's something of a rupture between generations of anarchism: between those whose political formation took place in the 60's and 70's—and who often still have not shaken the sectarian habits of the last century—or simply still operate in those terms, and younger activists much more informed, among other elements, by indigenous, feminist, ecological and cultural-critical ideas. The former organize mainly through highly visible Anarchist Federations like the IWA, NEFAC, or IWW. The latter work most prominently in the networks of the global social movements, networks like Peoples Global Action, which unites anarchist collectives in Europe and elsewhere with groups ranging from Maori activists in New Zealand . . . . The latter—what might be loosely referred to as the "small-a anarchists," are by now the far majority. But it is sometimes hard to tell, since so many of them do not trumpet their affinities very loudly. There are many, in fact, who take anarchist principles of anti-sectarianism and open-endedness so seriously that they refuse to refer to themselves as anarchists for that very reason. (Graeber 2002, 3)

Graeber's view captures another aspect of the post-ideological tendency. And it chimes in with contemporary critiques of classical anarchists such as Mikhail Bakunin and the idea that the political and theoretical battles that these anarchists waged belong to the past. Barbara Epstein writes,

> The anarchist mindset of today's young activists has relatively little to do with the theoretical debates between anarchists and Marxists, most of which took place in the late nineteenth and early twentieth centuries. It has more to do with an egalitarian and anti-authoritarian perspective.

There are versions of anarchism that are deeply
individualistic and incompatible with socialism.
But these are not the forms of anarchism that
hold sway in radical activist circles, which have
more in common with the libertarian socialism
advocated by Noam Chomsky and Howard Zinn
than with the writings of Bakunin or Kropotkin.
Today's anarchist activists draw upon a current
of morally charged and expressive politics.
(Epstein 2001)

In a similar vein, Purkis and Bowen write,

Anarchist theory works on a number of different
levels. Because it proposes radical changes in
society, it is essentially idealistic. However, on
another level, it is firmly rooted in the here and
now with regard to practical examples of people
on all sides actively undermining power and
authority, sometimes in weird and wonderful
ways. The terrains of theory and action have
changed, and now there are generations of activists operating in many fields of protest for
whom the works of Kropotkin, Malatesta, and
Bakunin are as distant in terms of their
description of the world as the literary classics of
writers such as Charles Dickens. (Purkis and
Bowen 1997, 2)

The consensus seems to be that new anarchists have
next to nothing to learn from classical anarchism and
that they have little in common with classical anarchism.
In my view, the conscious effort to ignore or distance
contemporary anarchism from the classical anarchism of
the 19th century is a mistake.

To show why, I will probe a few staple questions
about Bakunin, since he is undoubtedly an important
figure in the historical canon that post-ideological anarchism rejects: Can we call Bakunin's thought ideologically dogmatic? Does he adhere to strict revolutionary
principles that must guide revolutionary activity? Does

Bakunin promote a fixed organization of society, which should be implemented as a formal ideology? The logic of "little a anarchism" is that the answer to these questions is "yes." I will argue that the answer is emphatically "no." I'd like to examine Bakunin's writings on science, authority, and spontaneity to illustrate why this is the case. To make the argument, I will be using texts that are easily available to ordinary readers and not restricted to specialists.

BAKUNIN AS A POST-IDEOLOGICAL THINKER

Bakunin looked at abstract ideas, particularly regarding humanity and human society, with a critical eye. Bakunin recognized that oppression and domination within the material world were most often carried out through some sort of abstract principles understood to be above humanity. This was because Bakunin, not unlike his modern day fellow anarchists, understood that to shape human action according to abstract principles was to stifle the voluntary and spontaneous associations that he held so dear. It was in essence a restriction of human freedom. Bakunin writes,

> Until now all human history has been only a perpetual and bloody immolation of millions of poor human beings in honor of some pitiless abstraction—god, country, power of state, national honor, historical rights, judicial rights, political liberty, public welfare. (Bakunin 1970, 59)

Bakunin understood that imposing abstract ideas on human behaviors was a constraint. Abstractions developed as expressions of particular interests and they resulted in domination. In particular, he recognized that they were rooted in conventional sources of power such as god and the state. However, he took this critique further by looking at the ways in which science was used as an analytical tool to understand the material world. He argued that science was a product of the human mind, and in consequence was subjectively restricted. Science could only grasp general ideas from the endless amount of specifics, and thus was incapable of understanding the individual experience of every human life:

> . . . human thought, and in consequence of this, science can grasp and name only the general significance of real facts, their relations, their laws—in short, that which is permanent in their continual transformations—but never their material, individual side, palpitating, so to speak, with reality and life, and therefore fugitive and intangible. (Bakunin 1970, 54)

Bakunin stressed the importance of spontaneous initiative in human interaction. For him, this spontaneity was something that couldn't be predicted, or couldn't be solidified into strict scientific formulas. Science worked from human thought, and was therefore capable of only understanding general ideas, but not the diversity and unpredictability of reality itself.

Recognizing this inherent flaw in science, Bakunin argued that maintaining spontaneous and free social life was more important than allowing it to be led by scientific theory. To guide action with science was to overlook its flaws and therefore threaten life with theoretical authority. He writes, "Life . . . alone spontaneously creates real things and beings. Science creates nothing; it establishes and recognizes only the creations of life" (Bakunin 1970, 55). For Bakunin, the material reality of human existence—including its diversity, spontaneity, aspirations, and overall freedom—was the real developmental force of human life. Science itself created nothing.

Bakunin's critique of science as an abstraction reflects his commitment to human freedom and spontaneity. For Bakunin, freedom existed in the unrestricted decision-making power that individuals exercised over their own lives, springing directly from their own consciousness. This meant that humans were truly free insofar as they could make decisions without any external coercion. Bakunin writes,

> I am a fanatical lover of liberty. I consider it the only environment in which human intelligence, dignity, happiness, can thrive and develop. I do not mean that formal liberty which is dispensed, measured out, and regulated by the State; for this is a perennial lie and represents nothing but the privilege of a few, based upon the servitude of the remainder. Nor do I mean that individualist, egoist, base, and fraudulent liberty extolled by the school of Jean Jacques Rousseau and every other school of bourgeois liberalism, which considers the rights of all, represented by the state, as a limit for the rights of each; it always, necessarily, ends up by reducing the rights of the individuals to zero. (Bakunin [1993] 2002, 261)

For Bakunin, freedom relied upon individual initiative, either developed from the individual consciousness itself, or freely accepted by the individual. Any restriction upon this threatened freedom and liberty and thus created an environment where domination would flourish.

Bakunin understood that individual freedom and liberty coincided with a society based upon mutual aid, voluntary association, and social freedom. He argued that only within society, and only through social cooperation, could human liberty and freedom be fully developed:

> Man completely realizes his individual freedom as well as his personality only through the individuals who surround him and thanks only to the labor and the collective power of society. Without society he would surely remain the most stupid and the most miserable among all the ferocious beasts . . . society far from decreasing his freedom, on the contrary creates the individual

freedom of all human beings. (Bakunin [1993] 2002, 271)

Bakunin recognized that free cooperation and social interaction amongst one another was necessary if humans were to develop to their full potential. It was only through social life that humanity could develop a consciousness of the world and produce the material required to survive in it.

Bakunin saw cooperation and mutual aid as synonymous with individual freedom, and as an essential component for human survival. He also believed that human beings would cooperate with one another freely and spontaneously because this was a "natural law," or essential to their existence. Without this free cooperation, human beings couldn't survive, let alone develop themselves. He writes,

> In human society, as in nature, every being lives only by the supreme principle of the most positive intervention in the existence of every other being. The character and extent of this intervention depend upon the nature of the individual. To abolish this mutual intervention would mean death. And when we demand the freedom of the masses, we do not even dream of obliterating any of the natural influences that any individual or group of individuals exercise upon each other. We want only the abolition of artificial, privyleged, legal, and official impositions. (Bakunin [1993] 2002, 257)

For Bakunin, it was a mistake to think that individual interests resulted in competition or antagonism. Instead, this idea was an abstraction imposed by authorities—the church and state—used to structure social life for the benefit of particular interests. Bakunin argued that it was important, then, to seek out and destroy these abstractions, which otherwise hindered the spontaneous functioning of social life. This was the role he gave to theory and its purpose was investigative.

Bakunin's critique of science can be applied to an understanding of ideology. He understood the importance of spontaneous life over any sort of pre-developed theoretical framework. Although not specifically addressing social or political theory, Bakunin's skepticism about the explanatory role of theory is captured in his comments on science:

> It would be sad for mankind if at any time theoretical speculation became the only source of guidance for society, if science alone were in charge of social administration. Life would wither, and human society would turn into a voiceless and servile herd. The domination of life by science can have no other result than the brutalization of mankind. . . . In opposition to the metaphysicians, the positivists, and all worshippers of science, we declare that natural and social life must always come before theory, which is only one of its manifestations but never its creator. From out of its own exhaustible depths, society develops through a series of events, but not by thought alone. Theory is always created by life, but never creates it. (Bakunin [1993] 2002, 327)

Bakunin's critique of science and the role gave to theory brings his work closer to post-ideological or "little a anarchism" than the critics admit. He understood that spontaneous life, when not interfered with by authoritarian ideologies, would function in a manner that was beneficial both to the individual and the society as a whole. Bakunin used theory not as a tool to guide human life, but to uncover the manifestations of authority and power that hindered this spontaneity. He understood that theory could be an emancipatory agent when defining particular ideologies that threatened human freedom. Theory wasn't to be used as ideology, but to identify and repel ideological authority.

Consistent with his understanding of freedom and ideological authority, Bakunin recognized the need to create organizations that were based upon free association and were carried out from the bottom up. For Bakunin, if organizations were based upon top-down hierarchy, then they would inevitably threaten the spontaneous and free development of the individuals who made up the organization. The goal for Bakunin was to create forms of organization that did away with authoritarian principles, and were based most importantly on freedom and autonomy. He writes,

> The political and economic organization of social life must not, as present, be directed from the summit to the base—the center to the circumference—imposing unity through forced centralization. On the contrary, it must be reorganized to issue from the base to the summit—from the circumference to the center—according to principles of free association and federation. (Bakunin [1993] 2002, 77)

Bakunin clearly recognized the need to eliminate structures of organization that were based upon authority. He saw these authoritarian principles to be inherent in organizations that were structured vertically, where decision-making power was cast from the top, down. The organization of social life developed from spontaneous social interaction based upon common need. It was not to be decided upon from outside social life, and then implemented in some sort of pre-determined fashion.

Consistent with his skepticism about ideological authority, Bakunin considered what a future society based on principles of voluntary association, mutual aid, and spontaneous organization might look like. In doing so, his intention was not to develop an authoritarian ideology, but to use theory in order to repel ideologies that might interfere with the natural functioning of social interactions. Bakunin even checked himself when developing such ideas:

It is impossible to determine a concrete, universal, and obligatory norm for the internal development and political organization of every nation. The life of each nation is subordinated to a plethora of different historical, geographical, and economic conditions, making it impossible to establish a model of organization equally valid for all. Any such attempt would be absolutely impractical. It would smother the richness and spontaneity of life which flourishes only in infinite diversity and, what is more, contradict the most fundamental principles of freedom. (Bakunin [1993] 2002, 77)

Bakunin understood that the role of theory was not to push general ideological frameworks onto human life. This ran counter to the free, spontaneous, and voluntary society that he supported. At the same time, however, he recognized that there was a need to experiment with forms of societal organization and to think about the ways in which voluntary and free association might be supported and enabled to flourish.

Bakunin looked to the basic tenets of federalism to develop his ideas. For Bakunin, federal organizations would be needed immediately following the social and political revolution to meet human needs. He thought of federalism as a form of organization; in economic terms, as units of production. Yet the federal system was not a fixed framework to be applied everywhere. Rather, it was a thought experiment designed to show that society could be organized to support free association and mutual aid.

For Bakunin the basic unit of political organization was the commune and he imagined that communes would co-operate on the basis of voluntary association in order to meet collective needs. In association, communes would remain autonomous and free in their functioning and decision-making. He writes, "all organizations must proceed by the way of federation from the base to the summit, from the commune to the coordinating association of the country or nation" (Bakunin [1993]

2002, 83). There would be no overarching authority to restrict the free development of each commune.

Another example of Bakunin's thoughts on organizational structure is how he compared and contrasted the International Workingman's Association with the state. This again illuminates Bakunin's use of theory in a post-ideological manner. Bakunin is using theory to highlight the authoritarian elements within the state, and compare it to what he saw as a voluntary organization (the International Workingman's Association). His thoughts weren't to promote a particular ideology. Rather, they were to critique an existing one (the state) and to exemplify a free association that came about through voluntary association and not through force (the International).

For Bakunin, the International Workingmen's Association was an example of the sort of organization he imagined. This had emerged from the material conditions of the workers' lives within capitalism and it was an attempt to unite a variety of different factions of the left and labor organizations. It has developed through their struggles, not from abstract principles. Bakunin writes,

> The International Workingmen's Association did not spring ready-made out of the minds of the few erudite theoreticians. It developed out of actual economic necessity, out of the bitter tribulations the workers were forced to endure and the natural impact of these trials upon them minds of the toilers. (Bakunin [1993] 2002, 252)

The International exemplified the type of voluntary cooperation that was essential to his anarchism and the common impulse for liberty that he believed to be natural. It was qualitatively different from the organization of the state:

> . . . for the essential difference between the organized action of the International and the action of all the states is that the International is not vested

with any official authority of political power whatsoever. It will always be the natural organization of action of a greater or lesser number of individuals. . . . Governments, by contrast, impose themselves upon the masses and force them to obey their decrees, without for the most part taking into consideration their feelings, their needs, and their will. (Bakunin [1993] 2002, 256)

Because the International was formed voluntarily around common aspirations, Bakunin argued that it was able to elaborate its own political program. In his view, there was no question of developing its own political ideology. The political program was fleshed out directly in the debates of the International. Any attempt to formalize this program in a political theory was an attack on spontaneity. For Bakunin the rejection of theory, in this sense, was the International's essential strength:

No political or philosophical theory should be considered a fundamental principle, or be introduced into the official program of the International. Nor should acceptance of any political or philosophical theory be obligatory as a condition for membership, since as we have seen, to impose any such theory upon the federations composing the International would be slavery, or it would result in division and dissolution, which is no less disastrous. But it does not follow from this that free discussion of all political and philosophical theories cannot occur in the International. On the contrary, it is precisely the very existence of an official theory that will kill such discussion by rendering it absolutely useless instead of living and vital, and by inhibiting the expression and development of the worker's own feelings and ideas. (Bakunin [1993] 2002, 302)

Bakunin's ideas about on authority and spontaneity in his discussion of science, and his analysis of organizational structures provide the answers to the questions posed at the start of this essay. Does Bakunin's philosophy promote a particular ideological framework, which should be replicated in human society? Is Bakunin's thought sectarian, dogmatic, or ideologically strict? Most importantly, does Bakunin's thought authoritatively push abstract principles onto the living diversity of human life? As I have shown, Bakunin was aware of the dangers of ideology taking the form of authority within society. He used his theory as a tool to uncover and dismantle ideologies that restricted the free social interaction of human existence. His intention was not to direct human life, but to explore how we could stop human life from being directed. Bakunin advanced anarchist theory to counteract the dangers authoritative compliance that seemed inherent in conventional theorizing; he was writing in a post-ideological manner.

CONCLUSION

Although Bakunin was clearly alert to the dangers of ideology, he straddled the division between the "big A" and "little a" anarchists outlined above. On one hand, there is a highly recognizable post-ideological tint to his work. On the other hand, Bakunin searched desperately for a unified international movement that would undermine the existing bourgeois and state directed order. This is where Bakunin is most important for contemporary anarchist activists and theorists. He imagined an international revolution, a destruction of the old order that would release creative processes of free initiative and direct democracy and the construction of new free societies.

Reading Bakunin, we are given an insight into how we might strengthen our post-ideological social movements, using theory, not jettisoning it. By recognizing the dangers of theorizing, Bakunin proposed a way to engage theory without restricting spontaneous social life. It seems that to ignore his work is to refuse an avenue that leads toward a form of structure without authority, or a method in which to engage theory without the effects of domination.

In what ways, then, is reading Bakunin helpful, and why am I even concerned with the dismissal or neglect of Mikhail Bakunin? I think Bakunin offers us a way to use theory as a critical lens to spell out and combat authoritarian structures. Drawing on Bakunin does not threaten to stifle our anti-authoritarian social movements, but to clarify the purposes of our struggles and identify our enemies. Contemporary anarchist activists can read Bakunin fruitfully to think about what's at stake when we struggle without a clear idea of the obstacles to transformation and when we engage in theorizing that stifles revolutionary practice.

This engagement with Bakunin points to a larger project of recognizing the continuity of anarchism as a body of thought and practice. It is quite often we hear of the diversity and inconsistency of anarchism. This is clearly the case and I don't wish to deny it. However, it is important to highlight consistencies in anarchist activity that self-identifies as anarchistic, particularly in regards to a libertarian socialist project, because these have played the most prominent role in the history of anarchist activity. Exploring this continuity isn't a project of reification, where we must somehow apply or implement classical anarchist ideas into today's movements. It is to celebrate a rich, still vibrant history of anarchism, one that bears scars of sectarianism and hallmarks of diversity, and which holds the hope of realizing a world free of domination and exploitation. Exploring the continuities of classical anarchist thought isn't to fall into the jaws of authority, but to remind ourselves of our past battles, to identify our past mistakes, and to ultimately learn from our complex history. To understand who we are, we must understand who came before us, and a look at classical anarchism might just help do that.

REFERENCES

Bakunin, Michael. 1970. *God and the State*. New York: Dover Publications.

Bakunin, Mikhail. [1993] 2002. *Bakunin on Anarchism*, ed. and trans. Sam Dolgoff. Montreal: Black Rose Books.

Epstein, Barbara. 2001. "Anarchism and the Anti-Globalization Movement." *Monthly Review*, September 1: http://monthlyreview.org/2001/09/01/anarchism-and-the-anti-globalization-movement.

Graeber, David. 2002. "The New Anarchists." *New Left Review* 13: http://newleftreview.org/ll/13/david-graeber-the-new-anarchists.

Graeber, David and Andrej Grubacic. 2004. "Anarchism; Or the Revolutionary Movement of the 21st Century." ZNet, January 6: http://www.zcommunications.org/anarchism-or-the-revolutionary-movement-of-the-twenty-first-century-by-david-graeber.

Neal, David. 1997. "Anarchism: Ideology or Methodology." *Spunk Library*: http://www.spunk.org/texts/intro/practice/sp001689.html.

Purkis, Jon and James Bowen. 1997. *Twenty-First Century Anarchism: Unorthodox Ideas for a New Millennium*. Herndon: Cassell.

Anarchist Developments in Cultural Studies
ISSN: 1923-5615
2013.1: Blasting the Canon

Black Flame
A Commentary

Robert Graham*

In their critique of the so-called "seven sages" approach to anarchism in *Black Flame: The Revolutionary Class Politics of Anarchism and Syndicalism, Counter-Power, Volume 1* (2009), Michael Schmidt and Lucien van der Walt claim that there "is only one anarchist tradition, and it is rooted in the work of Bakunin and the Alliance" of Socialist Democracy (71). This is the tradition of "class struggle" anarchism, which for Schmidt and van der Walt is not merely "a type of anarchism; in our view, it is the *only* anarchism" (19). This is an extraordinary claim

* Robert Graham is the editor of the three-volume anthology of anarchist writings from ancient China to the present day, *Anarchism: A Documentary History of Libertarian Ideas.* He has published many essays on the intellectual history of anarchism and contemporary anarchist theory, including the Introduction to the Pluto Press edition of Proudhon's *General Idea of the Revolution in the 19th Century,* 'The Role of Contract in Anarchist Ideology,' 'From the Bottom Up: The First International and the Origins of the Anarchist Movement,' 'Noam Chomsky's Contributions to Anarchism,' 'Communism and Anarchism: The Great Debate Between Two Bastions of the Left,' 'Reinventing Hierarchy: The Political Theory of Social Ecology,' and many other reviews and articles.

based upon a historicist definition of anarchism that excludes even Proudhon, the originator of the doctrine and the first self-proclaimed anarchist, from "the broad anarchist tradition," by which Schmidt and van der Walt really mean the more narrow tradition of class struggle anarchism (18). According to this approach, the "broad anarchist tradition" is really nothing more than a form of socialism, one that is libertarian and revolutionary (6). Anarchism, as a distinct doctrine, disappears, subsumed under the socialist rubric.

That there are different schools of anarchist thought does not mean that only one of them qualifies as "anarchist," no more than the fact that there are many different schools of socialist thought means that only one of them qualifies as "socialist," although the Marxists used to think so. Schmidt and van der Walt argue that their narrow definition of anarchism makes anarchism a coherent doctrine because differing conceptions of anarchism with contrary ideas are now excluded from the very definition of anarchism. But if anarchism is just a form of socialism, and there are differing conceptions of socialism, then any definition of socialism that encompasses these competing and sometimes contradictory conceptions of socialism is similarly deficient. If the demands of coherence mean that only one body of thought can qualify as anarchist, then it must also be true that only one body of thought can qualify as socialist. But Schmidt and van der Walt accept that there are competing and contrary conceptions of socialism, including anarchism and Marxism. If both anarchism and Marxism can be considered forms of socialism, despite their many differences, then there is no reason why there cannot be different forms of anarchism. On the contrary, if Marxism is understood as an internally coherent theory of one kind of socialism, and contrary conceptions of socialism, such as "class struggle" anarchism, are also defined as "socialist," different conceptions of anarchism are also possible. Even though they may be contrary to each other to greater and lesser degrees, they still remain "anarchist."

Schmidt and van der Walt then conflate anarchism with self-described anarchist movements, so that anarchism cannot but be the ideas expressed and embodied by these movements, all of which, they claim, trace their lineage back to Bakunin and the First International (44–46). Anyone who cannot trace his or her ideological roots back to this family tree does not qualify as an "anarchist." This is a completely circular argument and a problematic way to approach the study of anarchist ideas and movements.

If anarchism is whatever Bakunin and his associates said it was, then of course Bakunin and his associates qualify as anarchists. But if other people develop conceptions of anarchism contrary to that of Bakunin and the Alliance, then they don't qualify as anarchists, even if they did so around the same time as Bakunin, or even before him, as in the case of Proudhon (83–85). Gustav Landauer, whose communitarian anarchism was heavily influenced by Proudhon and Tolstoy, both of whom Schmidt and van der Walt exclude from the anarchist canon, cannot be considered an anarchist because he was not a Bakuninist. On their account anarchism must be constrained within a narrow body of thought, from which no significant departures or modifications can be made without risking one's "anarchist" status. This is like attempts to maintain a Marxist "orthodoxy," and similarly threatens to inhibit any significant innovation because anarchism must remain within the general confines of its "original" formulation. The argument echoes a similar idea within Marxism, and it threatens to inhibit any significant innovation because anarchism must remain within the general confines of its "original" formulation. This turns anarchism from a living tradition into an historical relic.

While Schmidt and van der Walt exclude Proudhon from the "broad" anarchist tradition, Bakunin and Kropotkin certainly did not do so. Bakunin praised Proudhon for "boldly [declaring] himself an anarchist," and described his own revolutionary anarchism as "Proudhonism widely developed and pushed right to these, its final consequences" (Bakunin, 1974: 100 & 198).

Kropotkin similarly observed that Proudhon "boldly proclaimed Anarchism and the abolition of the State" (Woodcock 1995: 56).

There are other ways of defining anarchism, ways that recognize the possibility of different "anarchisms" and which allow anarchism to be conceived as a truly "broad" tradition of thought comprising different schools, currents, and tendencies. This was something that Kropotkin acknowledged, having participated in the formulation and refinement of anarchist views: the movement away from Proudhon's mutualism and Bakunin's collectivism to anarchist communism, the debates between the insurrectionists and the syndicalists, the disagreements over direct action and propaganda by the deed, the role of technology and the nature of post-revolutionary society. Later anarchists, such as Landauer, were aware of these debates and participated in some of their own, developing new ideas and approaches, incorporating elements from the anarchists who preceded them, often in a very conscious manner, but also departing from them in significant respects. For them, anarchism was a broad and *living* tradition, always subject to change, not restricted to the general form initially developed in the particular historical circumstances of the First International.

REFERENCES

Bakunin, M. 1974. *Michael Bakunin: Selected Writings*, ed. A. Lehning. New York: Grove Press.

Schmidt, M. and L. van der Walt. 2009. *Black Flame: The Revolutionary Class Politics of Anarchism and Syndicalism, Counter-Power, Volume 1*. Oakland: AK Press.

Woodcock, G., ed. 1995. *Peter Kropotkin: Evolution and Environment*. Montreal: Black Rose Books.

Anarchist Developments in Cultural Studies
ISSN: 1923-5615
2013.1: Blasting the Canon

(Re)Constructing a Global Anarchist and Syndicalist Canon
A response to Robert Graham and Nathan Jun on *Black Flame*

Lucien van der Walt [*]

Robert Graham's and Nathan Jun's thought-provoking inter-ventions in this special issue on 'Blasting the Canon,' regarding Michael Schmidt and my *Black Flame: The Revolutionary Class Politics of Anarchism and Syndicalism* (2009), is welcomed. It is a pleasure to engage two thoughtful writers, and their considera-tions on the anarchist canon—i.e., the texts/thinkers/theories that (as Jun argues) should be 'regarded as authoritative for anarchist thought and practice or especially significant in the historical development of anarchism.'

GRAHAM'S AND JUN'S CRITICISMS—AND MY CORE RESPONSE

Black Flame made a wide range of arguments–about, for example, the social basis of anarchist peasant uprisings, the movement's anti-colonial/anti-imperialist struggles, approaches to gender and unionism, struggle for the city etc. It has, of course, also spurred

---

[*] Lucien van der Walt works at Rhodes University, South Africa. He is the author (with Michael Schmidt) of *Black Flame: The Revolutionary Class Politics of Anarchism and Syndicalism* (2009), and the editor (with Steve Hirsch) of *Anarchism and Syndicalism in the Colonial and Postcolonial World, 1880-1940* (2010). He has published widely on labour and left history and theory, and political economy. Involved in union education and working class movements.

debates on anarchist (and syndicalist) theory, history and canon —such debate was one of its stated intentions (van der Walt and Schmidt 2009: 26-27).

The argument that is at issue with Graham and Jun is a fairly small part of *Black Flame*—the claim that anarchism (and its offshoot, syndicalism) is a distinctly modern phenomenon, born in the international socialist/ working class movement—specifically, the First International (1864-1877).

Here, in debates with Marxists and others, anarchism emerged as a distinct current, centred on the Alliance of Socialist Democracy: core members included Bakunin, Kropotkin and Malatesta. Anarchism was a libertarian form of socialism, opposed to social and economic hierarchy/inequality, favouring international class struggle and revolution, from below, for a self-managed, socialist, stateless order; syndicalism is one anarchist strategy (van der Walt and Schmidt 2009: 71, 170).

Graham objects, claiming that *Black Flame's* approach is 'narrow' and 'extraordinary' (by excluding certain trends), 'circular' in approach, contradictory (for supposedly insisting that anarchism be 'internally coherent,' while tolerating an incoherent 'socialism' encompassing Marxism and anarchism), and closed to 'significant departures or modifications' or 'refinement' (thus, 'dogma').

Jun claims it is circular, with a 'No True Scotsman' fallacy (setting arbitrary, shifting standards for inclusion into 'anarchism'). He rejects its (supposed) claim that anarchism is 'whatever the mainstream' of 'historical anarchism' accepted (since this might leave out other 'anarchist' views). He claims this is like asking a medieval European Catholic for a general survey of Christianity.

Both favour a vague (they say, 'broad') definition: for Graham, this means the 'possibility of anarchist doctrines arising independently in different eras and circumstances,' with anarchism having 'different schools, currents and tendencies.' Jun is more sweeping: 'anarchism' is not a 'doctrine,' but an 'orientation' 'throughout human history,' while not admitting this entails 'mass excommunications.'

I suggest, however, that these are serious misrepresentations of the *Black Flame* methodology, claims and coverage—Schmidt and I provide a historically-based argument that *tracks* the rise of anarchism (and syndicalism), *summarises* its key claims, *traces* its evolution and spread, *analyses* its key debates and moments—this is a fairly standard social science approach, not an exercise in arbitrary boundary setting. And, rather than being 'narrow,' it uses a truly global history and analysis, placing the colonial and postcolonial world, and a wide range of mass movements, centre-stage.

Secondly, I demonstrate that Graham's and Jun's alternative approaches are far from satisfactory: both claims for multiple 'anarchisms' are simply assertions, resting on *a priori* positions that lack a clear methodological rationale or empirical basis, and that are constructed in ways rendering any falsification imposs-ible. Neither provides reasoned grounds, nor evidence, for the supposed superiority of their alternative definitions.

Both authors, in short, manifestly fail to apply to their own approaches the same standards of rigour they demand from *Black Flame.* I submit that a historical, as opposed to a speculative approach, is more justified, and more fruitful.

RESPONSE: A HISTORICAL AND SOCIOLOGICAL METHODOLOGY

Graham and Jun dispute dating anarchism to the 1860s.

It is a matter of record, however, that the anarchist movement appeared as something *new* to its contemporaries, rivals, and adherents; with this appearance, anarchism *first* became the topic of scholarly enquiry, police investigation, and media attention (Fleming 1979: 17–19). Even writers favouring exceedingly loose definitions of 'anarchism' concede that 'anarchism' did not previously exist as a 'political force' (see, for example, Joll 1964: 58, 82, 84; Woodcock 1975: 136, 155, 170)—as, so indeed, does Jun, with his allusion to 'historical anarchism' (is there a different kind?).

The very question of whether there were earlier or 'different schools, currents and tendencies' of anarchism (Graham), or an anarchist 'orientation' 'throughout human history' (Jun) could not even be *posed* before this moment.

It is, then, anachronistic to represent this new, specifically, consciously 'anarchist' movement (and its syndicalist branch) as but one in a number of anarchist 'schools' 'throughout history.'

It was, and is, one of several more-or-less *libertarian* 'currents,' including socialist variants like *autonomia* (van der Walt and Schmidt 2009: 71–71). But to conflate these very different approaches with anarchism is unnecessary.

It also requires gutting the 'anarchist' movement of its specificities, while forcing the others into a single 'anarchist' category. And to make the effort to include Stirner, Zerzan, etc.

into 'anarchism' has little real justification (besides a sort of dogmatic convention), yet is analytically costly.

By contrast, *Black Flame* consciously undertakes defining 'anarchism' (and thus, considering its ideology, history and canon) through a broad, global, representative overview of the history of this new worldwide historical and social phenomenon through examining a wide range of cases.

Building on the Age of Revolutions, located in the 'capitalist world' and the working class and socialism 'it created' (van der Walt and Schmidt 2009: 96), anarchism was 'simultaneously and transnationally' constituted by a radical network in North Africa, Latin America, and Europe (van der Walt and Hirsch 2010: liv). It then expanded globally, its first mass formations including Cuba, Mexico, Spain, and the United States.

By focusing on this movement, and taking a global view, *Black Flame* abstracts the core, shared features of its ideology, its often misunderstood relationship with syndicalism, unpacks its major debates, divisions and developments, and its core social features—for example, the class character of its urban mass base.

This historical and sociological approach forms the basis for the conclusion Graham so hotly rejects: there 'is only one anarchist tradition, and it is rooted in the work of Bakunin and the Alliance' (van der Walt and Schmidt 2009: 71).

To describe this methodology as 'completely circular' (Graham), or as entailing a 'No True Scotsman' fallacy, or 'excommunications' (Jun), is a complete caricature, a failure to take seriously the core analysis Schmidt and I developed.

Contra Graham, moreover, *Black Flame* does not require that anarchism be reduced to 'self-described anarchists': it only requires *ideological and organisational lineage*. The IWW thus fits in the broad anarchist tradition; Stirner does not. It does not *require* that anarchism be 'internally coherent' (Graham), but merely claims that it *was*; this was a description.

There is no contradiction between a focused, precise definition, and a rich, nuanced, and broad account; the bulk of *Black Flame* provides a detailed history of the anarchist/syndicalist tradition, past and present.

RESPONSE: 'NARROW'—OR GOING GLOBAL?

Graham's charge that *Black Flame* has a 'narrow' approach is unconvincing.

Black Flame is perhaps the only truly global, non-Eurocentric, survey of the theory and history of anarchism (and syndicalism), covering 150 years, and the only thorough survey of the tradition's internal debates, again with a global—not a 'narrow'— view.

Indeed, it is *precisely* this scope that makes *Black Flame* peculiarly central to any serious debate on the meaning of 'anarchism' and its canon.

This is radically different to the narrowly North Atlantic framing that dominates the standard English-language surveys— due credit must be given to Joll, Woodcock, and Marshall for their pioneering works, but it cannot be denied they almost entirely ignored the world outside of (only parts of) Western Europe and North America.[1]

Compounding this profound imbalance, such works discuss at length obscure Western figures like Stirner, whose historical importance is trivial, and links to anarchism doubtful. This problem continues today, with marginal Americans like Rothbard, Zerzan, etc., constituting common fare in 'standard' surveys—whilst major figures like Liu, Flores Magón, J.C. Mechoso, Shin, Szabó, Thibedi, etc. are (at best) passing asides.

But with a worldwide view, trivialities in the West fade away in the light shed by truly important moments elsewhere. It is, then, rather peculiar to present *Black Flame* as 'narrow,' because it has a global sense of perspective.

Yet Graham continues: *Black Flame* has a problematic focus on 'the more narrow' world of 'class struggle anarchism.'

What exactly is 'narrow' about this world? It is, by any measure, far larger and more influential than any other contender for the 'anarchist' label; a focus on it is *necessary*, not 'narrow.'

This is the anarchism of towering figures, from insurrectionists (who Jun incorrectly assumes are excluded from *Black Flame*) like Galleani, to mass anarchists and syndicalists like Bakunin, Chu, Durruti, Goldman, Gutarra, Kim Jwa-Jim, Kropotkin, Makhno, Malatesta, Ōsugi, Rocker, and every historically important anarchist/syndicalist formation, from the Argentinean FORA and *Voz de la Mujer*, to Spain's CNT and Mujeres Libres, to the global IWW, South Africa's ISL/IWA, the Hunan Workers' Association, FAU/OPR-33, the Korean *Ŭiyŏltan*, etc.

---

[1] Woodcock (1975) gave Latin America 3 pages, ignoring Africa, Asia, Australasia, and most of Eastern Europe; Joll (1964) gave the rest 9 pages; Marshall (1998) gave 2 of 41 chapters (33 of 706 pages) to Asia and Latin America.

What 'school' of significance is lost by this focus? This is the force that activated revolutions in Spain, Ukraine, and Manchuria, and demonstrated anarchism was a means to change the world.

RESPONSE: 'DOGMA' OR LIVING TRADITION, CENTRAL TODAY?

Does *Black Flame's* focus somehow turn 'anarchism from a living tradition into an historical relic or dogma' (Graham)? No, since 'class struggle anarchism' (his term) has a rich, powerful history, and is *also* a 'living tradition'.

This is the tradition represented today by such key examples as the Spanish CGT and CNT, the Chilean FEL, Brazilian FARJ and Uruguayan FAU, the IWA/AIT, Egyptian LSM and other Africans, Anarkismo.net, the Greek rebels, and innumerable local groups and projects worldwide. Notions popularised by certain academic texts—that worker-peasant anarchism has been superseded or overwhelmed by a post-1945 'new anarchism' (e.g., Woodcock, 1975)—are highly misleading, even for the West today.

Graham worries that a strict definition will mean that 'significant departures or modifications' will entail exclusion from 'anarchist status.' But *every* definition implies exclusion. Example: Russian 'anarchist' Bill Shatov's 'modifications' included, as Petrograd Bolshevik police chief in 1918, crushing anarchists (Bryant 1923). Must he perpetually retain 'anarchist status'?

Graham notes that some figures in the anarchist tradition (like Landauer) drew on other ideas (like Tolstoy). *Black Flame's* point, however, is that what a tradition *shares* constitutes its defining features, the parameters for 'refinement.' (And Landauer, Tolstoy aside, was an anarchist, who died for the Munich councils revolution.)

RESPONSE: ONE, TWO, THREE MANY "ANARCHISMS"?

Of course, there are probably libertarian elements in all cultures, religions and historical periods (and most modern political ideologies).

But are these all *anarchist*? Graham and Jun insist they are, and claim this approach has support from 'notable members' of 'historical anarchism' like Kropotkin and Rocker.

This latter claim is indeed true—but does not resolve the matter.

Is this not precisely the methodological error that Jun claims of *Black Flame*: asking a medieval Catholic for a survey of Christianity? Further, if anarchism arises 'independently in different eras and circumstances,' or 'throughout history,' why should Kropotkin have decisive weight? But if Kropotkin *does*, then why should his movement's politics *not* define the parameters of anarchism?

Yet Graham and Jun *must* invoke Kropotkin and Rocker, since it would be obviously anachronistic (and futile) to consult the works of those outside Kropotkin's tradition (e.g., Lao, Winstanley, Godwin, and Stirner) for opinions on the general history of 'anarchism.'

Graham and Jun are also engaging here in a rather selective reading, skipping over Kropotkin's and Rocker's writings that make claims *identical* to *Black Flame*: anarchism as new, revolutionary, socialism (e.g., Kropotkin 1927: 46, 289–290; Rocker [1938]1989: 23–24, 34–35). It was, indeed, Kropotkin—and not *Black Flame*, as Jun suggests—who termed Stirnerism 'misanthropic bourgeois individualism,' opposed to anarchism's 'communist sociability' (van der Walt and Schmidt 2009: 47–48).

What Graham and Jun also miss is that Kropotkin and Rocker were increasingly involved in manufacturing, for the controversial, embattled, anarchist movement, a legitimating propaganda *mythology*. This centred on precisely the claim that 'anarchism' existed 'throughout history' that Jun favours.

This myth-making was only possible once anarchism had *emerged* in the 1860s—it started around 40 years later. It is a claim to antiquity by a new movement, no more evidently true than equivalent nationalist myths. Both anarchist and nationalist myths have an obvious political function, but they are analytically misleading and often demonstrably false: Kropotkin's work in this genre was marked by contradictory claims and rather dubious readings of past trends.[2]

While many are (rightly) sceptical of nationalist mythologies, anarchist mythology continues to have a firm grip. Yet rather than interrogate such claims, many activists and scholars compound the problem by grouping widely different libertarian (and not so libertarian) strands into 'anarchism,' sometimes by

---

[2] For example, his 1905 'Anarchism' (in Kropotkin 1927) deploys quite contradictory definitions: anarchism as ancient philosophy (287–288), as 'first formulated' in the 1790s (289–290), as new, 19th-century, revolutionary socialism (285–287), as a scheme for peaceful reform (290–291) etc.

selecting an (arbitrary) group of writers (e.g., Eltzbacher's 'seven sages' approach: [1900] 1960), sometimes by creating vast compendiums of anything vaguely libertarian (Marshall [2008] starts with prehistory).

But this sort of exercise requires anachronistic, selective readings of the past, and such exceedingly vague (and often shifting) definitions of 'anarchism' as to render the term meaningless. For example, bringing Stirner into the same category as Bakunin requires eliding great differences, effectively reducing anarchism to 'negating the state' (Eltzbacher [1900] 1960: 189, 191, 201).

Two major problems then arise.

First, the boundaries such an exercise requires are necessarily shaky. For example, if anarchists are those who merely 'negate the state,' they must include Marxist-Leninists seeking the state's 'withering away' (e.g., Mao [1949] 1969: 411), and neo-liberals opposed to statism (e.g., Thatcher, 1996). Since neither trend appears in most surveys of anarchism (except Marshall 2008: xiii, 517–518, 560), their exclusion is arbitrary and/or a *de facto* admission of the stated definition's fallacy.

Either way, the loose definition is unjustifiable, lacking clear criteria for inclusion and exclusion.

RESPONSE: ON METHODOLOGY AND ALTERNATIVES

Secondly, the arbitrary nature of the loose approach to studying 'anarchism' is exposed. An approach that seeks to assimilate as much as possible to 'anarchism'—presenting 'anarchism' not as a concrete historical phenomenon, but as multiple 'doctrines arising independently' (Graham) or an 'orientation' 'throughout history' (Jun)—must *start* from an preset *definition* of anarchism in such terms by the writer. This definition is not tested, but assumed true; it is freed from the possibility of falsification.

Or, it must *start* from an arbitrary *selection* of cases, from which the definition is developed (e.g., Eltzbacher [1900] 1960). The problem here is that the selection lacks justification besides anecdote, convention, or personal preference (see van der Walt and Schmidt 2009: 35). The basis for the category is thus itself unreasonable; its boundaries end up equally so.

When Graham insists that anarchism has many 'schools,' he fails to provide a reasoned basis for this assertion. Having insisted *Black Flame* has a 'completely circular' methodology, Graham simply asserts his claim, and then finds data that fits. When the claim is disputed, he can invoke the data thus generated, as evidence to support the claim's veracity, thereby presenting alternatives as 'narrow'—a tautology.

Jun asserts, also without serious grounds, that 'anarchism' exists 'throughout human history.' Once this is taken as true, it is easy enough to find an anarchist 'orientation' everywhere. The problem is that the definition rests upon nothing solid. Jun's story of the medieval Catholic's limitations reveals his assumptions: anarchism self-evidently exists universally; disagreement is evidence of intolerant 'excommunication' or parochial ignorance.

But the basis for the superiority, even validity, of Jun's definition is never initially established.

To return to Jun's medieval Catholic: it is well-established that the Christian Church first appeared two thousand years ago, attracting police, public, and scholarly attention; also that Catholicism was one of its main branches. By contrast, it is hardly self-evident that 'anarchism' has existed 'throughout history,' or that the movement of Bakunin, Kropotkin, Kim, Makhno, Mechoso, Thibedi *et al.* was merely one isolated branch.

RESPONSE: THE MEANING OF A WORD

And what do Graham and Jun mean by 'anarchism'? For Graham, a 'doctrine' wanting society 'without government,' or 'formal structures of hierarchy, command, control and obedience' (Graham 2005: xii–xiv). For Jun, a loose 'orientation,' fusing 'radical antiauthoritarianism and radical egalitarianism,' opposing 'morally unjustifiable . . . authority and inequality,' and 'unnatural' or 'arbitrary' inequality, coercion or domination.

These are rather different claims, and in neither case is their validity obvious. Why is either better than that that of *Black Flame* or one another? Is anarchism a 'doctrine,' several 'doctrines,' or an 'orientation'? Opposed to hierarchy or inequality?

There is no way of really resolving these issues, since this is discussion of *a priori* assertions. And these are also replete with ambiguities: Is *informal* hierarchy acceptable to Graham's anarchists, or 'obedience' to agreed norms or essential 'control'? In Jun's case: what of 'morally' *justifiable* inequality, or the coercion and domination that is neither 'arbitrary' nor 'unjustified,' like the military actions of the 1936 Durruti Column?

And there is, again, the problem of arbitrary inclusion/exclusion. Both Graham and Jun include in their 'anarchist' gallery, figures that demonstrably do not conform to either definitions, such as Stirner—who rejected any constraints on individual's right to 'take' by 'might' whatever they wanted, regardless of 'justice,' 'truth' and 'equality' (Stirner [1844] 1907: 200, 339, 421, 472).

And here we come full circle on the problems of vague definitions.

RESPONSE: SOME NOTES ON ARGUMENTS BY LABELLING

Graham claims that insisting that anarchism has definite historical referents is 'analogous to reducing Marxism to canonical figures and texts'; he speaks of *Black Flame* as promoting 'dogma,' while Jun invokes spectres of 'mass excommunications.'

Such points are rather unpleasantly framed, tainting *Black Flame* with a scent of heresy—argument-by-labelling that does not take us anywhere. Graham's own anthology work, after all, is a definite attempt to construct a canon of 'figures and texts'; Jun, too, admits that all political traditions entail some exclusions. If this means 'dogma' or 'excommunication,' the charge must apply to Graham and Jun as well.

CONCLUSION: A CLASS STRUGGLE, GLOBAL CANON—AND WHY

The issue is not, then, *whether* anarchism has definite 'canonical figures and texts,' but *which* merit inclusion. Vague claims about the nature of anarchism, developed through weak methodologies, cannot provide an adequate basis, since they entail deeply flawed definitions.

For its part, *Black Flame's* approach suggests the need to throw overboard spurious canons like the 'seven sages,' and to instead develop a historically-based, global canon, an accurate reflection of anarchism (and syndicalism) as a historical and contemporary current.

This must necessarily include Bakunin and Kropotkin, and while Stirner, Tolstoy and Thatcher have no justified place, figures like Goldman, He Zhen, Infantes, Landauer, Liu, Flores Magón, Makhno, Mechoso, Osugi, Rouco Buela, Shin, Szabó, and Thibedi must surely be serious candidates for canonical status.

REFERENCES

Bryant, L. 1923. *Mirrors of Moscow.* New York: Thomas Seltzer.

Eltzbacher, P. [1900]1960. *Anarchism*. London: Freedom.

Fleming, M. 1979. *The Anarchist Way to Socialism: Elisée Reclus and Nineteenth-Century European Anarchism*. Lanham, MD: Croom Helm/Rowman Littlefield.

Graham, R., ed. 2005. *Anarchism: A Documentary History of Libertarian Ideas, Vol. 1: From Anarchy to Anarchism, 300 CE to 1939*. Montréal: Black Rose.

Joll, J. 1964. *The Anarchists*. London: Methuen and Co.

Kropotkin, P. 1927. *Kropotkin's Revolutionary Pamphlets*. New York: Dover.

Mao Zedong. [1949] 1971. "On the People's Democratic Dictatorship." In *Selected Readings from the Works of Mao Tsetung*. Peking: Foreign Languages Press.

Marshall, P. 1998. *Demanding the Impossible: A History of Anarchism*. New York: Harper Perennial.

Rocker, R. [1938] 1989. *Anarcho-syndicalism*. London: Pluto Press.

Stirner, M. [1844] 1907. *The Ego and His Own*. New York: B.R. Tucker.

Thatcher, M. 1996. "Speech at Poznan Academy of Economics," July 4: http://www.margaretthatcher.org/document/108362.

Van der Walt, L. and S.J. Hirsch. 2010, "Rethinking Anarchism and Syndicalism: The Colonial and Post-colonial Experience, 1870–1940," in Lucien van der Walt and S.J. Hirsch, eds., *Anarchism and Syndicalism in the Colonial and Postcolonial World, 1870-1940*. Leiden: Brill.

Van der Walt, L. and M. Schmidt. 2009. *Black Flame: The Revolutionary Class Politics of Anarchism and Syndicalism, Vol. 1.: Counter-Power*. Oakland: AK Press.

Woodcock, G. 1975, *Anarchism*, rev. edn. London: Penguin.

Interview with Jürgen Mümken

Conducted and translated by Gabriel Kuhn*

Jürgen Mümken lives in Kassel, Germany, works in a print shop, and is an anarchist theorist focusing on postmodernity and poststructuralism. He also writes about housing policies, related to his former studies of architecture at the University of Kassel, and he edits the *Libertäre Bibliothek*, a series of libertarian novels published by the German anarchist press Edition AV.

While the German-speaking world saw the first explicit connections between anarchism and postmodern/post-structuralist theory in the 1970's, most notably with the anarchist bookstore *Rhizom* in Berlin, the term *post-anarchismus* was not used before Jürgen Mümken introduced it in the mid-2000's. Mümken's 2003 book *Freiheit, Individualität und Subjektivität. Staat und Subjekt in der Postmoderne aus anarchistischer Perspektive* [*Liberty, Individuality, and Subjectivity: State and Subject in Postmodernity from an Anarchist Perspective*] remains the most ambitious theoretical application of postmodern/ poststructuralist thought for the German anarchist movement. Mümken also edited the influential 2005 anthology *Anarchismus in der Postmoderne. Beiträge zur anarchistischen Theorie und Praxis* [*Anarchism in Postmodernity: Contributions to Anarchist Theory and Praxis*], and he maintains the website *postanarchismus.net*.

---

*   Gabriel Kuhn is an Austrian-born anarchist author and translator. He lives in Stockholm, Sweden, where he is involved in various community projects. His publications include *Vielfalt, Bewegung, Widerstand: Texte zum Anarchismus* (Münster: Unrast, 2009), *Gustav Landauer: Revolution and Other Writings* (Oakland: PM Press, 2010), and *Erich Mühsam: Liberating Society from the State and Other Writings* (Oakland: PM Press, 2011).

His political background in the German autonomous move-ment and his academic background in architecture sets Mümken apart from other prominent representatives of postanarchism, many of whom are strongly rooted in the social sciences. Müm-ken's understanding of postanarchism differs, at times signifi-cantly, from notions of postanarchism in the Anglophone world. Gabriel Kuhn, who himself has worked on the intersections of post-modern/poststructuralist theory and anarchism, albeit from a more critical perspective, interviewed Jürgen Mümken for *Anarchist Developments in Cultural Studies* in the fall of 2012.

KUHN: You are the most prominent postanarchist theorist in the German-speaking world. What does "postanarchism" mean to you and when did you start using the term?

MÜMKEN: In order to answer the question, I have to go back to the early 1990's when I was studying architecture. While doing work on prison architecture and its history, I discovered Foucault's *Discipline and Punish*. Through Foucault I became interested in philosophy. When, during the winter of 1996-97, I wrote a Master's thesis entitled *Die Ordnung des Raumes. Die Foucaultsche Machtanalyse und die Transformation des Raumes in der Moderne* [*The Order of Space: Foucault's Analysis of Power and the Transformation of Space in Modernity*], I had reached a point where I wanted to link Foucault to anarchism. As a byproduct of my thesis, I wrote an article entitled "Keine Macht für Niemand. Versuch einer anarchistischen Aneignung des philosophischen Projektes von Michel Foucault" ["No Power for No One: An Attempt to Link the Philosophical Project of Michel Foucault to Anarchism"], which was published in the anarchist quarterly *Schwarzer Faden* [*Black Thread*] in 1998. This is when my thorough study of poststructuralism and, especially, of Foucault began, eventually leading to the publication of my 2003 book *Freiheit, Individualität und Subjektivität. Staat und Subjekt in der Postmoderne aus anarchistischer Perspektive.*

At some point after the book's release, I discovered a 1999 university paper online, entitled "Anarchismus in den USA und Deutschland" ["Anarchism in the USA and Germany"]. It stated that my work built on Todd May's and that I had used Judith Butler's deconstructivism to show that an anarchist society "is not characterized by the absence of power, but by keeping power structures flexible and preventing them from turning into fixed structures of domination," as I wrote in "Keine Macht für Niemand." However, I had never heard of Todd May. Doing some more online research, I saw that the North American anarchist Jason Adams was looking for information on two German-speaking anarchists, namely Jens Kastner, who had written a book about the libertarian aspects in Zygmunt Bauman's sociology, and me. That was the first time I encountered the term "postanarchism." The year was 2004. I continued my research and discovered the work of Saul Newman, Lewis Call, and Richard Day, as well as, and this was particularly important, the Turkish website *postanarki.net*, which gave me the idea to create a website for the German-speaking world. So, basically, I've been using the term "postanarchism" since 2005. For me, it indicates a label that is useful to spread new ideas and does not stand for a new current within anarchism. Postanarchism is a certain way of looking at things and of shedding new light on them. It opens up space to analyze social conditions, to question anarchist "truths," and, if necessary, to modify or abandon them.

KUHN: What are some of the key poststructuralist ideas that can inspire anarchism? What's the focus of your book *Freiheit, Individualität und Subjektivität*?

MÜMKEN: There are many ways in which poststructuralism can inspire anarchism. In my work, Foucault is central, in particular his analysis of power, that is, his rejection of the "repressive hypothesis," his claim that there is "no outside of power," and that he does not see power as purely negative, but also as productive. For me, an anarchist society is not characterized by the absence of power but, as I have hinted at above, by preventing shifting relations of power from becoming fixed conditions of domination. When conditions of domination are abolished, new fields of power emerge, which will then have to be kept in check by "practices of freedom," as Foucault puts it. Power and freedom are social relations that are co-dependent—you can't have one without the other. I also think that Foucault's analysis of neoliberal governmentality is important in order to understand contemporary capitalism, its effects on people, and the reasons why there is so little resistance. Likewise, Derrida's concept of deconstruction is important, and feminist poststructuralism inspired by Judith Butler and gender studies. The list goes on. Poststructuralism is full of interesting tools.

The central themes of *Freiheit, Individualität und Subjektivität* are the agency of the state and the question of the subject. I have looked at anarchist and Marxist state theory and analyzed the subject between heteronomy and autonomy. Stirner plays an important role. I have approached his work from a post-structuralist perspective. I wrote the book mainly because I wanted to clarify a few things for myself. The departure point was the question that Deleuze and Guattari ask in *Anti-Oedipus*: Why do so many people fight for their oppression as if they were fighting for their salvation? I have not found an answer, but we have to address the question if we want to build a liberated society. Maybe my book can make a small contribution. After all, the question goes back to the mid-16th-century *Discourse on Voluntary Servitude* by Etienne de la Boëtie.

KUHN: In the English-speaking world, for example in the work of Todd May or Saul Newman, it seems important to distinguish postanarchism from "classical anarchism," most commonly associated with Bakunin and Kropotkin. Where do you see the place of postanarchism in anarchist history? You have done a lot of work on Bakunin.

MÜMKEN: I never intended to distance myself from classical anarchism. All I'm interested in is to update anarchist theory and practice. This, however, I deem necessary. Contemporary anarchist debate must reflect on the social transformations, theoretical developments, and practical experiences of the last decades. I consider postanarchism to be a part of this process. Bakunin and Kropotkin are still very important to me—Bakunin as a radical philosopher and Kropotkin as an anarcho-communist visionary. At the same time, both must be investigated critically in order to tease out the best of their ideas and to develop them further.

KUHN: Another difference between your understanding of postanarchism and that of others seems to lie in your view of anarcho-syndicalism. While some postanarchists see anarcho-syndicalism as a product of the classical era, neglecting non-economic forms of oppression, you have close ties to the German anarcho-syndicalists in the *Freie ArbeiterInnen-Union* (Free Workers' Union, FAU). How do you see the relationship between postanarchism and anarcho-syndicalism?

MÜMKEN: In the early 1990's, I briefly worked with the Kassel chapter of the FAU, but I was never a member. At the time, my ideas of political practice were closer to the autonomous movement, especially because anti-fascism was a priority. After the so-called "reunification" of Germany, racist attacks were a daily reality. Ever since I got interested in anarchism at the age of 18,

communist anarchism was my utopia, and I have always seen
anarcho-syndicalism as a means to reach it. However, during the
last thirty years I have repeatedly redefined my understanding of
communist anarchism and anarcho-syndicalism. In my opinion,
an organization that focuses exclusively on economic struggles is
no real anarcho-syndicalist organization. Anarcho-syndicalism
means first and foremost to eradicate the liberal division of
politics and economics. (Unfortunately, the workers' movement
adopted this division by organizing in parties on the one hand
and in unions on the other.) An anarcho-syndicalist organization
needs to be involved in anti-fascist, anti-racist, anti-patriarchal,
anti-nuclear, anti-genetic engineering, and anti-landlord struggles. But it also has to adapt to the neoliberal transformation of
labor. Social struggles do not only occur at the workplace, but
also in neighborhoods, where they are directed against processes
of gentrification, rent increase, and poor living conditions. I think
that anarcho-syndicalism can benefit from postanarchist thought,
especially regarding processes of subjectification in neoliberal
global capitalism and regarding the rejection of all forms of
identity politics. As I said before, this is not about distancing
oneself from the anarchist tradition, it is about renewing it.
Anarchist and anarcho-syndicalist theory and practice are
constantly "becoming," and this process never ends.

KUHN: You are a trained architect and you have done much work
on housing and urban planning, theoretically and practically. Can
you tell us a little more about how this relates to postanarchist
themes? The question of space is much discussed among poststructuralist theorists and has apparently played an important
role in your own discovery of poststructuralism.

MÜMKEN: Just for clarification: it is true that I studied architecture
and that I got my degree, but since I have never worked as an
architect, I am not allowed to call myself an architect according
to German law. Right now, I do very "classical" anarchist work as
a printer in a print shop. It is hard for me to even distinguish
between studying space and poststructuralism, because it was
through Foucault and his analysis of power that I first combined
the notions of the city, space, and housing with those of
postanarchism. It is crucial to understand, even if it seems trivial,
that all social struggles happen in time and space. It is important
for these struggles that space in itself does not exist. Space is
produced by social conditions. Capitalism produces space, patriarchy produces space, laws produce space. This also means that

struggles intervene in the production of space. Spaces are contested, and the struggles are not merely economic, but also cultural and symbolic. Right now, I am studying the "society of control," as Deleuze called it. In such a society, control is executed in space and through space. It is no longer necessary to keep each individual under surveillance, as in a disciplinary society. "Space" is therefore an important analytical category. When we talk about the relationship between society and space, we ought remember that the French geographer and anarchist Élisée Reclus belonged to the founders of social geography in the second half of the 19th century; unfortunately, this is somewhat neglected in anarchism today, while much interesting work on society and space has been done in Marxism, for example by Henri Lefebvre who coined the phrase "right to the city," which has sparked urban protest movements worldwide.

KUHN: Can you give us a short overview of the current anarchist movement in Germany? Are your postanarchist ideas well received? Do you meet rejection?

MÜMKEN: I am no expert as far as the contemporary anarchist movement in Germany is concerned. The FAU probably has a bit over 300 members, and then there are the non-violent anarchists around the journal *graswurzel-revolution* [*Grassroots Revolution*], as well as many local and regional anarchist groups and projects, active in various social movements. Younger anarchists are interested in postanarchist ideas; that is obvious whenever I give talks. Of course there is also critique, but that's the way it should be. I mainly wish for a productive debate on anarchist theory and practice. Personally, I haven't encountered much rejection, rather disinterest and a lack of understanding. Some folks think that postanarchism is too abstract, too academic, too theoretical. Others consider the critique of the "autonomous subject" problematic, since it is the foundation of their anarchist politics and utopias.

KUHN: What are the future possibilities for anarchism, both in Germany and internationally?

MÜMKEN: Anarchism certainly won't be a mass movement anytime soon. But it will remain the current within the left that pursues change most radically. The change I would like to see would allow people to live in a society that is truly free. I am not interested in creating my own island of happiness or in retreating to a rural commune, while leaving the overall social conditions untouched. Whether anarchism will ever contribute more to the change I envision than it does now, I don't know.

Anarchist Developments in Cultural Studies
ISSN: 1923-5615
2013.1: *Blasting the Canon*

Unscientific Survey
7 Sages Of Anarchism

Participants at the Second Anarchist Studies Network (Loughborough University, 3-5 September 2012) were asked to select seven sages of anarchism, those they would include in the anarchist canon (if they had to make a choice, following the tradition pioneered by Paul Eltzbacher in 1911). Respondents were also asked to explain their selection and ordering. After the conference, the request for help in this unscientific survey was posted on the ASN list-serv. The results, commentary, and data are below.

The participants were:

Alex Prichard, André de Raaj, Anthony Fiscella, Benjamin Franks, Bert Altena, Bob Black, Dana Ward, Dana Williams, Danny Nemu, David Graeber, Deric Shannon, Duane Rousselle, Emily Charkin, Iain McKay, Jamie Heckert, Jason Adams,

Jesse Cohn, Jim Donaghey, John Clark, John Nightingale, Judy Greenway, Lewis Call, Lewis Mates, Lucien van der Walt, Mal function, Mario Bosincu, Matthew Wilson, Michael Harris, Nathan Fretwell, Peter Ryley, Roy Krøvel, Ruth Kinna, Saul Newman, Shannon Brincat, Sharif Gemie, Siegfried Bernhauser, Stephen Condit, Stevphen Shukaitis, Stuart Christie, Sureyya Evren, Tuli, Uri Gordon, Zarathustra, Zn, and six others.

DATA

SAGES	EXTRA VOTES	AUTHOR-SPECIFIC EXPLANATIONS	LINKS
A philosopher I have known for most of my life, from my home town.			

Anonymous (including pseudonyms)		Writes all the best things.	
Anzaldúa, Gloria			*Gloria Evangelina Anzaldúa Papers, 1942-2004*, Texas Archival Resources Online: http://www.lib.utexas.edu/taro/utlac/00189/lac-00189p1.html
Appeal to the Young			Peter Kropotkin (1842-1921), "An Appeal to the Young," *The Anarchist Library:* http://flag.blackened.net/daver/anarchism/kropotkin/atty.html
Ba Jin			"Ba Jin Archive," *Anarchy Archives,* http://dwardmac.pitzer.edu/Anarchist_Archives/bright/bajin/bajinarchive.html
Badiou, Alain			"Alain Badiou: Biography," *The European Graduate School:* http://www.egs.edu/faculty/alain-badiou/biography/
Bakunin, Michael	18	(i) Original and best. (ii) Thinker, inspirer, activist, commitment, affection, exemplary.	"Mikhail Bakunin Reference Archive, 1817-1876," *Marxists Internet Archive:* http://www.marxists.org/reference/archive/bakunin/
Bataille, Georges			Supervert, *Georges Bataille Electronic Library:* http://supervert.com/elibrary/georges

			_bataille/
Berardi, Franco 'Bifo'			"Franco Berardi Bifo: Writer, Activist, Philosopher," *dOCUMENTA (13)*: http://d13.documenta.de/#/no_cache/participants/participants/franco-berardi-bifo/?sword_list[]=Berardi
Berkman, Alexander	3	*ABCs of Anarchism*—Superb!	Alexander Berkman, *ABCs of Anarchism*, *Internet Archive.com*: http://archive.org/details/AlexanderBerkman-ABCof Anarchism
Berneri, Camillo		Clear-sighted and insightful.	"Berneri, Luigi Camillo (1897-1937), *LibCom*, Sep. 21, 2004: http://libcom.org/history/berneri-luigi-camillo-1897-1937
Bey, Hakim*		For helping anarchism to make its 'postanarchist' turn.	"Hakim Bey and Ontological Anarchy: The Writings of Hakim Bey," *The Hermetic Library*: http://hermetic.com/bey/
Bhave, Vinobha			"Associates of Ghandi: Acharya Vinobha Bhave," *Mahatmi Ghandi* [website]: http://www.mkgandhi.org/vinoba/vinoba.htm
Bookchin, Murray	12	(i) Still important as the one who made the link between	"Murray Bookchin," *Anarchy Archives*: http://dwardmac.pitzer.edu/Anarchist_

Name		Notes	Source
		green values and anarchism. (ii) For introducing anarchism to environmentalism (and vice versa).	Archives/bookchin/Bookchinarchive.html
Breton, Emilie			Cf., Chapter 13 of *Organize!: Building from the Local for Global Justice* (Brunswick Books, 2012): http://brunswickbooks.ca/Organize
Brown, Tom	2	Succinct exponent of anarcho-syndicalism.	Tom Brown, "Principles of Syndicalism," *LibCom*, Nov. 27, 2006: http://libcom.org/library/principles-of-syndicalism-tom-brown
Butler, Judith			"Judith Butler: Biography," *The European Graduate School*: http://www.egs.edu/faculty/judith-butler/biography/
Cafiero, Carlo			"Carlo Cafiero: Biography," *The Anarchist Encyclopedia*: http://recollectionbooks.com/bleed/Encyclopedia/CafieroCarlo.htm
Camus, Albert			"Camus," *BBC Radio 4: In Our Times* [podcast], Jan. 3, 2008: http://www.bbc.co.uk/programmes/b008kmqp
Chuang Tzu			"Chuan Tzu: Translations and Commen-

Chomsky, Noam	6	(i) More as an example of 'engaged' intellectual. Not always correct, but a marvellous model of 'speaking truth to power.' (ii) For being the most influential anarchist intellectual in the USA. (iii) Thinker, commentator, inspirer, commitment, respect, and affection.	taries by Derek Lin," *Trutao.org*: http://www.truetao.org/chuang/home.htm *The Noam Chomsky Website*, 2011: http://www.chomsky.info/
Class War			Ian Bone, "Class War," *Ian Bone* [weblog], May 10, 2011: http://ianbone.wordpress.com/2011/05/10/class-war/
Collaborative Earth First! Includes *Do or Die* magazine		Analysis and debate (UK mostly).	*Do or Die: Voices from the Ecologicial Resistance* [web archive], *Eco-action.org*: http://www.eco-action.org/dod/
Comfort, Alex			*Alex Comfort* [official website]: http://www.alexcomfort.com/

Cornelissen, Christiaan		"Christiaan Cornelissen," *Wikipedia*: http://en.wikipedia.org/wiki/Christiaan_Cornelissen
CrimethInc.		*CrimethInc.* [website]: http://crimethinc.com/
Day, Dorothy		"Dorothy Day Library," *The Catholic Worker Movement*: http://www.catholicworker.org/dorothyday/
de Cleyre, Voltairine	2	*Voltairine de Cleyre: The Exquisite Rebel*: http://www.voltairine.org/
de Sade, Marquis		"The Marquis de Sade," *Wikipedia*: http://en.wikipedia.org/wiki/Marquis_de_Sade
Deleuze, Gilles	1	"Gilles Deleuze," *Stanford Enclyopedia of Philosophy*, May 23, 2008 (rev. Sep. 24, 2011): http://plato.stanford.edu/entries/deleuze/
Der Arbeter Fraint		"Der Arbeter Fraint: The Worker's Friend," *Solidarity Federation*: http://www.solfed.org.uk/?q=taxonomy/term/483
Durruti, Buenaventura		Peter Newell, "About Buenaventura Durruti," *Modern American Poetry*: http://www.english.illinois.edu/maps/scw/durruti

Flores Magón, Ricardo	2		recollectionbooks.com/bleed/Encyclopedia/FerrerFrancisco.htm "The Writings of Ricardo Ricardo Flores Magón (in English and Spanish)," *waste.org:* http://www.waste.org/~road runner/writing/magon/main.htm
For Socialism			Gustav Landauer, *For Socialism* (Telos Press, 1978): http://www.telospress.com/store/#!/~/product/id=17898073
Foucault, Michel	1	(Being a bit provocative here . . .).	*Foucault Studies* [online journal]: http://rauli.cbs.dk/index.php/foucault-studies/
Fourier, Charles	1	Pleasure is the key to human life. Actually, a great satirist.	"Charles Fourier Archive (1772-1837)," *Marxists Internet Archive:* http://www.marxists.org/reference/archive/fourier/index.htm
Freedom Group			"A History of Freedom Press," *Freedom: Anarchist News and Views:* http://www.freedompress.org.uk/news/about/history/
Freud, Sigmund			"Sigmund Freud," *Wikipedia:* http://en.wikipedia.org/wiki/Sigmund_Freud
Galleani, Luigi	1	Commitment, commentator and inspirer, affection.	Raffaele Schiavina, "A Fragment of Luigi Galleani's Life," *Kate Sharpley Library:*

			http://www.katesharpleylibrary.net/d51cvp
Geddes, Patrick			"Patrick Geddes," *Wikipedia*: http://en.wikipedia.org/wiki/Patrick_Geddes
Gilbert, David			"Authors: David Gilbert," *PM Press*: http://www.pmpress.org/content/article.php?story=DavidGilbert
Godwin, William	8		"William Godwin, 1756-1836," *The History Guide*: http://www.historyguide.org/intellect/godwin.html
Goldman, Emma	21	For introducing anarchism to feminism (and vice versa).	"The Emma Goldman Papers," *Berkeley Digital Library*: http://sunsite.berkeley.edu/goldman/
Goodman, Paul	1		"Paul Goodman: Writing on the Web," *The Preservation Institute*: http://www.preservenet.com/theory/Goodman.html
Gordon, A.D.			"James Horrox on A.D. Gordon and Anarchism," *Anarchy Alive!* [weblog], Sep. 13, 2012: http://anarchyalive.com/2012/09/534/james-horrox-on-a-d-gordon-and-anarchism/

Garborg, Arne			"Arne Garborg," *Store Norsk Leksikon*: http://snl.no/Arne_Garborg
Graeber, David	2		"Interview with David Graeber," *The White Review*: http://www.thewhite review.org/interviews/interview-with-david-graeber/
Heath, Nick		No Nick Heath, no fun!	"Nick Heath" [online radio show], *Anarchist Federation*, April 17, 2012: http://www.afed.org.uk/component/conten t/article/300.html
Hegel, G.W.F			"Georg Wilhelm Friedrich Hegel," *Wikipedia*: http://en.wikipedia.org/wiki/Georg_Wilhelm_Friedrich_Hegel
Hiscocks, Mandy			*.bored but not broken.* [Mandy Hiscocks' personal weblog]: http://boredbutnot broken.tao.ca/
			"Hof, Jan" [online biography], *Biografisch Woordenboek van het Socialisme en den Arbeidersbeweging in Nederland*: http:// www.iisg.nl/bwsa/bios/hof.html
hooks, bell			bell hooks, "Cultural Criticism & Transformation" [video], *Challenging*

Name			Reference
Hudson, Helen			*Media:* http://www.youtube.com/watch?v=zQUuHFKP-9s; "Interview with Hegel Hudson from the Certain Days Collective: CKDU News Collective," *National Campus and Community Radio Association:* http://previous.ncra.ca/exchange/dspProgramDetail.cfm?programID=80059
IWW			*Industrial Workers of the World: A Union for All Workers:* http://www.iww.org/
Jünger, Ernst			John King, *Ernst Jünger in Cyberspace* [unofficial website]: http://www.juenger.org/
Kafka, Franz			"The Works and Life of Franz Kafka," *Franz Kafka Online:* http://www.kafka-online.info/
Kanngieser, Anna			"Anna Kanngieser," *Transversal Geographies:* http://transversalgeographies.org/
Kropotkin, Peter	27	(i) A rational, articulate defence of humanitarian anarchism	"Peter Kropotkin" [web archive], *LibCom:* http://libcom.org/tags/peter-kropotkin

		based on cooperation. I still like the idea that biology is on our side. (ii) For establishing the philosophical foundations of anarchism in the 19th century. (iii) Thinker, inspirer, vision, commitment, respect.	
Lacan, Jacques	1		"Jacques Lacan (1901-1981)," *Internet Encyclopedia of Philosophy:* http://www.iep.utm.edu/lacweb/
Lagalisse, Erica			Octavio Vélez Ascencio, "Amnesty for Loxicha People Will End Injustice: OPIZ," trans. Erica Lagalisse, *El Enemigo Común*, June 2 2011: http://elenemigocomun.net/2011/06/amnesty-loxicha-end-injustice/
Landauer, Gustav	11		"Landauer, Gustav (1870-1919)": *LibCom*, Sep. 22, 2004: http://libcom.org/history/landauer-gustav-1870-1919
Lao Tzu/Taoism	3	Difficult to follow, and there's such a conceptual chasm to cross. But they seem to be	*Lao Tzu Page* [website]: http://www.taopage.org/laotzu/

		saying something interesting about how to relate to the world.	
Le Guin, Ursula	2	For creating convincing, fully realized anarchist societies, as in *The Dispossessed.*	*Ursula K. Le Guin* [website]: http://www.ursulakleguin.com/
Lee, Richard B.		Very important source on hunter-gatherer life.	"Richard Borshay Lee," *Wikipedia:* http://en.wikipedia.org/wiki/Richard_Borshay_Lee
Makhno, Nestor	2		*The Nestor Makhno Archive:* http://www.nestormakhno.info/
Malatesta, Errico	12	(i) Pragmatic, principled. (ii) Commitment, commentator, activist, inspirer, respect, and affection.	"Errico Malatesta," *LibCom:* http://libcom.org/tags/errico-malatesta
Marx, Karl	1		*Marx and Engels Internet Archive:* http://www.marxists.org/archive/marx/index.htm
Mella, Ricardo			"Ricardo Mella," *Wikipedia:* http://en.wikipedia.org/wiki/Ricardo_Mella
Meltzer, Albert	1	Untiring propagandist, thinker, commentator, activist, inspirer,	Stuart Christie, "Albert Meltzer, Anarchist," *The Kate Sharpley Library:*

Michel, Louise	commitment, respect and affection.		http://www.katesharpleylibrary.net/w9gk1g "Louise Michel Biography," *International Institute of Social History*: http://www.iisg.nl/collections/louisemichel/biography.php
Miller, Henry			Valentine Miller, *Henry Miller: Personal Collection* [website], 2005-2012: http://www.henrymiller.info/
Mirbeau, Octave			"Octave Mirbeau," *Wikipedia*: http://en.wikipedia.org/wiki/Octave_Mirbeau
Morris, William	(i) Still like those ideas of aesthetics as part of life. Not so keen on the medievalism. (ii) *News From Nowhere*, wonderful anti-industrial classic.		*William Morris Society, UK* [website]: http://www.williammorrissociety.org/
Müsham, Erich	Important but underrated.	1	Erich Müsham, *Wikipedia*: http://en.wikipedia.org/wiki/Erich_M%C3%BChsam
My anti-anarchist friend that I talk to at the local coffee shop			

Myself		
Naess, Arne		ReRun Productions, *The Call of the Mountain: Arne Naess* [video documentary excerpt]: http://www.youtube.com/watch?v=llvnEaLUOac
Nettlau, Max		"Max Nettlau Papers," *International Institute of Social History:* http://www.iisg.nl/archives/en/files/n/ARCH01001.php
Nguyen, Mimi Thi		"Mimi Thi Nguyen, Assoc. Professor of Asian American Studies," *University of Illinois at Urbana-Champaign:* http://www.aasp.illinois.edu/people/mimin
Nietzsche, Friedrich	1	*The Friedrich Nietzsche Society* [website]: https://fns.org.uk/
Nieuwenhuis, Ferdinand Domela		"Ferdinand Domela Nieuwenhuis," *Wikipedia:* http://en.wikipedia.org/wiki/Ferdinand_Domela_Nieuwenhuis
Ortt, Felix		"A Brief Look at the Life of Felix Ortt: Prominent Dutch Christian Anarchist," Portrettengalerij [weblog], April 4, 2007: http://portrettengalerij.blogspot.co.uk/2007

Paasche, Hans			/04/brief-look-at-life-of-felix-ortt.html; *Hans Paasche* [unofficial weblog]: http://en.hanspaasche.com/
Pelloutier, Fernand			"Fernand Pelloutier," *LibCom*: http://libcom.org/tags/fernand-pelloutier
Perlman, Fredy		*Against His-story, Against Leviathan*	Fredy Perlman, *Against His-story, Against Leviathan* (1983), *The Anarchist Library*, http://theanarchistlibrary.org/library/fredy-perlman-against-his-story-against-leviathan
Post Colonial Anarchism			Roger White, "Post Colonial Anarchism," *Colours of Resistance*: http://www.coloursofresistance.org/344/post-colonial-anarchism/
Proudhon, P-J	16	For developing the anarchist critique of property.	"Pierre-Joseph Proudhon," *Anarchy Archives*: http://dwardmac.pitzer.edu/Anarchist_Archives/proudhon/Proudhonarchive.html
Ramus, Pierre			"Pierre Ramus," *Wikipedia* [German]: http://de.wikipedia.org/wiki/Pierre_Ramus
Read, Herbert	1		"Herbert Read, (1893-1968)," *The Anarchist Encyclopedia*: http://recollectionbooks.com/

			bleed/Encyclopedia/ReadHerbert.htm
Reclus, Elisée	3		"Elisée Reclus," *Anarchy Archives*: http://dwardmac.pitzer.edu/Anarchist_Archives/bright/reclus/reclus.html
Riot, Coco		queer Spanish artist	*Coco Riot* [website]: http://cocoriot.com/
Riste, Synnøve			"Sunnmørsposten: Eternally Yours," *Historieportal*: http://www.pergjendem.com/?p=151
Rocker, Rudolf	7	For *Nationalism and Culture*—thinker—commitment, respect.	*Rudolf Rocker* [website]: http://flag.blackened.net/rocker/
Rousseau, J-J			*The Rousseau Association* [website]: http://rousseauassociation.ish-lyon.cnrs.fr/
Sahlins, Marshall		*The Original Affluent Society* is indispensable.	Marshall Sahlins, "The Original Affluent Society" [abridged], in *The Politics of Egalitarianism: Theory and Practice*, ed. Jacqueline Solway (NY: Berghahn, 2006): http://www.vizkult.org/propositions/alinei nmature/pdfs/SahlinOriginalAffluent Society-abridged.pdf
Sakae, Osugi			"Osugi Sakae, 1885-1923," *LibCom*:

		http://libcom.org/library/osugi-sakae-biography
Schürmann, Reiner		"Reiner Schürmann: A Shrine," *presocratics.org*: http://www.presocratics.org/?page_id=588
Shakyamuni (Gautama Buddha)		"The Life of Buddha," *The Buddhist Society*: http://www.thebuddhistsociety.org/resources/Buddha.html
Situationist International	1	*situationist international online* [website:, Center for Digital Discourse and Culture, Virginia Tech University]: http://www.cddc.vt.edu/sionline/
Solidarity Federation		*The Solidarity Federation* [website]: http://www.solfed.org.uk/
Spence, Thomas		*Thomas Spence Society* [website]: http://thomas-spence-society.co.uk/
Spinoza, Baruch		Steven Nadler, "Baruch Spinoza," *Stanford Encyclopedia of Philosophy*: http://plato.stanford.edu/entries/spinoza/
Stirner, Max	8	Svein Olav Nyberg, *Max Stirner* [website]: http://i-studies.com/stirner/
Subcomandante Marcos		*Writings of Subcommander Marcos of the*

		EZLN [website]: http://flag.blackened.net/revolt/mexico/marcos_index.html
The Bund		"Bund," Jewish Virtual Library: http://www.jewishvirtuallibrary.org/jsource/judaica/ejud_0002_0004_0_03730.html
The emerging 'para-academics' publishers, within and without the university		
Thoreau, Henry David	1	"Henry David Thoreau," Wikipedia: http://en.wikipedia.org/wiki/Henry_David_Thoreau
Tolstoy, Leo	2	Alexandre Christoyannopoulos: Publications and Other Research Dissemination [including works on Tolstoy]: https://sites.google.com/site/christoyannopoulos/publications
Traven, B		B Traven [unofficial website]: http://www.btraven.com/
Tucker, Benjamin		Wendy McElroy, "Benjamin Tucker and Liberty: A Bibliographical Essay" (1981),

			The Forum: The Online Library of Liberty: http://oll.libertyfund.org/index.php?option=com_content&task=view&id=796&Itemid=259
Tucker, Kevin		*Species Traitor* editor	"Kevin Tucker: Essays from Species Traitor," *The Anarchist Library*: http://theanarchistlibrary.org/library/kevin-tucker-essays-from-species-traitor
uprising			
Walia, Harsha			"Harsha Walia," *Rabble*: http://rabble.ca/taxonomy/term/1843
Ward, Colin	11		"Colin Ward," *The Anarchist Library*: http://theanarchistlibrary.org/authors/Colin_Ward.html
Weil, Simone			*Simone Weil* [website archive]: http://simoneweil.net/home.htm
Werbe, Peter		*Fifth Estate* editor, many key insights in the '80s.	*Fifth Estate* [magazine]: http://www.peterwerbe.com/estate.htm
whoever set up *Adbusters*			*Adbusters* [website]: http://www.adbusters.org/
Wilde, Oscar			*Oscar Wilde* [website]: http://www.cmgww.com/historic/wilde/

Williamson, Robin	"If you know how to wonder you will know how to pray." Can't say fairer than that.	Pig's Whisker Music: The Official Website of Robin and Bina Williamson: http://www.pigswhiskermusic.co.uk
Wilson, Peter Lamborn*		"Hakim Bey and Ontological Anarchy: The Writings of Hakim Bey," *The Hermetic Library:* http://hermetic.com/bey/
Woodcock, George		"George Woodcock," *The Anarchist Encylopedia:* http://recollectionbooks.com/bleed/Encyclopedia/WoodcockGeorge.htm
work		
You Can't Blow Up a Social Relationship		Libertarian Socialist Collective, "You Can't Blow Up a Social Relationship," *LibCom:* http://libcom.org/library/you-cant-blow-up-social-relationship
Zapata, Emiliano		"Emiliano Zapata," *Indigenous Peoples Literature:* http://www.indigenouspeople.net/zapata.htm
Zinn, Howard		*Howard Zinn, 1922-2010* [unofficial website]: http://www.howardzinn.org/

* Hakim Bey and Peter Lamborn Wilson appear separately, as nominated.

	COMMENTS ON ORDERING
1	Personal preference, not necessarily only those who identify as anarchists but also including intellectuals/activists who escape labelling.
2	My favourite anarchists, inspired by my work with children and communities.
3	Basically, I ordered them in terms of their contribution to anarchist ideas and the movement as well as how much they impacted my own political development over the last 25 years. Also, if the list were for libertarians rather than just anarchists, I would have to have added Maurice Brinton and Cornelius Castoriadis. And, in terms of favourite anarchists and influence, I would list Makhno and Durruti—but do they count as 'sages'? Anyways, I've included Makhno—he wrote a bit after all. As for Bookchin, well, the last few years of his life seemed to be about destroying his own legacy and annoying anarchists, but you cannot dismiss his decades of work because of that.
4	The ordering is more or less random, based perhaps on those to whom I have most often referred in my own work. It is not an order of preference, significance, or anything else systematic. Tomorrow I would probably draw up another list, so I am sending this before second, third, etc. thoughts make too much noise.
5	Order they came to me.
6	I guess it's based on how much their writings and life stories touched and influenced me.
7	Chronological order.
8	I ordered them according to personal significance and preference. I started with Stirner, but later on I noticed that it is impossible to be a Stirnerian and start with Stirner. You have to start with yourself. So my most favourite sage is myself.
9	I excluded many people who are also influential in my thinking as an anarchist—Foucault, Castoriadis, Butler, Debord, Vaniegem, etc. Also excluded influential novelists—Piercy, LeGuin, Moorcock. Also excluded

	organisations/collectivities and those who are influential because of what they did, rather than what they wrote. The notion of a specifically 'anarchist' canon is highly suspect—most anarchists draw on a range of influences outside the main theorists.
10	Fairly random order.
11	Chosen by who I reckon is the most influential rather than those I personally prefer. Also ranks Rocker, Zinn, Ward, Parsons, Reclus.
12	I take a sage to be someone who has thought deeply and at length about a given topic and expresses an idiosyncratic view ('wisdom' is too subjective a category, and no one is truly original). The names above are not in any particular order, except for Proudhon's, which could inevitably come first since his prolific output is both uniquely original and unlikely to be surpassed in range, depth, or sheer volume. The rest are essentially derivative.
13	Chapter plan.
14	I'm unfortunately very ignorant about anarchists but the order reflects the order in which I discovered them.
15	No real reason, but they are the ones that stand out for me, and [that] I have done the most work on.
16	Anti-colonialism, spirituality, nature. 1 & 2 [are] first order preferences; the others are random.
17	Largely chronological. Groups, not individuals, that produced significant works and theory.
18	Chronological, all emphasised that anarchism is 'not Marxism.'
19	Chronological.
20	Stirner puts us on a higher pov [point-of-view] altogether and helps put man's other brilliant thoughts in perspective.
21	Bakunin is barely an anarchist, but not to include him would immediately mark one out as a loon amongst

	anarchists. Graeber's work on debt places him in an exclusive group of anarchist political economists, but the rest of his output is fairly standard and inter-changeable with innumerable others.
22	Historical order, loosely. It's tempting to want to jettison the triad of Proudhon-Bakunin-Kropotkin for the sake of novelty (and to avoid the pitfalls of a "canon" as such), but they're all three so indispensable for their interventions in actual living movements, for the differences they made in the tradition (delineating the differences between mutualist, collectivist, and communist economics, etc.), and for the sheer still-unexhausted novelty of their thought. Malatesta is useful to study as someone who is deeply involved in practice, someone for whom practice revises theory, a kind of pragmatist in the sense of Charles Peirce or William James. I significantly omit Stirner, not because he's uninteresting, but because I find the relations between his thought and the rest of the anarchist tradition to be somewhat thin, and because its practical uses are less apparent. Landauer, Goldman, and Goodman might be my three controversial inclusions—three astonishingly creative Jewish activist-thinkers. Landauer's work has never gotten the kind of uptake it deserves in the English-speaking world because of the translation barrier, but his peculiar blend of speculative philosophy and engaged praxis left us with a lot to think about (and work with). I think Kathy Ferguson makes a good case that Goldman's "political thinking in the streets" deserves more careful attention and thought than it usually gets, and it would be criminal not to have someone on this list represent the incredibly crucial opening of anarchism onto feminism and of feminism onto anarchism. She also stands for my wish to shrug at the very idea of a list of "seven sages" (why seven? And, more importantly, why conceptualize anarchism primarily in terms of a series of Great Thinkers, even if there's a dose of irony administered with it? It almost inevitably marginalizes the usually marginalized—both in terms of race/gender/sexuality/etc. and also in terms of genres of practice: syndicalism has many fine thinkers, from Émile Pouget to Judy Bari, but few really representative "sages"). Finally, Goodman did so much to bring anarchism into relation with a post-WWII world, to draw out its applications in fields ranging from sexuality to urbanism to anti-racism to culture, and to renew anarchism in the fallow "valley

	time" of the 1940s-1950s—well, it's hard to find a more prolific and fruitful political imagination in any one person, period. Landauer and Goodman (as inheritors to Proudhon) also reflect my ideological biases toward what some have tried to call "practical anarchism," emphasizing the patient, peaceful construction of alternative systems to meet everyday needs in existing communities over dramatic moments of insurrection or radical breaks with the totality of the past.
23	Texts that I've found provocative, insightful, and enduring in their concerns. If anyone asks me about anarchism, it's texts I think of, not people. Though I'm very fond of a number of contemporary and historical figures (and have spent my adult life with a number of those in the latter group), it's the ideas that matter to me. Texts can present some of the same problems as the 'canon'—reification, abstraction etc.—but the recommendation to read 7 texts is probably less likely to result in these problems than one to examine the work of 7 individuals.
24	I'm not numbering . . . I suppose the list would be the thinkers who I've found most useful in elaborating an anarchist politics, one which is focused on questions of autonomy, cultural subversion, affect, and self-reproduction . . . or something like that.
25	1. Anarchism 2. is 3. not 4. about 5. great 6. men 7. (or women).
26	Commitment and intelligence were my criteria, but they are not in hierarchical order; they are all equally sage and awesome in a horizontal way.

27	I picked people who represent some of the main currents within communist anarchism, since it's the dominant category of anarchists active today. I suppose a list of 'seven sages' (surely a problematic notion to begin with) should reflect that. These folks, in their own ways also represent discrete poles within some of the major debates among anarchist communists, including ecology, organizationalism, the role of class struggle, questions around gender and sexuality, insurrection v. revolution, anarchism as a critique of structures/institutions v. daily life, etc.
28	My order is alphabetical; I learn from them all and I find them all stimulating sages.
29	Writers who I've read and influence my thought.
30	Personal preference, not necessarily only those who identify as anarchists but also including intellectuals/activists who escape labelling.
31	Order of significance and personal preference regarding links between environment, the social, and politics.
32	I began bottom up, as the ones I knew were not top were easier. It is an honest attempt. Not to chart intelligence, but guidance.
33	This is a list of classic figures anarchists should read as sources of anarchist *sagesse*. The greatest contributions to the anarchist project lie in the most radical and critical dimensions of Buddhist, Daoist, Hegelian-Marxist, and Freudian-Lacanian thought. This explains six of the seven. Reclus is included because he first synthesized the anarchist critique of domination and introduced the ecological dimension into radical social thought. The listing is chronological.
34	#1[Kropotkin] is the most 'central' to modern anarchists, #7 [Bakunin] less so. Of course, if I could go off-list, I'd also include Voltairine de Cleyre, Gustav Landauer, Ricardo Flores-Magon, Tolstoy, etc. I like Bakunin's biography, but I've always thought of him more as an activist than a unique thinker (which is surely not the case, though). Since a "canon" is socially constructed, anarchist sages are very Euro-centric. Malatesta and

	Bakunin's impact upon the South is huge, and they deserve a place simply for their work in promoting anarchist thinking elsewhere. Kropotkin was the widest (imho) thinker, who wrote the most, and still most relevant for people today. Goldman and Reclus were both good at acknowledging the multiple ways in which domination and inequality effect people (above and beyond capitalism and state domination), including race, gender, and sexuality (and animals, in Reclus's case). I'm not a big Proudhon fan (maybe as a result of writing-style, perceived scatteredness, non-anarchist nature, and other factors), but his impact has been huge and to leave him out would be like leaving out Comte from a discussion of Sociology's roots (although Comte matters very little for explaining social phenomenon today). My ideological commitment is towards thinkers who are more social in-nature (thus Stirner and individualists don't appeal to me), perhaps those who tend towards anarcho-communism (but, then again, that's probably the majority of the anarchist pantheon and movement, even today). Not sure if my rankings are very meaningful, since—like any social theory—it is always more useful to pick and choose based on the situation at hand (thus Kropotkin is not always going to be the best pick . . . sometimes Bakunin might be).
35	Impact on movement globally. Insights on core issues.
36	The order is simply date of death—only one is still alive. The choices are a representative of the different periods of anarchist history. They were chosen (rather too quickly and with a lousy gender balance) as they are interesting thinkers in their own right, though they also challenged anarchist orthodoxies from a number of different perspectives. People like these are important if a tradition like anarchism is not to ossify into a dogma, especially as it becomes more fashionable. So, with the exception of Proudhon, they are not the founders of the tradition, but those who elaborated on it and took it in interesting directions.
37	Such fun, I feel like we could play with these names all night long. I imagine having cards with these names on them and experimenting with numerous juxtapositions . . .

38	No particular ranking and no particular explanation.
39	To be honest, I can't actually get to seven . . . not sure whether that says something about the state of anarchist thought, or the state of my thought . . . the only two I know I'd definitely add are Landauer and Ward . . . anyway, will get back to you when I can think of five more.
40	Names in no particular order, and Robin Williamson included to deliberately bugger up your classification system.
41	Order in which they came to my mind.
42	I chose Marx for number one because I believe his central contention with 'anarchism,' or what is called anarchism, has little to nothing to do with hierarchy, coercion, or authority. Many secondary texts claim that it has everything to do with that, but my own research, influenced by Maximilien Rubel and others, suggests this is not accurate. Rather, I believe he is, essentially, an anarchist, even if he calls himself a communist. Another way to describe what he "is", might be to say that he is a materialist anarchist. Marx's central contention had much more to idealism vs. materialism, rather than anti-authority vs. authority. Emma Goldman and Stirner are sages because they both resist the more subtle forms of hierarchy, coercion, and authority and make them much more explicit than most anarchist thinkers. Rudolf Rocker figures for me because he was a syndicalist who embraced Nietzsche and Nietzschean threads, which most anarchists haven't done historically. Schürmann, Deleuze, and Agamben are all well known radical philosophers who might not specifically identify as anarchist, but whose philosophies are nevertheless, amongst the most important for anarchism in the contemporary period.
43	This is a list of anarchists whose work I would recommend to others who wanted to know more about anarchism. All have influenced my own life and thinking in different ways at different times; the chronology is personal. Many others who have contributed to my own development as an anarchist would not necessarily call

	themselves/be called anarchists at all (e.g. bell hooks, Audre Lorde). I don't think anarchism has or needs 'sages,' nor a 'canon.' That's the other guys' game. No Gods, no masters, no cannons, no canons!
44	Chronological order.

www.ingramcontent.com/pod-product-compliance
Lightning Source LLC
Chambersburg PA
CBHW050648270326
41927CB00012B/2925